Moore and Wittgenstein
on Certainty

Moore and Wittgenstein on Certainty

AVRUM STROLL

New York   Oxford
OXFORD UNIVERSITY PRESS
1994

Oxford University Press

Oxford   New York   Toronto
Delhi   Bombay   Calcutta   Madras   Karachi
Kuala Lumpur   Singapore   Hong Kong   Tokyo
Nairobi   Dar es Salaam   Cape Town
Melbourne   Auckland   Madrid

and associated companies in
Berlin   Ibadan

Published by Oxford University Press, Inc.
200 Madison Avenue, New York, New York 10016

Oxford is a registered trademark of Oxford University Press

Library of Congress Cataloging-in-Publication Data
Stroll, Avrum, 1921–
Moore and Wittgenstein on certainty / Avrum Stroll.
p.   cm.
Includes bibliographical references and index.
ISBN 0-19-508488-8
1. Moore, G. E. (George Edward), 1873–1958.   2. Wittgenstein,
Ludwig, 1889–1951. Über Gewissheit.   3. Certainty.   4. Skepticism.
I. Title
B1647.M74S86   1994   121'.63—dc20   93-22633

2 4 6 8 9 7 5 3 1

Printed in the United States of America
on acid-free paper

For Mary

Acknowledgments

There is an unforgettable entry in *On Certainty*—it is just one of many—where Wittgenstein writes: "Light dawns gradually over the whole." I should like to take this passage out of its original context and apply it to myself. The passage implies, of course, that before there was a shimmer of light there was darkness. These are, in fact, good descriptions of the process I went through in writing this book. Wittgenstein, as all exegetes know, is a notoriously obscure writer, and *On Certainty* is especially difficult to understand. It consists of a set of notes composed in the last eighteen months of his life and is unfinished, unpolished, and kaleidoscopic. When I first studied it the outcome was darkness, and even after a couple of readings there was only a glimmer of illumination. But light gradually dawned over the whole, and by time I had rewritten the manuscript five or six times I felt that I had some inkling of what Wittgenstein was up to. Whether that impression is well-founded readers will have to judge for themselves.

I was greatly assisted in this process of progressive enlightenment by a large number of persons. It would be impossible to describe the nature of their observations and suggestions in this limited space. Let me just say that I found them invaluable. I therefore wish to thank Henry Alexander, Georgios Anagnostopoulos, Marco Borioni, Paulo Dau, Guido Frongia, Christopher Latiolais, Marianne McDonald, A.P. Martinich, Robert Nozick and Barry Smith. To these names let me add that of my wife, Mary, who took time away from her own research on medieval papal politics to read each draft of the manuscript. Her acute and constructive recommendations greatly improved the style and organization of the work. This book was mainly written during three lengthy stays at the American Academy in Rome in the period 1989–1992. Without the hospitality and generosity of the then director, Dr. Joseph Connors, and his wife, Françoise, and of the assistant director, Pina Pasquantonio, it would have taken me much longer to complete this study.

I also wish to thank Timothy Moore, who owns the copyright to his father's *Philosophical Papers*, for permission to quote from that work and Basil Blackwell for permission to quote from their edition of *On Certainty*, which was translated from the German by Denis Paul and G.E.M. Anscombe.

La Jolla, California   A.S.
October 1993

Contents

*Moore and Wittgenstein
on Certainty*

Isn't the question this: "What if you had to change your opinion even on these most fundamental things?" And to that the answer seems to me to be: "You don't have to change it. That is just what their being 'fundamental' is." (*O.C.*, 512)

1

Why Moore and Wittgenstein?

This book is almost entirely about Moore and Wittgenstein, and its concentration is on a spectrum of topics that they explored in the latter stages of their careers: whether there is a common sense view of the world and if so what it is; whether the propositions comprising such a view are known to be true, and known to be true with certainty; whether the common sense view is a specimen of folk thought—folk psychology, folk physics, and folk semantics—and accordingly whether it will and should be replaced by a world picture deriving from scientific inquiry. Each of these topics splinters into an array of others—when it is true and/or appropriate to say one knows, when doubting has or fails to have a point, what counts as a proof, and when the adducing of evidence is apposite—so that the range we shall ultimately be dealing with covers most of the classical subject matter of epistemology and some aspects of metaphysics.

The question may well be asked: Why Moore and Wittgenstein as the foci of this study? With Wittgenstein especially, a positive response, half answering the question, is fairly obvious. There is a second positive response to the other half that is less so. Obviously, Wittgenstein is one of the great philosophers of the twentieth century, perhaps the greatest; indeed, a reasonable case can be made for the claim that he may be the greatest philosopher since Kant. Of himself he said that his most important contribution was to have introduced a new method into philosophy, and as we shall see, there is considerable merit, as well as self-insight, in this remark. But in addition, his substantive contributions to the theory of meaning, the philosophy of mind, epistemology, aesthetics, ethics, and the philosophies of psychology and mathematics have been enormously influential, though in each of these cases the results he achieved can hardly be disassociated from the method itself.

But that, as is well known, is one of the features of philosophy: that its greatest advances, or at least changes in perspective, are often functions of new procedures. From Plato through Descartes and Spinoza to the present this has been the case. In the twentieth century, we can associate such changes, for instance, with the approaches that derive from developments in mathematical and symbolic logic: The achievements of Frege, Russell, and Quine are examples of how a new methodology can transform an ancient subject. With J.L. Austin and the intensive concentration upon ordinary language another breakthrough was achieved whose results in such papers as "A Plea for Excuses" and "Three Ways of Spilling Ink" arise from the unique techniques that Austin employed.

What often makes for dispute in philosophy and for differences in the estimation of philosophers by other philosophers are differences in judgments about the merits of the methodology being invoked. So there is, as one might well expect, dispute about Wittgenstein's place in the pantheon of philosophical gods. Wittgenstein never expatiated on what that method was: he seemed to imply that others would pick it up in the course of reading his works. In the preface to the *Philosophical Investigations* he says that he felt his thoughts would be crippled if he tried to force them in any single direction against their natural inclination. So the method is displayed by strings of aphoristic remarks, a technique that, as he writes, "is connected with the very nature of the investigation." These remarks, often jumping from one topic to another, he characterizes as "sketches of landscapes which were made in the course of these long and involved journeyings." We shall have more to say about his method in the chapters that follow. But whatever history's ultimate judgment about Wittgenstein and the style of doing philosophy that he introduced, there is no doubt that he was an original and profound investigator whose way of exploring philosophical problems has no exact precedent.

Unlike some disciplines in which it is the answers that count, in philosophy genius is often measured by the questions that are asked. By that measure Wittgenstein has no equal. He posed a host of queries that no one had asked before and that no one might ever have asked had he not lived. "If you are whistling a tune and you are interrupted, how do you know how to go on?" "Why is the alphabet like a string of pearls in a box?" "Does my telephone call to New York strengthen my conviction that the earth exists?" "Why would it be *unthinkable* that I should stay in the saddle however much the facts bucked?" "Are we to say that the knowledge that there are physical objects comes very early or very late?" And he was unbelievably productive. Of what are estimated to be some ninety volumes of materials in the Wittgenstein *nachlass*, only a dozen or so have now been edited and published. Some of the manuscripts in the collection are, to be sure, variants of others, and some are composed of non-philosophical correspondence, but the quantity of the purely philosophical material is staggering.

Ironically enough, during Wittgenstein's lifetime only two authorized works were published, the *Tractatus* and a short paper on logical form in the *Proceedings of the Aristotelian Society*. The full impact of all that he wrote has thus yet to be felt. If one adds to his philosophical power an unusual personality and life style, we encounter a certain kind of mystique that no other philosopher of our time has possessed. In terms of the effect he had on those around him the closest analogue is possibly Socrates. Norman Malcolm's *Memoir* heightens the analogy; it depicts a philosophical personality who might well have been the protagonist of the *Crito* and the *Phaedo*. We can thus easily see why one would choose to write about him.

The second positive response is less obvious. Since Wittgenstein's death in 1951 there has been a vast outpouring of articles, monographs, collections of essays, some biographies, and even some novels, devoted to his work and his life. In the past decade the flow has become a torrent. In 1987, for example, there appeared a fifteen-volume collection, edited by John V. Canfield, consisting of more than 250 previously published articles about Wittgenstein. Three of these volumes deal with the *Tractatus*, and the others with his later work after his return to Cambridge in 1929, with the *Blue and Brown Books*, the *Investigations*, *Remarks on the Foundations of Mathematics*, *Last Writings on the Philosophy of Psychology*, and so forth.

Furthermore, since the middle 1980s the literature devoted to Wittgenstein's philosophy has been augmented by new books by Cora Diamond, Rudolph Haller, G.P. Baker and P.M.S. Hacker, Gertrude Conway, Marie McGinn, Ronald Suter, S. Stephen Hilmy, Fergus Kerr, Norman Malcolm, Jaako and Merrill B. Hintikka, Jonathan Westphal, Oswald Hanfling, Colin McGinn, David Pears, E. von Savigny, and Anthony Kenny, to mention only a few. One can add to the burgeoning corpus three biographies (a new edition of W.W. Bartley's controversial *Wittgenstein*; Volume 1 of a projected three-volume biography by Brian McGuinness dealing with the period up to 1921; and a one-volume, synoptic biography by Ray Monk, published in 1990) and even a (somewhat scurrilous) novel, *The World As I Found It* by Bruce Duffy in which Wittgenstein is the main character.

So this plethora of recent studies, added to an earlier torrent of scholarly materials, makes it sensible to ask: Why propose to do another book on Wittgenstein? To this question, as I have said, the answer though positive is not obvious. But it is simple. In the Wittgensteinian materials that have been published to date, two of his works are generally regarded as masterpieces, standing out from the others: the superlative contribution of Wittgenstein's early period, the *Tractatus*, and the even greater achievement of his maturity, the *Philosophical Investigations*. But a consensus is growing among exegetes that a third work must be added to this pair, namely, *On Certainty*. Yet this work has not received the intensive scholarly treatment it deserves.

Some of the books I have referred to above, for example, Oswald Hanfling's excellent *Wittgenstein's Later Philosophy*, devote some space to *On Certainty* (a whole chapter in Hanfling's case), but in general their focus is elsewhere. More important, they tend to interpret *On Certainty* in the light of Wittgenstein's approach in the *Investigations*, thus minimizing the originality of the later work. Moreover, when contrasted with the flood of treatises on the *Tractatus* and the *Investigations* the studies devoted to *On Certainty* are surprisingly few, though growing in number. These fall into two groups, separated by nearly a decade of silence. There were five books in what might be called an extended first phase, or those published between 1971 and 1981: *Intentionality and Knowledge: Studies in the Philosophy of G.E. Moore and Ludwig Wittgenstein* by Helge Malgren, 1971; *Certainty: A Discussion of Wittgenstein's Notes in On Certainty* by Carolyn Wilde, 1976; *Paradoxes of Knowledge* by Elizabeth Wolgast, 1977; *Wittgenstein and Knowledge* by Thomas Morawetz, 1978; and *On Doubting the Reality of Reality:*

Moore and Wittgenstein on Sceptical Doubts by Gunnar Svensson, 1981. This brief, concentrated flurry stopped suddenly, and no books on the Wittgenstein opus appeared until 1989 when *Sense and Certainty* by Marie McGinn and *Wittgenstein On Foundations* by Gertrude Conway emerged.

These are both interesting contributions that attempt to grapple in new ways with some of the fundamental themes of *On Certainty*. Conway, rightly in my opinion, sees Wittgenstein as offering a new type of foundationalism, rejecting the sort of categorization of Wittgenstein as an anti-foundationalist that has received its most explicit formulation in *Philosophy and the Mirror of Nature* by Richard Rorty (1979). She appeals to many passages in *On Certainty* in support of her view, but much of the evidence derives from Wittgenstein's other writings. In effect, then, her scope is the whole Wittgensteinian corpus, beginning with the *Tractatus*. The work is thus not a study of *On Certainty* per se.

In contrast, Marie McGinn's book has exactly this concentration. McGinn argues that unlike Moore, Austin, Stroud, and Cavell, it is Wittgenstein who has provided a philosophically satisfactory rebuttal of scepticism. This essay sees deeply into the nature of scepticism and into Wittgenstein's treatment of it. Her thesis that Wittgenstein has shown why no justification that the external world exists is needed is a persuasive one and on the right track. But McGinn's approach has serious shortcomings as well, which I shall mention in a moment.

So, to date (1993), we have seen only a handful of books dedicated to *On Certainty*. To this literature we can add a small number of articles, most of them written in the past few years, whose focus is *Uber Gewissheit*. I should add, of course, that there is a staggering number of papers dealing with the relationship between Wittgenstein's views in *On Certainty* and such topics as religion, psychology, and culture; but in most of these the concentration is not upon *On Certainty* itself. Much of this literature either assumes that Wittgenstein's views are obvious and thus gives a superficial treatment of very subtle material, or simply misrepresents Wittgenstein in the course of arguing some theses of special interest to the authors, many of whom are not philosophers.

Without discussing in detail the seven specifically philosophical books I have mentioned it is difficult to make a convincing case that there is more, and indeed more of importance, to be said about *On Certainty* than we can find in the existing, specialized literature. But at least two general points can be made now in support of this judgment. First, only a handful of these materials deals with the relationship between Moore and Wittgenstein, and with the exception of Svensson's and McGinn's studies, none of them explores it *in extenso*. But even Svensson's understanding of Moore is flawed, so that the power and depth that Wittgenstein felt in Moore's treatment of the topic of certainty is not fully communicated. In most of the other writers Moore turns out to be merely a stalking horse for Wittgenstein, or the author's emphasis is upon the differing treatments of the phrase "I know" *as this appears in propositional contexts*. McGinn's monograph is marred by both of these features. In a book of eight chapters, three are devoted to "I know," an emphasis that illustrates her belief that Wittgenstein is offering a different analysis of the status of the propositions she calls "Moore-type propositions."

What McGinn fails to see is that as *On Certainty* progresses, Wittgenstein is steadily moving away from thinking of certainty in propositional terms at all. In contrast, he is better understood as driving a wedge between the concepts of knowledge and certainty, as "arguing" in his peculiar aphoristic way that these play different roles in human intercourse. One might say that for him propositions evincing knowledge claims *belong to* the language game, whereas certainty *grounds* the language game and is a condition of its possibility. What "stands fast for us" are not propositions but deeper sorts of commitments, both to non-human reality and to the human community. As Wittgenstein puts it:

> Giving grounds, however, justifying the evidence, comes to an end; but the end is not certain propositions' striking us immediately as true, i.e., it is not a kind of *seeing* on our part; it is our *acting* which lies at the bottom of the language game.
>
> If the true is what is grounded, then the ground is not *true*, nor yet false.

(*O.C.*, 204, 205)

Wittgenstein italicizes both "seeing" and "acting" in the first passage. He does so in order to delineate certain seminal differences between the concepts of knowledge and certainty: the former is tied to proposition making and has its turf within the language game, whereas the latter is connected with action and underlies the language game. One of his constant themes, mainly a negative refrain, is that Moore conflates these notions. But the main burden of his book is to give a positive characterization of certainty that radically disassociates it from knowing, that makes it "something animal as it were" (*O.C.*, 359).

To depict Wittgenstein's discussion of "I know" as if it were limited to the propositional making uses of language is to miss the originality of his approach, which lies in the powerful alternative to any propositionally oriented way of thinking about certainty. That alternative becomes, as the book proceeds, the basis for a new diagnosis of what is wrong with scepticism and a new prescription for neutralizing it. McGinn's interpretation remains fixed at the propositional level and does not carry us to this deeper dimension. My discussion attempts to provide this shift in perspective.

The second general point is that most of the earlier literature I have referred to has the character of reworked doctoral theses. These works not only suffer from the usual defects of dissertations. They also tend to be dominated, as I have mentioned, by a treatment of *On Certainty* that sees its main ideas as an extension of those in the *Investigations*. (The latter comment is true, for instance, of Morawetz's *Wittgenstein and Knowledge*, and I suspect, though I do not know for sure, that the former comment is as well.)

A corrective is needed that represents both mature scholarship and the recognition that *On Certainty* is a highly original work, in many fundamental ways quite different from the *Investigations*. In particular, the highly therapeutic thrust of the *Investigations* is much diminished in *On Certainty*. Wittgenstein is himself caught up in relatively straightforward, classical philosophical concerns about the nature of certainty and its relationship to human knowledge. One must, of course, not go overboard in stressing this difference.

As many commentators have correctly indicated, there is considerable continuity in Wittgenstein's writings, from early to late. Thus, in the *Tractatus* we
find in 4.1272, an analysis of the sentence "There are objects" that prefigures his
discussion of entries 35–37 in *On Certainty* (see chapter 7, which deals with
those passages). Further, as I point out in chapter 6, Wittgenstein's "method" of
dealing with philosophical problems, which reached its most mature form in the
Investigations, is carried over without much change in *On Certainty*. Yet sometimes where there appears to be continuity there is difference. In 6.51 of the
Tractatus we find the following remark about scepticism: "Scepticism is not
irrefutable, but obviously senseless, when one wishes to doubt that which cannot
be questioned. For doubt can only exist where a question exists; a question only
where an answer exists, and these only where something can be said."

One might take this comment to be a prescient reference to scepticism as
that is treated some thirty years later in *On Certainty*, and to do so would not be
wholly wrong. The two treatments agree that scepticism is senseless. But the
grounds offered for this judgment differ enormously; and, in fact, the later
analysis is deeper and more sophisticated (see chapter 10 for details). So while
not denying a degree of continuity in Wittgenstein's thinking, one is still justified in saying that there are significant differences between *On Certainty* and his
earlier work, including the *Investigations*.

The simple answer, then, to the query of why another book on Wittgenstein
is that it is about time the important but comparatively underground status of
this work should be surfaced and its fundamental ideas be brought out in a way
that focuses upon the relationship between Moore and Wittgenstein; hence this
endeavor, which attempts to take some steps in those directions.

On Certainty has a dramatic history: how it came to be written in the first
place, the timing and mode of its composition, the role it plays in the Wittgensteinian corpus as a new venture, and its unfinished, probative, Socratic character. Let me briefly speak to these matters in order to justify the attention it will
receive in this book. As I pointed out earlier, Wittgenstein died in 1951, and
given the vast amount of material that the executors of his *nachlass* had to work
through it was not until 1969 that *On Certainty* was published. The fact that it
appeared so late and that so much attention was still being paid to the *Philosophical Investigations* (published in 1953) explains to a great extent why the book was
neglected until fairly recently. There is also another factor. *On Certainty* is a
running commentary on three of G.E. Moore's greatest papers, "A Defense of
Common Sense," "Proof of an External World," and "Certainty," which were
published between 1925 and 1941.

Moore, who died in 1958, was one of the most celebrated philosophers of
the pre-World War II period. But he had long since fallen out of favor by the
time *On Certainty* was published. Consequently, many scholars did not fully
grasp the importance of *On Certainty* because it can be understood only by reading it through the filter of Moore's essays, written more than a quarter of a century earlier, and this they had no interest in doing. To some degree this
situation has been reversed. Moore's status in the past four or five years has
begun to improve, and there is a greater awareness that he is a major figure in
twentieth century philosophy.

With the growing appreciation of Moore, Wittgenstein's interpretation took on a new significance; a small but growing coterie of scholars now see it as the most profound examination of Moore's contributions to epistemology. But in the process of reading *On Certainty*, they have also come to realize that there is more to *On Certainty* than merely a commentary on Moore. They now realize that it contains a novel approach to the problem of certitude and to the sceptical challenges that any defender of certitude must face. My study emphasizes this feature of the book, which makes it of direct relevance to current issues in epistemology.

That scepticism continues to bedevil contemporary philosophers is attested to by the large number of books recently devoted to this subject: Barry Stroud's *The Significance of Philosophical Scepticism* (1984), P.F. Strawson's *Skepticism and Naturalism: Some Varieties* (1985), Robert Fogelin's *Hume's Scepticism in the Treatise of Human Nature* (1985), Thomas Nagel's *The View from Nowhere* (1986), Marjorie Clay and Keith Lehrer's *Knowledge and Scepticism* (1989), Kai Nielsen's *God, Scepticism and Modernity* (1989), and Leo Groarke's *Greek Scepticism* (1990).

On Certainty differs from any of Wittgenstein's other works in the way it came to be written. In 1949, two years before his death, and before it was diagnosed that he was suffering from cancer of the prostate, Wittgenstein visited his former student, Norman Malcolm, at Cornell. Some years earlier Malcolm had written an essay, "Moore and Ordinary Language," for a volume that appeared in 1942 in the Library of Living Philosophers series, edited by P.A. Schilpp, entitled *The Philosophy of G.E. Moore*. In that essay Malcolm argued that Moore's defense of the common sense view of the world was really a defense of the ordinary employments of language as against the extended and paradoxical uses that philosophers made of these idioms.

But some seven years later Malcolm changed his mind. In a paper entitled "Defending Common Sense," he claimed that in the philosophical contexts in which he was speaking, Moore had misused the expressions "I know," "I know with certainty," "It is certain," and "I have conclusive evidence." Malcolm contended that Moore's employment of these expressions ran counter to their ordinary and correct use and gave a number of powerful arguments in support of this contention. When Wittgenstein arrived at Cornell, Malcolm read him this paper, which was soon to be published in the *Philosophical Review*.

Wittgenstein had long been interested in Moore's defense of the common sense view of the world, and according to G.E.M. Anscombe and G.H. von Wright, had told Moore that "A Defense of Common Sense" was his best paper. Wittgenstein was impressed by Malcolm's claim that Moore was misusing such expressions as "I know that" and "I know that with certainty." When he returned to England, he began to write in his characteristic, apothegmatic fashion about the correct use of these expressions and then more extensively about the topic of certainty itself. These remarks formed an autonomous collection that was later published as *On Certainty*.

Scholars find a special fascination in this collection, which in its original, unedited form can be found at the recently opened Wittgenstein archives at the University of Bergen in Norway. The material is in an untitled notebook and without numbered entries (both of which were added by the editors). The pages are lined, and one can distinguish the entries from one another because each is separated by a space of one line. The material, all handwritten, is in first draft form and unpolished, with all of the later entries dated by groups. It thus allows one to follow the progress of Wittgenstein's thought on the topic of certainty, which, in the shadow of death, occupied the last two years of his life. The progression shows a deepening sensitivity to its complexities and, unexpectedly, an increasing (though still critical) respect for Moore, the sort of respect that most of the commentators I have mentioned fail to notice.

That Wittgenstein became obsessed by the topic is clear: The last seven comments (670–676) were entered into his notebook two days before he died (April 29, 1951). *On Certainty*, which I shall discuss later, begins with the sorts of issues about Moore's use of "I know" that Malcolm had raised; the influence of Malcolm's paper on Wittgenstein is patent. For instance, in the sixth entry, Wittgenstein writes: "Now, can one enumerate what one knows (like Moore)? Straight off like that, I believe not—For otherwise the expression 'I know' gets misused. And through this misuse a queer and extremely important mental state seems to be revealed."

But, as I indicated above, Wittgenstein carried the issues surrounding the notion of certainty much farther than either Malcolm or Moore, and it is in the depth and originality of his inquiry that the importance of *On Certainty* lies. The outcome of that inquiry was a philosophical masterpiece comparable to the *Tractatus* and the *Philosophical Investigations*.

Let's assume that we have made a reasonable case for writing another book about Wittgenstein. We now face the questions: Then why a book that is almost equally about Moore? Why not deemphasize Moore, referring to him only where necessary, and concentrate on Wittgenstein, patently the greater figure? To these queries a compelling response is more difficult, but I believe the case can be made. A little history will help us see how.

I have mentioned that *On Certainty* is a running commentary on three of Moore's essays. Moore lived for another seven years after Wittgenstein had inserted its final seven entries, but Moore probably never saw it. It lay unedited, buried in the huge Wittgensteinian *nachlass* until the late 1960s. Apart from his interest in the conceptual issues those papers raised, Wittgenstein might well have had another motive for writing about Moore. In the 1930s Moore had written an extensive, highly critical commentary on a set of lectures Wittgenstein had given shortly after his return to Cambridge, and Wittgenstein might have used *On Certainty* to respond to them. That commentary, entitled "Wittgenstein's Lectures in 1930–33," was included in Moore's *Philosophical Papers*, posthumously published in 1959.

The period 1930–1933 represented a transitional epoch in Wittgenstein's philosophical development. At the time he was struggling to create a new method for dealing with philosophical problems. In these lectures the nature of philosophical activity was thus a dominant issue; it had also been, of course, a central theme in the *Tractatus*. In the Tractarian view philosophy has nothing to do with the natural sciences. Scientific activity issues in significant sentences about the world, but philosophical activity does not. Philosophical pronouncements say nothing: they are "pseudo-propositions," or utterances that appear to be significant propositions but are "senseless" (*Sinnlos*). Wittgenstein was repeatedly to return to the issue about the nature of philosophy; it is a dominant theme even in his final writings. From the *Tractatus* on, the issue turned on the question of how philosophical *utterances* were to be construed. Were they covert necessary statements, to be analyzed as if they were types of logical or even mathematical propositions? This was not implausible since Wittgenstein at that time held that such logical and mathematical statements said nothing. Or did they have a different status, and if so, what was it?

Moore's commentary, of monograph length, not only described Wittgenstein's various conjectures in this connection but dealt with them critically, showing in detail and with compelling logical force that his thinking was confused on many of these matters. Moore even wrote a short paper, which he gave to Wittgenstein, summarizing some of his objections; so Wittgenstein was well aware of the difficulties Moore had detected. In *On Certainty*, Wittgenstein returns to the problem. He still describes philosophical pronouncements, including some of those made by Moore in his three papers, as "senseless." But he no longer calls them "pseudo-propositions." Now he characterizes them as "grammatical rules" (a notion he had first proposed in the lectures of the 1930s), but meaning by this locution something new—what he calls "pieces of instruction." In *On Certainty* they are analyzed as "senseless" for reasons that differ from those he had offered earlier. His discussion of Moore can thus be regarded as a delayed response to Moore's earlier objections. Their differing approaches to the nature of philosophical practice are both instructive and interesting, and Moore's contribution to the debate cannot be ignored.

In addition, as I said earlier, Moore was regarded as one of the foremost philosophers of his time, though as we shall see he also had his detractors. In any case, it is no accident that the Library of Living Philosophers series published a volume on Moore before commissioning such a tribute to Russell. And it never published a work on Wittgenstein, an omission that in hindsight is difficult to explain but that at the time might have been justified by the paucity of material Wittgenstein himself had published. But the esteem in which Moore was generally held in the first half of the century was not misplaced. At the beginning of the century, in what was to be the philosophically significant year 1903, Moore wrote a book and a paper that revolutionized twentieth century thought in two of its main fields: ethics and epistemology.

The book was *Principia Ethica*, which via its diagnosis of the so-called naturalistic fallacy vigorously defended the autonomy of ethics, that is, the non-reducibility of ethics to any scientific or naturalistic conception. *Principia* had an enormous influence not only on philosophers but on intellectuals in general, in particular on the members of the Bloomsbury group—Virginia Woolf, Lytton Strachey, John Maynard Keynes, and others—who spoke of it as having transformed their lives.

Tom Regan has argued in his *Bloomsbury's Prophet* (1986) that the Bloomsberries, as they were known, saw in *Principia Ethica* a philosophy emphasizing liberation of the individual and rejecting a life led in conformity with the rules of conventional morality. To interpret *Principia* as conveying this message has struck many scholars as misguided, but Regan defended their interpretation as accurate. Whether Regan is right in his own reading of Moore is a complex question. The issue has been carefully and judiciously analyzed in a paper by Ray Perkins Jr., entitled "Moore's Moral Rules," that appeared in the *Journal of the History of Philosophy* (October 1990, No. 4, pp. 595–599).

Whether the Bloomsberries understood Moore is also a debatable issue. But that they were "liberated" by the standards of their time is not, a point that is well documented in the spate of recent books about them by Edel, Levy, and Skidelsky. Strachey and Duncan Grant were lovers. Grant abandoned Strachey for Keynes and then rejected him for Vanessa Bell, Virginia Woolf's sister, who had herself broken off an extramarital affair with Roger Fry to join Grant. Both within the groves of academe and without, Moore's book was a bombshell, and its powerful effect on moral philosophy has lasted to the present time. For example, in a lengthy essay on the history of moral philosophy in this century entitled "Toward *Fin de siècle* Ethics" that appeared in *Philosophical Review* (Vol. 101, 1992), co-authors Stephen Darwall, Allan Gibbard, and Peter Railton said:

> The *Philosophical Review* is a century old; so too—nearly enough—is a certain controversy in moral philosophy, a controversy initiated by G.E. Moore's *Principia Ethica*. Both centenarians are still full of life. (p. 115)

And:

> Why, then, isn't Moore's argument a mere period piece? However readily we now reject as antiquated his views in semantics and epistemology, it seems impossible to deny that Moore was on to something. (p. 116)

While Darwall, Gibbard, and Railton rightly see Moore as of central importance in twentieth-century ethics, their views about his contributions in the areas of "semantics and epistemology" are less well considered. To a great extent the first five chapters of my book, which focus on Moore's epistemological writings, are designed to show why they, like those in moral philosophy, are still of current significance. We can start with Moore's famous paper of 1903, "The Refutation of Idealism," whose impact was at least as great as that of *Principia Ethica*.

Before this paper was written the prevailing mode of philosophy both on the Continent and in the English-speaking world was idealism, a complex philosophy taking many different forms, some post-Kantian, some post-Hegelian, but all of them having in common the notion that reality was ultimately mental. Moore's refutation was of the form of subjective idealism that derived from Bishop Berkeley and that rested on the idea that to be is to be perceived. Moore's criticism of the notion that *esse is percipi* was devastating.

Idealism, in that form, has more or less vanished from the Western philosophical scene as a result of his critique. Moore had himself been an idealist as a young philosopher at Cambridge, so the essay represents a radical break with deep past commitments. Under Moore's influence, Russell also abandoned idealism. In place of it Moore substituted a tough-minded, realistic philosophy which maintained that various kinds of things exist independently of being perceived.

Moore called these things "material objects," or "physical objects," and distinguished them from *mental* entities (such as ideas, after-images, and desires) whose existence does depend on their being perceived. In time he buttressed this form of realism by his defense of common sense, though, of course, the two conceptions are not identical: one can be an epistemological realist without being a defender of the common sense view of the world. Many contemporary philosophers of science exemplify the distinction. They hold that there are mind-independent objects but also that common sense must be supplemented by the findings of science or even discarded entirely in arriving at a true theory about the nature of reality.

Beyond these contributions, Moore made a number of major philosophical discoveries for which he is not always given sufficient credit. The distinction between asserting and expressing which is found in his little book *Ethics* (1912), became one of the basic ideas that led to speech act theory in the work of J.L. Austin just after World War II. Austin's "Other Minds" and *How to Do Things with Words* were followed in 1961 by John Searle's *Speech Acts*, in 1984 by A.P. Martinich's *Communication and Reference*, and in 1989 by Paul Grice's *Studies in the Way of Words*.

Moore's original insight thus spawned a virtual industry in philosophy and linguistics that is still with us. What is called *Moore's Paradox* is exhibited by a sentence like "Smith left the room but I don't believe it," an oddity that Moore first discovered and that, when exploited by others, generated another continuing enterprise in the philosophy of language—presupposition theory. The paradox is not a formal contradiction but involves some sort of tension or incompatibility between what is presupposed as background information when a statement is made and what is explicitly asserted by the statement.

Moore first discussed this paradox in a paper he read to the Cambridge Moral Sciences Club in 1944. Wittgenstein was at the talk and wrote to Moore the following day, saying that Moore had made a philosophically important "discovery" to the effect that contradiction "isn't the *only* logically inadmissible form." The more general notion of *philosophical paradox* that Wittgenstein himself and such Wittgensteinians as J.T. Wisdom, O.K. Bouwsma, Norman Malcolm, Alice Ambrose, and Morris Lazerowitz later made so much of probably appeared first in Moore's "A Defense of Common Sense." One could add more to this distinguished list of contributions. Much that Moore touched turned to philosophical gold either in his hands or in those of individuals he influenced.

In the light of these achievements why should there be a question about giving virtually equal time to Moore in this book?

The fact is, as I remarked earlier, that even before his death in 1958 Moore's reputation had been eclipsed; except for a few acolytes who continued to treat him as an important figure, his work in epistemology was no longer widely discussed. Why was this so? And was such neglect justified? At least one recent commentator has said yes. In *G.E. Moore* (1990) Thomas Baldwin contends that Moore's final papers "end in failure" and that his "failure is symptomatic of his persistent unwillingness to address directly epistemological implications of his philosophy of perception" (268–269). I will argue against that judgment, but first let us see what factors led to the decline in his reputation.

Part of the answer, of course, is that philosophical fashions and reputations tend to fade once a thinker has died. This is true of most of the "giants" of twentieth-century philosophy. Over a thirty-year period, beginning in 1939, the Library of Living Philosophers series published thirteen books about the most illustrious philosophers of the era. Yet Dewey, Santayana, Whitehead, Cassirer, Jaspers, Broad, C.I. Lewis, and Sarvepalli Radhakrishnan are hardly discussed today. Even Russell, the author of some eighty books and the co-author of one of the great achievements of modern logic, *Principia Mathematica*, is now mostly referred to only in connection with the theory of descriptions. So after nearly a half century as a leader in the field, it was not surprising that Moore suffered the same fate as some of his distinguished contemporaries.

But there are several other reasons as well. A pervasive criticism of Moore even before World War II, and certainly afterward, was that much of his work was either trivial or inconclusive. Rudolf Metz complained:

> Though we may call Moore the greatest, acutest, and most skilful questioner of modern philosophy, we must add that he is an extremely weak and unsatisfying answerer. When questioning is excessively luxuriant, answering must naturally be scanty. Solutions and results are hardly to be expected from Moore, and if they occasionally appear, they are only like crumbs that fall from the master's table. (quoted by Susan Stebbing in *The Philosophy of G.E. Moore*, 521)

The triviality issue was also non-trivial. For example, after sixty pages of ana-lyzing Russell's theory of descriptions in the Russell volume of the Library of Living Philosophers series, Moore arrived at the judgment that Russell's analysis of such a proposition as "Scott is the author of *Waverley*" was wrong. According to Russell, this sentence means the same as "Exactly one person wrote *Waverley* and that person was identical with Scott."

Moore's subtle linguistic sense led him to the conclusion that a person could be the author of a book without having written it, for that person might have dictated it. Therefore, since Russell claimed that to be an author entails having *written* the work in question, Russell was mistaken. The theory of descriptions that Frank Ramsey in the 1920s called "that paradigm of philosophy" has been on center stage for nearly one hundred years. It is probably the single most important contribution to analytical philosophy in this century. By comparison with the brilliant work that has been done on this theory, it seemed that Moore's welter of words had produced a conceptual gnat.

In addition, readers found that Moore's obsessive concern with accuracy of statement led to a complicated writing style that was tortuous to read. Some blamed this on Moore's so-called analytic method. No philosopher before Moore had so carefully examined what others had said, drew such fine distinc-tions, and wrote such painstakingly careful papers.

Here's an example of Moore at the height of his most excruciating analytical exactness. He is responding to a criticism by O.K. Bouwsma:

> Immediately after giving this description which is analogous to the descrip-tion I gave, Mr. Bouwsma (p. 206) makes an assertion which has puzzled me very much. He asserts: "Professor Moore says there is something about which you

first feel sure and then about which you doubt." I think he must mean that in describing the object which I say the reader will be able to pick out, I imply that the reader will first feel sure of something and then feel doubtful of the very same thing. But *what* is the thing which Mr. Bouwsma thinks I imply that the reader will first feel sure of and then doubt? I *do* imply that the reader will feel sure, with regard to some object which he is seeing, that it is *natural* to take that object to be identical with a part of the surface of his right hand; since I imply that he will *see* it to be natural to do this, and to say that he will *see* this is to say that he will feel sure of it. But this, that it is *natural* to take that object to be thus identical, is a thing which I don't imply that he will ever feel doubt about: what I imply that he will feel doubt about is the very different proposition that the object in question *is* identical with part of the surface of his right hand. If, therefore, Mr. Bouwsma thinks I imply that the reader will ever doubt that it is *natural* to take this object to be identical with part of the surface of his right hand, he is making a sheer mistake as to what I imply. But I do not think that he is making *this* mistake. I *think* he means that I imply that the reader will at first feel sure of the very thing which I *do* imply that he will subsequently doubt of—namely that the object in question *is* identical with part of the surface of his hand. But do I imply this? Why does Mr. Bouwsma think I do? I *think* that the reason he thinks so is as follows. He thinks I imply that the reader will feel sure, with regard to an object which he is seeing, and which is in fact part of the surface of his hand, that it *is* part of the surface of his hand. And I *think* I do imply this. (*The Philosophy of G.E. Moore*, 633–634)

But apart from the factors I have mentioned, there is one overwhelmingly important reason for the decline in Moore's reputation: his adherence to sense-data theory. Under the powerful assaults of such writers as G.A. Paul, W.H.F. Barnes, and J.L. Austin, sense-data theory lost its grip on epistemology, and with its disappearance there was concomitantly a loss of interest in Moore's papers. Moore himself never abandoned the theory. His last paper, published in 1957, a year before he died, was called "Visual Sense-Data." But it, like the theory itself, was a fading echo of past concerns.

What then is responsible for the recrudescence in Moore's reputation? I think there are two factors, and chapter 3 will expatiate on these. First, in contrast to the rampant scientism in philosophy today, typified by Quine's naturalized epistemology, which holds that philosophy is just an extension of science, or even more radical variants that deny it any descriptive validity whatever, Moore presents a powerful defense of the autonomy of philosophy as capable of giving us a true description of the world.

Moreover, the common sense view of the world, *as he depicts it*, has the feature that it is not open to revision by science. Indeed, the position Moore espouses implies that this pre-technical, pre-scientific outlook, which nearly all of us share, is deeper, more primitive, conceptually prior to, and the basis for the refined and regimented descriptions of reality that science and mathematics provide. Accordingly, whatever science tells us about the world must be compatible with the common sense view. Moore's papers thus give us a different picture of the world, one that is both familiar and compelling. A simple example of a proposition that is part of the common sense view is *people die*. This is a proposition virtually every adult knows to be true, but it is not one belonging to any science. One might say that it stands in a presupposition relation to such sciences as biology and medicine. It is not something scientists *merely assume* as a hypothesis; rather they, like everybody else, *know* it to be true. But presupposing it, they may ask such questions as, How and why do people die? Such questions and their answers belong to science; but those answers must be consistent with the knowledge that people do die. No scientific theory that denied such a proposition is acceptable; and that, in effect, is what it means to say that the common sense view is not open to scientific revision. A larger, indefinite list of such propositions is what Moore meant by the common sense view of the world. In a somewhat different vocabulary a similar characterization is found in Wittgenstein's *On Certainty*. Although neither of them denigrates science, they are saying something enormously important: here is an *autonomous* picture of the world, a product of philosophical inquiry. This is one reason Moore's "deep epistemology," when contrasted with the pervasive scientism I have mentioned, is worth exploring in further detail in this study.

Second, in Moore's writings on certainty we find one of the two major contemporary alternatives to what is today the most commonly received theory of knowledge—a theory that received an explicit formulation in Hume and has been widely accepted since. According to this "official theory" all knowledge claims are expressible as propositions that fall into two categories which are *exclusive* and *exhaustive*. These terms mean that no proposition can be a member of both categories and that the two categories, taken in conjuction, include all possible knowledge claims. We thus have a synoptic theory covering all possible cases. One complication in describing the theory is exactly how each category is to be defined or characterized.

Historically, there have been different names and frequently different conceptions associated with each category. For instance, Hume himself distinguished between propositions expressing a relationship of ideas to one another and propositions about matters of fact. In Leibniz we find a related, though different, distinction, between necessary and contingent propositions. Kant discriminated between analytic and synthetic propositions. Both Kant and Hume distinguished a priori propositions from those that are a posteriori.

In the twentieth century we find philosophers employing all of the above plus other discriminations—L-determinate propositions from F-determinate, tautologies from significant statements, and so on. In a longer essay, each of these different pairs would have to be distinguished from one another. For instance, to say that a proposition is necessary is not identical to saying that it is analytic. To say the former is to say that the proposition holds (is true) in all possible worlds; to say the latter is to say that the predicate term is part of the meaning of the subject term and in that sense gives us a (partial) analysis of the meaning of the subject term. Some philosophers have maintained that "Every event has a cause" is necessary because it holds in all possible worlds, but that it is not analytic because "being caused" is not part of the meaning of "event." Some propositions, however, are both analytic and necessary, for instance, "All husbands are married." It is necessary because it is true in all possible worlds, and it is analytic because "being married" is part of the meaning of "being a husband." Similar differences hold between the other pairs of notions I have mentioned.

But historically, all of the propositions belonging to the a priori (necessary, analytical, L-determinate, tautology) side of the distinction have been thought to possess an important epistemological characteristic that marks them off from those belonging to the a posteriori (synthetic, contingent) side of the distinction. The characteristic is that they can be determined to be true without reference to experience. The operative point can be brought out by considering how we come to establish the truth of the following propositions:

(i) All husbands are married.

(ii) Before 1930 all new Model-T Fords were black.

It is clear at some relevant time in the past we could have determined whether (ii) is true only by an appeal to experience, that is, by examining the automobiles in question or by checking the records of the Ford Motor Car Company. The point is that in order to determine the truth of (ii) some research into the way the world is—what records show, what an observation of cars reveals, and so on—would have been requisite; it is not enough merely to have understood the proposition. This is what it means to say that (ii) is a posteriori, namely, that its truth can be ascertained only *after* some resort to experience. This proposition also has the feature that it might have been false: One can imagine that the Ford Motor Car Company made some experimental cars in other colors that it did not sell to the public.

So to say that (ii) might have been false is equivalent to saying that it is not a necessary truth, since there are describable circumstances in which it might not have been true. But now let us contrast (ii) with (i). We can tell without any research into the nature of the world that (i) is true. We know this *prior* to any sort of research into the facts of the matter. All we have to do is understand the proposition and we can *see* that it is true. Moreover, it is not merely true; it is necessarily true. For it is impossible to imagine or describe any circumstances in which, as those terms are customarily used, someone could be a husband without being married. So (i) is both a priori and necessary.

Now Hume and some subsequent philosophers saw this exclusive-exhaustive division, however it was expressed, as having important and highly paradoxical implications for the theory of knowledge. They contended that propositions belonging to the category of the a posteriori (synthetic, contingent, etc.) *were never certain*, and they bolstered this inference with the argument that all such propositions could be determined to be true only on the basis of past experience. And since past experience, being only a sample of all experience, might turn out in the light of future happenings to have been unreliable, such propositions could never be certain. At most they could be known to be true with some degree of probability.

In contrast, a priori (analytic, necessary, tautological) propositions are certain. To say that they are "certain" entails that they hold in all possible circumstances, so that no future experience can run counter to them; and this, in turn, entails that a person asserting them cannot be mistaken. But such certitude produced no information about the world; it was a product of the special, usually definitional, relationships holding between the terms in a proposition. From the truth of the sentence "All giants are tall," it does not follow that there are giants. Or as Wittgenstein pointed out, one who knows that it will either rain or not rain knows nothing about the weather. Such propositions thus provide information about conceptual relationships, not about matters of fact. Accordingly, this Humean analysis issued in a paradox about knowledge, namely, that insofar as propositions were descriptive of the world they could never be certain; and insofar as they were certain they were devoid of information about the world. The theory thus supported a kind of scepticism since it maintained that one could never have information about the world that was certain.

In the twentieth century this Humean theory has had two major challenges, both having important implications for epistemology. In "Two Dogmas of Empiricism" (1950), W.V. Quine rejected the claim that the propositions falling into these two categories differ in kind—that is, that one was dealing with an exclusive distinction. He argued that the difference between so-called synthetic propositions and so-called analytic propositions is not a difference of *kind* but a difference of *degree*. Analytic propositions are those that can be constructed from uninterpreted logical laws by substituting synonyms for the logical constants that occur in those formulas. But synonymity itself is a matter of degree, so that the supposed contrast between these two categories of propositions is not one of kind. According to Quine, all propositions, whether analytic or synthetic, are in principle susceptible to modification or even rejection in the light of future experience; they merely differ in the degree of their susceptibility to such changes. For example, the basic laws of physics are less susceptible to revision than scientific conjectures or hypotheses, but in principle (depending on the evidence) any proposition may be given up or altered. It seems a straight implication from such an analysis that there is no such thing as absolute certainty, since any p that is certain will hold come what may.

Despite this approach to the analytic-synthetic distinction, Quine does not at first glance appear to be a sceptic. By "knowledge" he means those bits of information that are the products of scientific inquiry at some specific historical stage, so unlike the sceptic he cannot be interpreted as holding that knowledge does not exist. Yet this initial impression is misleading in my judgment since his position does entail a rejection of certitude. In effect, Quine is offering a "persuasive definition" of "knowledge"—that is, recommending that any conception of knowledge which ties certitude to knowledge should be abandoned. Therefore, when assessed from the standpoint of the classical debate between sceptics and their opponents, his denial of certitude seems to place him with the sceptics, and as we shall see, in considerable opposition to Moore. I conclude that his challenge to the traditional interpretation of the analytic-synthetic distinction separates him from the Humean tradition in one sense but unites him with it in another.

But Moore's challenge was of a completely different order. He thought, unlike Quine, that the traditional distinction between contingent and non-contingent (synthetic/analytic) propositions was defensible. What he denied in "A Defense of Common Sense," "Proof of an External World," and "Certainty" was that contingent propositions could not be known to be true with absolute certainty. Indeed, Moore asserted the exact opposite—for instance, that he knew the propositions "I am a human being" (said about himself) and "The earth has existed for many years past" to be true with certainty.

Though Moore does not say explicitly that Hume is his target, in effect he was issuing a profound challenge to the official theory deriving from his eighteenth-century predecessor and, of course, to its sceptical underpinnings. That Moore had made such statements is well known, but why he made them is less known. The answer, I believe, has to do with a special strategy he developed for dealing with scepticism. It is this second feature that makes Moore of contemporary interest. That, at least in part, is why we shall be exploring his views in the chapters that follow. But it also provides an additional reason for explaining why almost as much of this book is about Moore as it is about Wittgenstein.

2

Is There Such a Thing As Certainty?

Under the heading "Shaking Us Up" there appeared in the *Los Angeles Times* of June 18, 1988 the following editorial:

> Among the many surprises that the 20th century has produced is the discovery that there is no certainty—not even in mathematics. From the time of the ancient Greeks until 1931 it had been assumed that mathematics, a purely logical system based on self-evident axioms, was as solid as anything could be. Mathematics was taken as the epitome of thought and as a model for what thinking should be. At the turn of this century the great number theorist David Hilbert declared, "In mathematics there is no *ignorabimus*. . . . We *must* know, we *will* know."
>
> Boy, was he wrong. Thirty years later Kurt Goedel made one of the most amazing and unsettling discoveries in history. He showed that any formal system, like mathematics, contains true statements that cannot be proved and other statements whose truth cannot be decided. Goedel's incompleteness theorem showed that it is impossible *in principle* to know everything.
>
> Now comes Gregory J. Chaitin of the IBM Thomas J. Watson Research Center in Yorktown Heights, N.Y., who has taken Goedel's work one step further. In an article in the July issue of *Scientific American* titled "Randomness in Arithmetic," Chaitin writes, "I have shown that there is randomness in the branch of pure mathematics known as number theory. My work indicates that—to borrow Einstein's metaphor—God sometimes plays dice with whole numbers!"
>
> In other words, anyone who thought that Goedel's theorem applied only to the fringes and unimportant areas of mathematics was wrong. The numbers themselves—the most fundamental and self-evident area of mathematics—are not safe. "Incompleteness and randomness are natural and pervasive," Chaitin says. . . . reading Chaitin's article makes the world shake just a little. It is a reminder that things are never quite as they seem.

The writer of the editorial is correct in his or her assessment of the significance of the Goedel theorem for formal systems, but philosophers and no doubt many others would indeed be "shaken up" to hear that it has been discovered that "there is no certainty," and especially to hear that this remarkable achieve-

20

ment was first accomplished in the twentieth century. Since this book is all about certainty, we had better consider carefully what the writer is claiming; if the editorial is right, there will be nothing for us to write about or to describe. Still, before we give up the ghost both the editorial writer and Chaitin say some reassuring things. Note that both of them seem assured—we might even say they speak as if they are absolutely certain—there is no certainty. For example, in commenting on Hilbert's remark that "We *must* know, we *will* know," the editorial writer says, "Boy, was he wrong." And Chaitin is quoted as saying, "I have shown that there is randomness in the branch of pure mathematics known as number theory." To *assert*, as the editorial writer does, that Hilbert is wrong and to *assert*, as Chaitin does, that he has *shown* such and such surely implies that each speaker is certain about what he or she is averring. So it is not implausible to suggest that their practice contradicts the very thesis they are advancing.

There is a second feature of the editorial worth commenting on. Its author seems to believe that the issue of whether there is such a thing as certainty turns on the question of whether it is possible to know *everything*. As the writer indicates, "Goedel's incompleteness theorem showed that it is impossible *in principle* to know everything." If it is true that some things cannot be known, it follows that not everything can be known. But historically speaking, the matter of whether everything can be known has not been a central concern of philosophers. That it has been *a* concern is, of course, well known. It is the sort of issue sometimes discussed in the philosophy of religion, for example. Some theorists in that field have held it to be impious to claim that anyone other than God could know everything. But it is dubious that anyone in the philosophy of religion has produced a proof to that effect as elegant or as convincing as Goedel's.

Of course, whether there is such a thing as certainty has been a central philosophical concern, but the emphasis has been different from that indicated by the editorial writer in several respects. For instance, there is a barrage of arguments, traceable at least to the famous sceptic Pyrrho of Elis (360–270 B.C.), whose import is that certainty by human beings is unattainable. Given this hoary tradition, philosophers would find it peculiar to hear that it is a twentieth-century discovery that there is no certainty. Moreover, this sceptical tradition does not challenge persons to prove that everything can be known with certitude; indeed, it poses a stronger challenge. It demands that it be demonstrated that at least something, even one thing, is certain. The central epistemological tradition of the West has understood the challenge in this way. Those who have taken up the gauntlet, believing certitude to be possible, have tried to show that *something* (but surely not everything) is incontestably beyond doubt. Descartes is a good example. His famous *cogito* ("I think, therefore I am") is a paradigm of the sort of principle for which philosophers have searched, a principle that could be relied on come what may. Descartes believed that such a principle, in this case the *cogito*, would provide the basis or the foundation for an entire structure of other knowledge claims—for example, that there is an external world, that there are other minds, that there is a God, and so forth. He was convinced that without a secure foundation the entire scaffolding of knowledge would collapse.

Descartes is hardly unique. Though the sceptical tradition in various forms continues today to be a viable option for many thinkers, many other philosophers, past and present, have believed or now believe that certitude is attainable. That so-called dogmatic tradition is probably even older than its sceptical rival, since scepticism is essentially a reactive attitude following upon what are judged to be insupportable claims to knowledge. The most famous ancient dogmatic view of the kind in question is found in Plato's *Republic*. Plato believed that a highly trained, carefully selected few might acquire knowledge, and he described the sorts of conditions that would have to be satisfied for this to be so. As we shall see in later chapters, the meaning of "knowledge" that Plato was working with is still considered the correct or ordinary sense of that term, or at least closely to approximate it. According to Plato, a person, A, can correctly be said to know that p if and only if (i) p is true, (ii) it is impossible for A to be mistaken, and (iii) A has the "right sort" of supporting reasons for p. These three conditions, especially the second, connect knowledge with certainty. One implication following from this usage is that if A claims to know that p and is found to be mistaken, A will have to withdraw the claim to know. This is the sense of "know" that Descartes was employing, and it is the sense that many contemporary philosophers also accept. Wittgenstein encapsulates the whole tradition in a characteristically concise passage: "For 'I know' seems to describe a state of affairs which guarantees what is known, guarantees it as a fact. One always forgets the expression 'I thought I knew'" (*O.C.*, 12).

This tradition, whose proponents hold that certitude is possible, unquestionably constitutes the mainstream of Western epistemology. Scepticism, despite its importance, is seen from this perspective as derivative or parasitic. Furthermore, it is thought to be counter-intuitive on the ground that it is obvious that we do possess knowledge, indeed plenty of it. Yet even in this camp scepticism is seen to have a point. It gets its importance in two ways: first, by forcing dogmatists to face certain awkward, paradoxical, or unforeseen implications of the conception they are working with; and, second—and more important—by forcing them to sharpen their arguments in support of the position that certitude is not only attainable but is in hand. The latter has turned out to be an exceedingly difficult task whose best efforts are frequently undermined by clever sceptics. Since time immemorial the battle between these competing factions has seemed to many to be irresolvable, given the apparently endless capacity by each side to mount new and powerful assaults upon the other. Since antiquity some writers have used this conceptual deadlock itself as an argument in favor of scepticism. As Sextus Empiricus put it in the third century A.D., "To every argument investigated by me which establishes a point dogmatically, it seems to me there is opposed another argument, establishing a point dogmatically, which is equal to the first in respect of credibility and incredibility." Benson Mates echoed Sextus in 1981. Here is what he said in defense of a version of scepticism: "The scepticism expressed in the following essays goes beyond the traditional form in certain respects. . . . it argues that the reasons given on both sides of the issue are equally good and not, as suggested in antiquity, equally bad" (*Sceptical Essays*, ix–x).

Despite such pessimistic assessments, opponents of scepticism continue the quest for certitude and believe that a resolution of the issue is possible. A good example of this approach, arriving at a conclusion opposed to that of Mates, is found in "Scepticism and Dreaming: Imploding the Demon" by Crispin Wright (*Mind*, January 1991, 87–115). Wright's conclusion, after a meticulous examination of the demon hypothesis, is that "there is actually no method of sceptically undermining our right to rely on any of our cognitive faculties using a fantasy." The debate is thus well worth studying, and to a great extent that is what this book is all about.

More specifically, our route into this battlefield is via the thought of Moore and Wittgenstein, who, as I indicated previously, expressed—though in quite different ways—the view that certitude is possible. From their perspective, as representatives of the anti-sceptical tradition that begins with Plato, the so-called twentieth-century discovery that the editorial writer refers to is perhaps not so much a discovery as a claim of a startling, counter-intuitive sort.

That the claim is startling is beyond question. The issue of certitude is not merely a technical concern, debated abstractly by philosophers, mathematicians, and other theorists. Like some philosophers, the plain man would also be surprised and shocked to hear that there is no certainty. To be sure, whether the ordinary man has a specific view about this question is perhaps debatable: he may never have thought about the issue at all. So it is hard to predict how he would repond to the question, Do you believe that there is no such thing as certainty? No doubt, the way the question was posed, the context in which it was raised, and other factors would condition the types of responses he would give. But independently of what such a person would say, we can infer from his everyday practice and from his everyday speech that he acts *as if* he believes that some things are certain. When in ordinary circumstances one says to another, "Open that door for me, please" or "The door is open, please shut it," that person is not merely supposing or assuming there is a a door there. Instead, certitude seems to be manifested by, or perhaps even embedded in, the person's actions. So if a philosopher were to say to the speaker in that context, "You don't know or can't be sure there is a door there," the ordinary man would be perplexed by the remark.

There are certain other indications in what I have called this *as if* way that support the notion that the ordinary man would be suprised to hear there is no such thing as certainty. There is the palpable fact that the word "certain" is used in everyday discourse, along with many cognates, equivalents, and grammatical variants; and it would be exceedingly odd if this set of locutions had no application—that is, that nothing corresponds to these idioms—so that they are literally empty of content. The alternatives to the supposition that the word "certain" does have application to mental states, actions, and even features of the world would be the notions that persons do not really mean what they say or that what they say is never to be taken literally or that they are simply confused since there is no such thing as certitude, and so forth. Philosophers have, to be sure, argued for each of these theses, but they are prima facie counter-intuitive and less persuasive than the simple suggestion that since most people use words like "certainty" there must be something that corresponds in human life to that locution and its congeners.

But, of course, the sceptics have known these things all along. They have known that most persons do not doubt the existence of chairs and doors as they go about their daily rounds, and they have known that such avowals as "I feel certain that" or even such stronger utterances as "It is certain that" and "There is no doubt that" are frequently employed in everyday speech; and yet these features of common life have not produced in the sceptic's the conviction that there is such a thing as certainty.

The acknowledgment that many philosophers have not been convinced by facts such as these raises a serious methodological question about our inquiry in this book. What would it take to produce such conviction? That is, what sort of evidence or proof would one have to produce to convince these doubters that there is such a thing as certitude? In raising this question, we face a highly paradoxical situation. It is a common conception about philosophy that its essence is argument. That is, it is commonly supposed that a philosopher is someone who provides reasons in support of some thesis or proposition he or she is asserting. The process of providing such reasons is argumentation; and it is considered to be the task of the philosopher to argue a case rationally—that is, to give cogent reasons for a position one adopts.

But it is this view of philosophy that leads to a paradox with respect to our subject here. If the sceptic is right and there is no such thing as certainty, then there can be no such thing as a proof to the contrary, and it would be fruitless to attempt to find one. But why should this be so? The matter is complex and turns on the relationship between knowledge and certitude. These are often not distinguished. A glance at the quotations just cited from Sextus Empiricus and Benson Mates reveals that they put the sceptical challenge in terms that mention neither knowledge nor certainty. Sextus speaks about arguments that "establish a point dogmatically" and about such arguments being "credible" or "incredible," and Mates talks about "the reasons given on both sides as being equally good."

These writers seem in different ways to be suggesting that it makes no difference whether it is the existence of knowledge or the existence of certainty that is being denied. Other writers have even more explicitly conflated knowledge and certainty, asserting that A knows that p is equivalent to saying that A knows that p with certainty—the Platonic definition above comes close to suggesting this equipollence. Yet other writers—Moore, for instance—distinguish knowledge from certitude. But even Moore holds that knowing is a necessary condition for certitude; so that without somebody's knowing that p it is not the case that p is certain. Wittgenstein, in contrast, regards the concepts as logically independent of one another.

Our paradox goes through on any of the above positions because a proof is not merely a valid argument; it is a valid argument whose premises are known to be true. If one holds, as Mates, Sextus, and Plato seem to, that one could without a change of meaning add to the previous sentence the words "with certainty," we could say equivalently that a valid argument is one whose premises are known to be true with certainty. So if there are no such things as knowledge or certainty, there could be no such thing as a proof. Accordingly, it would not be possible to prove the thesis that certitude exists. If that were so, how could one go about the business of confuting the sceptic? If one can't argue one's case, what other resources remain?

The dilemma faces not only a prospective dogmatist but should be troublesome to the reflective sceptic as well. As we have seen, Goedel's work culminated in a proof that there are undecidable propositions. But if he did produce a *proof* to that effect, then he advanced an argument whose premises were not merely highly probable but were known to be true with certainty. Therefore his work, contrary to what the editorial writer claims, cannot be used to support the notion that certainty is impossible. In a similar fashion, Chaitin's proof concludes that *it is certain* that numbers have an inherent randomness. But that result, even if correct, does not allow one to infer that certitude is impossible since the result itself implies that certitude exists. How then does one prove that certitude is impossible? Clearly, nothing analogous to the Goedel theorem will suffice. And in parallel fashion, one cannot prove that certitude exists without using an argument which is viciously circular, since, as a proof, it presupposes the conclusion it wishes to establish. Given the nature of this difficulty, how can one sustain the conviction that there is certitude without employing modes of reasoning whose very structure either viciously entails the conclusion or eventually begs the question?

I have emphasized this perplexing situation because it provides a useful transition for studying the approaches of Moore and Wittgenstein. Neither ever attempts to *provide an explicit argument to the effect that certainty is possible.* Though they do not mention the paradox I have described, they provide clues of varying degrees of strength that any attempt to provide such a proof would be the wrong way to proceed. In such famous papers as "A Defense of Common Sense" and "Certainty," Moore simply asserts that he knows some propositions to be true with certainty, but without in any way defending this claim. In "Proof of an External World," however, we find his one extensive discussion that bears upon the point at issue. In this essay he explains why he has not attempted to (and indeed cannot) give a proof of that claim. Here, in part, is what he says:

> How am I to prove now that "Here's one hand, and here's another"? I do not believe I can do it. In order to do it, I should need to prove for one thing, as Descartes pointed out, that I am not now dreaming. But how can I prove that I am not? I have, no doubt, conclusive reasons for asserting that I am not now dreaming; I have conclusive evidence that I am awake; but that is a very different thing from being able to prove it. I could not tell you what all my evidence is; and I should require to do this at least, in order to give you a proof. (*P.E.W.*, 148–149)

In the passage Moore draws a distinction between one's having conclusive evidence that a proposition is true and one's proving that it is true, and at the end of the essay he distinguishes between knowing certain propositions to be true and proving they are true. He says: "I can know things which I cannot prove; and among things which I certainly did know, even if (as I think) I could not prove them, were the premises of my two proofs" (150).

Moore's discussion in this essay (and indeed in some of the other essays I have alluded to) raises all sorts of exegetical and philosophical questions, some of which he never answers. How does he know that the evidence he has is conclusive without being able to tell us what it is? What is the difference, if any, between having conclusive evidence for a proposition and knowing that proposition to be true? And even more important, what is the relationship between such concepts as knowledge and certainty? Are they the same? In "Certainty" Moore does explicitly address the last question, saying: "It is, indeed, obvious, I think, that a thing can't be certain, unless it is known: this is one obvious point that distinguishes the use of the word 'certain,' from that of the word 'true; a thing that nobody knows may quite well be true, but cannot possibly be certain'" (240). He adds, "We can then say that it is a necessary condition for the truth of 'It is certain that p' that somebody should know that p is true." Moore then gives a subtle argument to show that though knowing is a necessary condition for p's being certain, it is not a sufficient condition (240), which makes it clear that for him the two concepts are not identical.

Thus, accepting Moore's thesis that the concepts are not identical and that knowing is a necessary condition for certainty, one can draw an important implication about Moore's philosophical views from his conception of this relationship. I submit that one is entitled to infer that just as Moore would say he cannot prove that he knows "Here is one hand and here is another" to be true, so would he say that he cannot prove that he knows this proposition to be true with certainty. Indeed, the whole thrust of his discussion is that no such proof is possible. Yet he insists, as we have seen, that this position is consistent both with his knowing that p is true and in being certain that p is true. We thus have strong reasons for believing that Moore would have stated, if asked, that any attempt to prove that certitude is possible will be abortive.

Wittgenstein's last work, On Certainty (Uber Gewissheit), is a running commentary on the three previously mentioned essays by Moore; it is devoted to the concept of certainty. Yet, like Moore, Wittgenstein never provides an argument to demonstrate that certitude is possible. Instead, the book is full of comments which verge on being such arguments without reaching that degree of explicitness. For instance, Wittgenstein says: "If you tried to doubt everything you would not get as far as doubting anything. The game of doubting itself presupposes certainty" (O.C., 115). Or again, "If you are not certain of any fact, you cannot be certain of the meaning of your words either" (114).

In the following passages, Wittgenstein distinguishes between giving a proof and our being rightly convinced that a proposition is true. In the context he is discussing, such idioms as "our being rightly convinced" and "our right to assume" are roughly equivalent to "our being certain of." Thus, like Moore, he seems to hold that we can be certain of things we cannot prove.

> This is how we acquire conviction, this is called "being rightly convinced."
> So hasn't one, in this sense, a *proof* of the proposition? But that the same thing has happened again is not a proof of it; though we do say that it gives us a right to assume it. (O.C., 291–295)

Clearly, none of these apothegms, and they are typical, contains an explicit argument whose conclusion is that certainty exists. This is typical of Wittgenstein's procedure throughout *On Certainty*. It is, of course, possible to construe the set of maxims, apothegms, questions, and other literary devices he employs as being instances of non-standard modes of argumentation; and we shall indeed interpret him in such ways in later chapters. But these are interpretations of what he might have said rather than descriptions of what he did actually say. For instance, when Wittgenstein writes, "If you are not certain of any fact, you cannot be certain of the meaning of your words either," we do not have an argument proving there is certainty, though one seems to be lurking just beneath his words.

To produce such an argument one would first need to prove that one is certain of the meaning of one's words, and then it would follow that one can be certain of something—but then how would one prove that one can be certain of one's words without begging the question at issue? Nevertheless, the text makes it plain that Wittgenstein believes we can be certain of our words and, accordingly, that certainty is possible: Indeed much of *On Certainty* is devoted to an attempt to characterize its nature. Nevertheless, Wittgenstein does not argue the case. But why not? And how can he (and Moore) deal with those of a sceptical persuasion who think nothing is certain?

To answer that question, to illustrate the sorts of strategies that Moore and Wittgenstein follow—strategies that are wholly different from one another and yet have in common that they do not depend on proofs or even on explicit argumentation—is what we shall now try to show in the succeeding chapters. As our paradox evinces, and as Moore and Wittgenstein seem to sense, conventional modes of argumentation will beg the question and may suffer from other liabilities. It is surprising that the most profound and knowledgeable interpreters of Moore and Wittgenstein have not noted this peculiarity in their approaches. I believe they developed their techniques through the growing realization that scepticism could not be met by conventional modes of argumentation—that is, that there was something different about scepticism which required new approaches to it.

For Wittgenstein the challenge could be met only by the creation of a new method of doing philosophy (see chapter 6 for its description). The depth of their respective contributions to modern philosophy cannot be fully appreciated without beginning with this awareness. We can think of these strategies as new types of defenses of the idea that certitude is attainable—defenses that are designed to produce conviction without explicit argumentation. In their different ways, they each thus transformed, or at least broadened, the traditional Anglo-American conception that argumentation is the essence of philosophy. Since Moore is the twentieth-century originator of the genre, let's begin by trying to understand how and why he developed such an approach.

3

Moore

As I pointed out in chapter 1, in such papers as "A Defense of Common Sense," "Proof of an External World," and "Certainty," Moore was *in effect* challenging the received opinion that no contingent statements can be certain. I say "in effect" because he never explicitly states that he has in mind the traditional doctrine deriving from Hume. However, the caustic, at times sarcastic, way in which he speaks indicates that there is a specific theory he is opposing, a theory which he believes some philosophers have actually held and which he finds absurd. He is so emphatic in asserting a contrary view that it is difficult to resist the inference that the Humean doctrine is the target of his comments. Here, for example, is a shortened version of what he says at the beginning of "Certainty":

> I am at present, as you can all see, in a room and not in the open air; I am standing up, and not either sitting or lying down; I have clothes on, and am not absolutely naked; . . . there are a good many other people in the same room in which I am; and there are windows in that wall and a door in this one.
>
> Now I have here made a number of different assertions; and I have made these assertions quite positively, as if there were no doubt whatever that they were true. . . . By asserting them in the way I did, I *implied*, though I did not say, that they were in fact certain—implied, that is, that I myself knew for certain, in each case, that what I asserted to be the case was, at the time when I asserted it, in fact the case. And I do not think that I can be justly accused of dogmatism or over-confidence for having asserted these things positively in the way that I did. In the case of some kinds of assertions, and under some circumstances, a man can be justly accused of dogmatism for asserting something positively. But in the case of the assertions such as I made, made under the circumstances under which I made them, the charge would have been absurd. On the contrary, I should have been guilty of absurdity if, under the circumstances, I had *not* spoken positively about these things, if I spoke of them at all. Suppose that now, instead of saying "I am inside a building," I were to say "I *think* I'm inside a building, but perhaps I'm not: it's not *certain* that I am." . . . Would it not sound rather ridiculous for me now, under these circumstances, to say "I *think* I've got some clothes on" or even to say "I not only think I have, I know that it is very likely indeed that I have, but I can't be quite sure"? For some persons, under some circumstances, it

28

might not be at all absurd to express themselves thus doubtfully. . . . But for me, now, in full possession of my senses, it would be quite ridiculous to express myself in this way, because the circumstances are such as to make it quite obvious that I don't merely think that I have, but know that I have. For me now, it would be absurd to say that I *thought* I wasn't naked, because by saying this I should imply that I didn't know that I wasn't, whereas you can all see that I'm in a position to know that I'm not. But if *now* I am not guilty of dogmatism in asserting positively that I'm not naked, certainly I was not guilty of dogmatism when I asserted it positively in one of those sentences with which I began this lecture. I knew then that I had clothes on, just as I know now that I have.

Passages in the other essays make similar claims; therefore, as I have said, a strong case exists for holding that Moore had the traditional theory in mind. But whether this exegetical point is correct or not is a matter we can set aside here. There is no doubt that since the traditional view maintains that no empirical statement can be known to be true with certainty, Moore's position stands in sharp contrast to that doctrine. As I indicated in chapter 1, this is one of two theses he advanced that makes his work of contemporary interest. We must thus try to understand why he makes these claims and then later decide, if we can, whether he is right or not.

The other important thesis for contemporary philosophy is Moore's defense of the common sense view of the world. This thesis is intimately tied to the first, since Moore thinks that the propositions comprising the common sense view are both contingent and are known to be true with certainty. In particular, however, what makes Moore's version of the common sense view apposite here, as I said earlier, is that it runs counter to a highly popular outlook in contemporary analytical philosophy today; namely, the notion that with respect to our description and understanding of the world there is no such thing as certainty, even in mathematics or in logic. We have seen that this is a position taken by Chaitin, who finds randomness even in number theory; but Chaitin is a late arrival on the philosophical scene. The notion has been around for a long time, and its most famous contemporary proponents are W.V. Quine and Karl Popper. According to Quine, for instance, whatever knowledge we have or will come to have about the world is or will be based upon scientific inquiry. But science is never wholly settled, since it depends on experiment and observation; and future experiments and observations may require revisions in even the most solidly grounded existing theories about the nature of reality. In principle, then, even the best-confirmed scientific laws may ultimately have to be abandoned or revised in important ways.

One consequence which such a form of scientism has widely been thought to entail is that all forms of "folk theory" will have to be abandoned—folk psychology, folk physics, folk semantics, and so on—and among these we can include what Moore called the "common sense view of the world.

A forthright expression of this point of view is found in Paul Churchland's *Matter and Consciousness* (1988):

As the eliminative materialists see it, the one-to-one match-ups will not be found, and our common-sense psychological framework will not enjoy an intertheoretic reduction, *because our common-sense psychological framework is a false and radically misleading conception of the causes of human behavior and the nature of cognitive activity.* . . . Accordingly, we must expect that the older framework will simply be eliminated, rather than be reduced, by a matured neuroscience. (43)

I discuss folk theory and philosophy in more detail in chapter 10, where the emphasis is upon Wittgenstein's treatment of that relationship; but Moore is equally important. Since Moore contends that the common sense view is wholly true, is known to be so with certainty and is not open to revision or replacement, there is a direct conflict between these prevailing forms of scientism and Moore's outlook. Accordingly, we need to try to understand why Moore makes such claims and then try to decide whether he is right or not.

Now obviously both of the preceding theses run counter to any form of scepticism, including those mitigated or moderate forms which maintain that some propositions about the world can be determined to be true with varying degrees of likelihood, though none of them can be known to be true with certainty. We can thus add a third respect in which Moore's philosophy has a significant bearing upon the contemporary scene in which forms of relativism, probabilism, and outright scepticism are in fashion. In Moore's work we find a major philosopher who rejects all forms of scepticism. And once again we need to try to determine whether Moore is right in doing so.

In what follows, then, I shall address these three issues, beginning with what Moore means by the common sense view of the world. This view was first propounded by Moore in his Cambridge lectures of 1911, which were first published in book form in 1953 at the instigation of John Wisdom as *Some Main Problems of Philosophy*. The view was modified in important ways when Moore wrote "A Defense of Common Sense," and it is this document we shall use as containing the best and most mature version of his position. As we shall see, it will be important to distinguish—as Moore fails to do—his view in "A Defense" from that he advanced in "Certainty" some fifteen years later, although, of course, the papers have in common the doctrine that so-called contingent statements can be certain.

Moore begins "A Defense of Common Sense" by stating two propositions he knows to be true with certainty. The first consists of a heterogeneous and presumably indefinitely long list of other propositions Moore also states he knows to be true with certainty. Among these are such propositions as:

There exists at present a living human body which is *my* body. Ever since it was born it has been either in contact with or not far from the surface of the earth; and at every moment since it was born, there have also existed many other things, having shape and size in three dimensions (in the same familiar sense in which it has). . . . There have, at every moment since its birth, been large numbers of other living human bodies, each of which has, like it, (a) at some time been born, (b) continued to exist from some time after birth, (c) been, at every moment of its life after birth, either in contact with or not far from the surface of the earth; and many of these bodies have already died and ceased to exist. But the earth had existed also for many years before my body was born; and for many of these years, also, large numbers of human bodies had, at every moment, been alive upon it; and many of these bodies had died and ceased to exist before it was born.

... I am a human being, and I have, at different times since my body was born, had many different experiences, of each of many different kinds; e.g., I have often perceived both my own body and other things which formed part of its environment, including other human bodies. (33–34)

This list forms one half of the common sense view. Moore says three things about it that immediately catch the exegetical eye. First, he claims to know each of these propositions to be true with certainty, but adds that he either does not know how he knows them or at least is less sure how he knows them than that he does. We shall see that these are not casual remarks but key elements in his treatment of scepticism. Second, he calls these propositions "obvious truisms" and adds that they may seem, at first sight, not to be worth stating. The list thus differs from the list of the seven propositions he asserted at the beginning of "Certainty"; for surely those propositions cannot be described as "obvious truisms." That Moore is standing up and not sitting or lying down, and that there are windows in that wall and a door in this one, are neither obvious nor truistic. I doubt that Moore himself recognized the difference between the propositions in the two lists; but I believe the difference is important. If I am right, a distinction must be drawn between propositions that are both contingent and certain and that form part of the common sense view of the world and those that, while also being contingent and certain, do not. That is, my position is that certainty is a necessary but not a sufficient condition for a proposition's belonging to the common sense view. This distinction, which I shall expand upon later, will give us a clue as to what might be meant by the common sense view of the world.

The third striking remark Moore makes is this. Commenting on the list of propositions in "A Defense of Common Sense," he says, "they are, in fact, a set of propositions, every one of which (in my own opinion), I *know* with certainty, to be true." Why, the exegete must ask, does he add the phrase "in my own opinion" to what is otherwise a very strong statement? And why does he not add this phrase to the seven propositions he asserts at the beginning of "Certainty"? Wittgenstein, I believe, was also struck by this addendum. It led him to an interpretation of Moore according to which Moore thought that *knowing* was an internal psychological state. Such a view implied that whether one knew something or not was a matter that could be determined by introspecting one's own state of mind. Introspection would allow one to decide whether one really knew that p or, for example, merely believed that p. Wittgenstein thus portrays Moore as if Moore thought that the difference between knowing and believing was somehow a function of one's personal experience and that this difference would be immediately apparent if one looked inward, as it were. As the following passage indicates, Wittgenstein interprets Moore as confusing internal questions (those about one's own pains) with external questions (those about whether the object we are looking at is really a tree):

> Moore wanted to give an example to show that one really can *know* propositions about physical objects.—If there were a dispute whether one could have a pain in such and such a part of the body, then someone who just then had a pain in that spot might say: "I assure you, I have a pain there now." But it would sound odd if Moore had said: "I assure you, I know that's a tree." A personal experience simply has no interest for us here. (*O.C.*, 389)

Thus, according to Wittgenstein, Moore is a kind of Cartesian, locating knowing in a private realm that is accessible to its proprietor only. In *On Certainty* Wittgenstein produces a barrage of arguments, some of them familiar from the *Investigations,* to demonstrate that this conception is radically mistaken and that it gives rise to an untenable subjectivism. But it is possible that he over-reacted to Moore's use of the phrase "in my own opinion," reading too much into it (though I shall later argue that he was right). Admittedly, it is difficult to understand why Moore said what he did since nearly everything else he asserted about the common sense view made many of its component propositions objective in character and part of a public fund of knowledge. When Moore asserts, for example, that ever since he was born (he actually says "since my body was born") there have also existed many other things having shape and size in three dimensions, he is describing a truth that in no way depends upon his own opinion.

That he is generally thinking of knowing as being something objective and interpersonal is clearly brought out by the second proposition that he asserts to be part of the common sense view. Unlike his first proposition, which was composed of a host of substatements, this second statement is a single proposition, though a lengthy one. Moore's statement of it is convoluted. But to simplify we can say that this proposition maintains that very many human beings who now live or who have lived on the earth know with certainty propositions that correspond to those Moore has asserted he knows. That is, each of them knows, for instance, that since being born he or she has been in contact with or not far from the surface of the earth, that he or she knows that other persons exist, and so forth. The importance of this second principle is not only that Moore is claiming that other persons know or have known truths corresponding to those he is asserting he knows but that in many of these instances, the *content*—that is, what they all know—is the same; for instance, that the earth is very old. There is thus an objective character to the common sense view that is directly connected with what nearly everybody knows. This is why, as I have indicated, Wittgenstein's interpretation of Moore may seem at first glance to have missed the mark.

The key to understanding the common sense view and to providing a defense of it thus lies, as I see it, in identifying the special attributes that certain propositions must possess if they are to be constituents of the common sense view. As I have just pointed out, not all propositions that are both contingent and certain possess these characteristics. Our task, then, will be to identify and describe these features. In chapter 9 I shall list a number of them, but in this chapter I shall identify and describe only one: *the feature that some empirical propositions which are known to be true with certainty are such as not to be known to be true only in certain circumstances or under certain conditions.* I call this the attribute of being *circumstance-* or *context-independent.*

I shall argue that a proposition must possess this feature if it is to be a constituent of the common sense view. Let us begin by forming two lists of propositions. List I will in turn be divided into two groups of propositions, A and B. All the propositions in both groups are contingent and all are true, but only those in group B are part of the common sense view. Some of the propositions in A are of special interest to us here. By analyzing them, we can eliminate some features they possess that one might intuitively think belong to the common sense view, in particular that common sense must embody well-established scientific laws. List II will also be divided into two groups of propositions, C and D. All of the propositions in both groups are contingent, and all of them, but in different ways, can be said to be certain. Those in C, for instance, can be said to be known to be true with certainty *under certain conditions or in certain contexts*. But this cannot be said of those in D, and therefore those in D, but not those in C, are components of the common sense view. Via these two lists, then, we shall be distinguishing two ways in which the propositions comprising the common sense view differ from other contingent propositions and in so doing come to understand what I take the common sense view to be. Since Moore never sets out the defining features of the common sense view, some reconstruction of his practice is necessary here. I believe that the conception we shall arrive at is a purified and simplified version of what he had in mind.

In giving this interpretation, I shall refer to and work with Moore's use of the phrase "under certain circumstances" and with certain roughly equivalent expressions. If readers will turn back to the long quotation from "Certainty" that opens this chapter, they will notice that this phrase occurs five or six times. One of the common equivalents of "circumstance" is "condition," but the English idioms that contain these terms differ slightly. We say "*in* certain circumstances" or "*under* those conditions," but hardly ever "*under* certain circumstances," which is the phrase Moore actually uses. His ear seems to have failed him here; but the liability has no philosophical significance and we can ignore it.

Apart from that minor deviation from standard usage, Moore is otherwise using the term "circumstances" in an ordinary way. In that usage, a circumstance is a condition (and circumstances are conditions) surrounding and affecting an agent. Thus a worker who loses his or her job is forced by that happening (circumstance) to live in a reduced way. Circumstances surround and thus affect an agent (or a group of agents, such as a family). The important point for our purposes here, as we shall see, is that the surrounding circumstances are always distinguished from the agent or agents per se. Thus they are in some sense "external" to the agent. An agent thus might find himself or herself caught up in unforeseen circumstances, forced by those circumstances to do such and such, and so on. These could be any set of contingencies, for example, the weather or changes in the economy. In the analysis that follows, we shall also be using the term in this, its ordinary, sense, in which a distinction is presupposed between the agent and the conditions that affect the agent. Let us now turn to our two lists:

LIST I

Group A

1. The earth is 4.5 billion years old.
2. There exist many different kinds of things on the earth and all of them are formed from the elements mentioned in the Periodic Table.
3. I live at 1750 Valdes Drive.
4. The Investiture Contest began in the year 1111.

5. The most common reaction to continuously suppressed anger is depression.

6. $S = \frac{1}{2}gt^2$.

Group B

1. The earth is very old.
2. There exist many different kinds of things on the earth.
3. I am a human being.
4. Human beings live in various different places on the earth.
5. Human beings have feelings: At various times they are sad, elated, in pain, in love.
6. Some things existing on the earth die, and humans are among the things that die.

Before presenting List II, I shall compare and contrast the propositions in Groups A and B. As I said earlier, the two groups have in common that each proposition in each group is contingent (factual, synthetic, empirical, etc.). Of each we can say that its negation is not self-contradictory, that the propositions if true do not hold in all possible worlds, and so forth. Moreover, we can say that, in fact, each of the propositions in both lists is true. It is true, for instance, that all of the differing things that exist on the earth are formed from the elements mentioned in the Periodic Table and that the Investiture Contest began in the year 1111. The two lists also contain singular statements and general statements. It follows that if there is a special feature possessed by the propositions in B not possessed by those in A, that feature cannot be contingency, singularity or generality, or being true, since those attributes are exhibited by the propositions in both groups. We shall thus have to look elsewhere for the differentiae.

Now one important difference between the two groups is that some of the propositions in A are straightforwardly, or are in some defensible sense, scientific statements. Number (6), for instance, is the usual formulation of the law of falling bodies. Perhaps propositions (1) and (5) could be considered to be scientific propositions as well. Why would one classify them as such? A plausible response is that such propositions are the products of specialized, technical research programs. It is not part of the general fund of pre-scientific knowledge that the earth is 4.5 billion years old. This is a piece of information that has emerged as a result of the complex investigations engaged in by geologists and astrophysicists. Neither is it part of the common fund of pre-analytical knowledge that the common reaction to suppressed anger is depression. That idea is again the product of sophisticated, experimentally based inquiries by pychologists and psychiatrists. The average person comes to acquire these pieces of information not by any investigation he or she has pursued but secondhand, as it were, for example, by hearing or reading news accounts of such inquiries. Accordingly, whether such pieces of information are true or not cannot in general be determined by non-experts. Instead, they represent the best judgments of scientists, and their truth can be ascertained only by the collective judgment of such specialists.

In contrast, the propositions in Group B are not the products of specialized investigations. They can be known to be true by virtually all adults either on the basis of their own experience or on the basis of information transmitted to them by others, the "others" in these cases also being non-specialists who have themselves either acquired such information directly or indirectly. That human beings have feelings; that at various times they are sad, elated, in pain, in love, and so forth, are things known to be true with certainty and without engaging in a technical investigation. If a science were to develop, as some eliminative materialists suggest, which flatly denied that people have feelings, are or have ever been in love, and so on, such a "science" would be discredited. Here common sense is dominant. If there is a role for science in this domain, it is to add to and not subtract from that which everyone knows.

Now each of the sentences in Group B has a conceptual content that is arrived at by non-scientific, or even more generally, by non-technical investigations. Shall we say, then, that the unique feature which identifies propositions as being part of the common sense view is that they are non-scientific, or at least non-technical? The suggestion is persuasive, but it is a little too weak. What we can say is that it is a necessary but not a sufficient condition that such propositions be non-scientific or non-technical. That is, there are non-scientific, non-technical, contingent propositions that are known to be true with certainty and that, nevertheless, are not part of the common sense *weltbild*. We can see this by considering the two groups of propositions in List II. All of them, with some qualifications, are both certain and non-technical; yet we shall see that there are strong reasons for denying that those in Group C belong to the common sense view. This implies that we shall have to look still further to discover the distinguishing characteristics of those propositions that are constitutive of the common sense view. Let us now look at List II in order to make such a discrimination.

LIST II

Group C

1. I am in a room and not in the open air.
2. I am standing up.
3. There are some people in the same room as I am.
4. There are windows in that wall and a door in this one.

Group D

1. I am a human being.
2. There exists at present a living human body which is my body.
3. At every moment since it (my body) was born, there have also existed many other things, having shape and size in three dimensions.
4. There have, at every moment since its (my body's) birth, been large numbers of other living human bodies, each of which, has like it at some time been born and continued to exist for some time after its birth.

The propositions in Group C are taken from "Certainty" and those in Group D from "A Defense of Common Sense." The two groups have in common that Moore claims he knows each of these propositions to be true with certainty. But there is an importance difference: with respect to the propositions in Group C he states that he knows them to be true when asserted in the circumstances in which he did assert them. Clearly, he does not hold that in any circumstance one could with truth assert that there is a door in that wall (said while pointing to a particular wall). But he does not add such a qualification to the propositions in Group D. The fact that he does not I find significant. I submit that the truth of those propositions, given the conceptual content they express, does not depend on the circumstances in which they are made. This suggestion runs counter to some of the best-established views held by philosophers today, but I think I can defend it. If I am right, by means of this notion we can distinguish propositions that are both contingent and certain from those that are also contingent and certain and yet are part of the common sense view.

To get at what is at stake here let us take a step backward and ask: What does Moore mean by saying that the propositions in Group C are known to be true with certainty *in certain circumstances?*

Moore is not unique in holding that certitude is achievable in certain circumstances: Malcolm and Austin also make similar claims. But the supporting reasons these philosophers give often differ. Moore claims that it would be absurd in normal circumstances to qualify the assertion "I am inside a room" by such phrases as "I think" or "perhaps," that is, saying "I think I am inside a room, but perhaps I am not" or "It's likely I am inside a room, but I can't quite be sure." His point, however, is not merely that it would be *odd* to say such things in those circumstances; but it is a deeper point connected with truth. *He asserts that in adding such modifiers one would not correctly be describing the existing state of affairs* (228).

Moore is thus asseverating that certain idioms are used in the process of describing the world, and *depending on the context* these idioms either describe the world correctly or they do not. He can thus be taken to be making a semantic point as well as a pragmatic one about the oddity of the utterance. So when one says, "I think I am inside a room," that utterance, made in that context, either correctly describes a state of affairs or it does not. It can be true, for instance, even if one is not in a room but thinks one is or false if one is in a room but thinks one is not. "I know I am in a room" may also describe a state of affairs, but if it is true, then one *must* be in a room; so the two propositions have different truth conditions. Moore is thus talking about what it is true to say in certain circumstances. Hence one who says "I think that p" is depicting a different state of affairs from one who says "I know that p." If in the circumstances in which he made the assertions in Group C Moore had added the rider "I think" to those propositions, he would have been misdescribing the situations he was trying to depict. His defense of the claim that the propositions in Group C are certain is thus that, when made in the particular circumstances in which he made them, they are true descriptions of the existing state of affairs.

But now let us look at the propositions in Group D. Are they, in the same way, true *only* in certain circumstances? I submit that they are not—that, for example, the truth of the utterance "I am a human being" does not depend on the particular circumstances that prevail when one utters it. We can contrast it in that respect with a sentence like "There is a door in that wall." One can falsify "There is a door in that wall" by moving to a different room and then pointing to a wall that has no door. But one can't falsify "I am a human being" by doing something analogous to moving to a different room. One who moves to a different room, or indeed *into an entirely different environment*, is still a human being. What change in circumstances would falsify "I am a human being"? It is very difficult to say.

Suppose it were discovered that I had come from Mars and had not been born on the earth. Would that count as a change in my circumstances? Presumably it would, just as if I had been born in a barrio instead of in suburbia. But would my being born on Mars *prove* that I was not a human being? Surely not. No more than my being born in a barrio instead of in suburbia would *prove* that. But, you say, the earth is the place where humans are born, and that is why it makes no difference with respect to your humanity whether you were born in a barrio or not. But does being born on Mars make a difference in that respect? I submit that it does not. If in all other respects, including my genetic make-up, I resembled a human being, was indistinguishable from humans born in barrios, talked and acted like a human being, and so forth, it would be more sensible to conclude that some human beings come from Mars than to conclude that I am not a human being.

Suppose that like the protagonist of Kafka's *Metamorphosis* I gradually began to change into a bug-like creature. And let us suppose it were known that this change occurred because of exposure to a form of radiation but without affecting my genetic code. Would my exposure to radiation count as a change in my circumstances? Let us assume that it does. Suppose I could not speak or write as a result of this transformation. Then, in that case, I could not utter the sentence "I am a human being," and accordingly there would be nothing to disconfirm. Let us instead suppose that I could still speak, and I insisted that I am a human being despite those outward changes. What would one say about such a case? Would my utterance be false? Would it be true? My intuition is that most persons who were aware that no genetic transformation had taken place would say of me that I am human but that my appearance had been radically altered by exposure to the radiation. This sort of assessment would assimilate the case to other deformations, some of them severe, as with the Elephant Man. The fact that I could continue to speak would be strong support for this judgment.

Let's change the scenario and suppose that because there had been a radical change in my genetic constitution it was now generally agreed that I was no longer human and that a new type of animal had been created. But then what relevance would an appeal to the circumstances have in that case? Do we decide that a parrot which can say "I am a human being" is a parrot in some circumstances and is not a parrot in other circumstances? Would it be true, after my metamorphosis had rendered me non-human, that I would be a human being in other circumstances? What would they be? In what circumstances am I not a human being, and in what circumstances am I one? Suppose one answered these questions by arguing as follows:

> A philosopher has written: "A being alone is either a beast or a god, but not a man." Let's assume that humans are political animals, as this statement suggests. Wouldn't an isolated person not be a human? So wouldn't that change in his circumstances affect his humanity? More generally, can we not say that some objects, perhaps not human beings, are what they are in virtue of the context? A certain divot of grass is part of a football field because it lies within certain boundaries; outside of those it is not part of the field.

The objection is interesting but mistaken; it rests on the wrong analogy. Take the question of the isolated human being. In isolation that individual is not a member of a society and therefore not a citizen. But because of his genetic constitution he is still human. Being a citizen is analogous to a divot of grass being part of a football field; in isolation it is not part of a football field, but it is still a piece of grass. A human being in isolation is thus still a human being.

The appeal to *circumstances* thus seems misplaced with respect to the question of whether I am a human being or not. What the issue should properly turn on *is the sort of entity I am*. If it is the genetic changes that are decisive, then they have caused a change *in me* and not in my circumstances. That is why it makes no difference with respect to my being human where I was born or whether I was recently irradiated.

Similarly, whether something is a parrot or not has nothing to do with the circumstances in which it says "I am a human being." Its circumstances can change drastically, but it will still be a parrot. The issue concerning my humanity after my metamorphosis will likewise have nothing to do with the circumstances in which I continue to assert "I am a human being," but will be resolved only when it is determined what kind of creature I now am. But that is also true of me in my normal state. "I am a human being" is judged to be true not by the circumstances in which I utter this remark but by other considerations, such as whether I have a human genetic constitution, can speak a natural language, was born of other human beings, and so on. Accordingly, I submit that the truth of "I am a human being," uttered by any human being, is not affected by the circumstances in which it is made.

Similar remarks apply to the other propositions in Group D. For example, what change in circumstances would affect the truth of the claim that the earth existed long before I was born?

Now it is important to stress here that the *context-independence* of such propositions should not be confused with their *contingency*. Their contingency lies in the fact that their negations are not self-contradictory or inconceivable. There is no logical contradiction in asserting that I am not a human being or that the earth did not exist long before I was born; such claims if taken literally are simply false. But contingency must be distinguished from context-independence. What we are now claiming is that, unlike the propositions in Group C, those in Group D are not only contingent but context-independent as well. Being context- or circumstance-independent is a feature, though not the only one, as I shall argue in chapter 9, that distinguishes propositions that constitute our common sense view from those that do not. Further, I contend that this feature arises because of the nature of the conceptual content expressed by those propositions. With respect to each of the propositions in Group D, we find that its content is such as to render it context-independent in the above sense. But that is not true of the propositions in Group C, and it is this feature that differentiates the propositions in the two groups from one another.

Of course, the distinctions we are drawing here are not found in Moore, so a considerable amount of interpretation and reconstruction is now being developed. But I think we have arrived at another way of explaining what Moore's thesis about the nature of the common sense *weltbild* amounts to. My way of putting his point is to say that the common sense view of the world consists of propositions having the characteristic that virtually everybody knows them to be true. This is not true of the propositions in Group C. Not everybody knows that Moore is standing up or that there is a door in that wall. But you and I know that every human being was born, that the earth existed long before anybody alive today was born, that at various times everyone is or has been been sad, elated, in pain, and aware of certain sensations. You and I know that other human beings and animals die. The proposition "All animals die" does not depend for its truth on any special set of circumstances, though, of course, some animals die because of the special circumstances in which they find themselves. "All animals die" and "The earth is very old" are propositions having the sort of conceptual content that renders them circumstance-independent. That content will vary from proposition to proposition, but each such proposition will exhibit the feature of context-independence.

But besides context-independence there are other indexes for identifying such propositions, and I shall discuss these in later chapters. I call such propositions primordial and designate the sort of knowledge they express as primordial knowledge. An indefinitely long list of such propositions embodies a kind of pre-technical knowledge that, I take it, is what Moore means by the common sense view of the world. With certain important qualifications, we can also say that some such conception is what Wittgenstein has in mind when he says that there is something that "stands fast for all of us."

4

Moore's Strategy

Given this characterization we are now in a position to make a run at deciding whether Moore is right in holding that such propositions are known to be true with certainty, and this is the issue that I will focus on here. The matter is complex and raises all sorts of related and important conundra. It is obviously impossible to address all of these in this chapter, but I will at least touch on some and defer others until later. Among these are: In the situations in which he utters the words he does, is Moore really expressing a proposition? Clearly, the words "I am a human being" said by him without the accompanying scenario in which they would ordinarily make sense raises an issue of this sort—and indeed both Malcolm and Wittgenstein challenge him on this point. But keeping their caveats in mind for later discussion, I will here assume that Moore is right in thinking that there is a proposition these words express in their literal lexical use, and more generally that all the locutions he uses in his main papers are propositions. Further, is Moore *justified* in claiming to know that he is a human being when no doubt has been raised about this matter by others? This question I will table for the nonce. Is he justified in claiming to know something without being able to give supporting reasons for his claim? This is a major question of this book, so I will say a few words about it below.

There is also the issue of whether such primordial propositions as "I am a human being" and "The earth existed long before I was born" are indeed true as Moore and I have been claiming. We can also set this question aside on the ground that whether such propositions are true or false is subsidiary to our present concern, which is an epistemological one—that is, whether one can *know* whether any p is true or for that matter whether any p is false. Still, let us further pare down the complexities and stipulate that all the propositions comprising the common sense view are true. We do so on the ground that it is difficult to believe that anyone could provide a compelling argument to the effect that such statements as "I am a human being" (said by Moore about himself) and "The earth exists" are false. And in order to make matters still simpler, I will assume what would otherwise be debatable, namely, that if it is true that A knows that p, *where p is primordial,* then A knows that p with certainty. We can even take a further terminological step to minimize divagations and stipulate that if A knows that p is true with certainty, p is certain.

The central issue we wish to address can now be stated. It is *whether any primordial p is certain*.

In trying to resolve this issue, we must come to grips with two other questions: Is Moore merely *saying* that he knows that p, or does he really know that p? And, second: *How* does Moore know that p is true? The first issue is key; for if *he*, Moore, really knows that p with certainty, it follows by our stipulation above (and independently of that by existential generalization) that p is certain. But it is, of course, possible that Moore is mistaken when he *says* he knows that p, and if so, that leaves it open whether p is known (e.g., by someone else) or not known at all. Let us begin by discussing the question of whether Moore is merely saying he knows but is, in fact, mistaken. We shall attempt to show that Moore is not mistaken, that indeed he does know that he is a human being, and, accordingly, that the proposition in question is certain. Moore, as I indicated previously, never offers a *proof* to that effect; he simply states that he knows that p and adds that either he doesn't know how he knows or at least is less sure how he knows than that he knows. We can begin our task by asking whether these claims are defensible.

Many philosophers have denied that they are, including Wittgenstein and Malcolm. But Moore has a point. Even Wittgenstein expresses a similar point of view in at least one place in *On Certainty*. In the following passage, for instance, he caricatures the sort of philosopher who seems to be urging that the statement "I am a man" is open to investigation, and, accordingly, to possible disconfirmation: "That I am a man and not a woman can be verified, but if I were to say I was a woman, and then tried to explain the error by saying I hadn't checked the statement, the explanation would not be accepted" (79).

Wittgenstein's comment that "the explanation would not be accepted" is relevant to our issue. As Moore indicates with respect to the question of whether one is a human being or not (a peculiar question for Wittgenstein and Malcolm, but not for Moore, as we have stipulated), one would be inclined to say—"But of course I am." If asked how one knows, one might say, following Moore, "I don't know; I just do." If asked whether one had conducted an investigation into the matter, the reply might well be that an investigation is not needed. One simply knows that one is a human being; and indeed, one simply knows that the persons one meets in daily life are human beings as well. Moore seems to have a good case when he asserts both that one knows this sort of proposition with certainty and yet may not be sure how one knows. Both Wittgenstein and Moore would agree that one can't seriously entertain the suggestion that Moore, in the full possession of his senses, would need to verify that he is a human being and that in the process could somehow make a mistake. Moore uses the word "absurd" to describe such a philosophical conceit. The suggestion that an investigation is needed at all and that one might be mistaken in carrying it out thus also seems to deserve Wittgenstein's rebuke.

These sorts of responses raise the general question of whether one is justified in claiming to know that p without being able to explain how one knows.

The question is intricate. To begin to answer it properly would require a number of distinctions: does it refer to the genesis of knowledge or to reasons that give logical support to a claim, and so forth? But without opening that Pandora's box, we can give some arguments that provide prima facie support for Moore's claim. A person with absolute pitch knows that such and such a sound is E flat. But few such persons could answer the question, How do you know that? Or if they attempt to answer the question they are likely to say "I just do." Again, there are idiot savants who can correctly add enormous lists of long numbers. They know the answer with certainty. But how do they know it? They cannot tell us. So there are cases in which it is perfectly in order to claim to know that p while also admitting that one does not know how one knows that p. But conceding this, the question is whether in most situations when we are playing the ordinary language game and make a claim, we can avoid, if pressed, giving the supporting reasons for it. This is what Wittgenstein is concerned to deny. Still, with respect to the question of whether it would be absurd to require supporting reasons for the claim that one is a human being, Moore and Wittgenstein are in accord.

But absurd though it may seem to Moore and Wittgenstein, some philosophers persist in pressing home the notion that one can imagine scenarios in which such an inquiry is not out of place: indeed, Moore (in some sentences I omitted from the long passage quoted earlier) conceded that a blind man, suffering from certain sorts of medical problems, might not know with certainty that he had clothes on. So, these philosophers ask, isn't it possible that one could be mistaken in thinking one was a human being? Suppose that our metamorphosized bug believed incorrectly that it was a human being; wouldn't it at least make sense for the bug to conduct an investigation into the question? In effect, what these philosophers are suggesting is that: if it is even possible one is mistaken about p, then it follows that we do not know p with certainty. It is this sort of objection which poses the central difficulty for Moore's contention that he knows this p or that p to be true with certainty. After all, isn't it possible with respect to any of these so-called primordial propositions that he could be mistaken about them? Couldn't Moore be wrong in holding that he had two parents, that the earth is very old, and that all of us have lived at or near its surface?

This kind of philosophical move, which can be formulated as an argument that turns on the possibility of error, is historically of enormous importance and is one of the moves central to scepticism. Without attempting to prove that he knows, Moore attacks and I believe disposes of this argument. The effect is to leave his claim to know without knowing how he knows unimpaired.

Let us now look at how Moore deals with this sceptical argument, which we shall call the argument from possibility. It maintains that in any given case in which a factual claim is being made it is possible that one could be mistaken. And if it is possible that one could be mistaken, it follows that one can't be said to know that the claim is true. This argument turns on the notion of possibility and on the conception of knowledge which entails that if one knows that p it is impossible that one could be mistaken about p. Moore also accepts this conception of knowledge, but rejects the argument. He shows, via a brilliant counterargument insufficiently appreciated in the contemporary literature, that this sceptical line of reasoning rests upon a modal fallacy, an equivocation upon the term "possible." The following passage contains his analysis:

> But what Russell means is quite clearly not self-contradictory. What he means is roughly: In dreams we often feel as if we were remembering things which in fact never happened. And that we do sometimes, not only in dreams, but also in waking life, feel as if we remembered things which in fact never happened, I fully grant. That this is true I don't feel at all inclined to question. What I do feel inclined to question is that this fact is in any way incompatible with the proposition that I do now know for certain that I heard a sound like "Russell" a little while ago. Suppose I have had experiences which resembled this one in the respect that I felt as if I remembered hearing a certain sound a little while before, while yet it is not true that a little while before I did hear the sound in question. Does that prove that I don't know for certain now that I did hear the sound "Russell" just now? It seems to me that the idea that it does is a mere fallacy, resting partly at least on a confusion between two different uses of the words "possible" or "may."
>
> What really does follow from the premiss is this: That it is possible for an experience of a sort, of which my present experience is an example, i.e., one which resembles my present experience in a certain respect, not to have been preceded within a certain period by the sound "Russell." Whereas the conclusion alleged to follow is: It is possible that this experience was not preceded within that period by the sound "Russell." Now in the first of these sentences the meaning of "possible" is such that the whole sentence means merely: Some experiences of feeling as if one remembered a certain sound are not preceded by the sound in question. But in the conclusion: It is possible that this experience was not preceded by the word "Russell"; or This experience may not have been preceded by the word "Russell"; "possible" and "may" are being used in an entirely different sense. Here the whole expression merely means the same as: "It is not known for certain that this experience was preceded by that sound." And how from "Some experiences of this kind were not preceded" can we possibly be justified in inferring "It is not known that this one was preceded"? The argument seems to me to be precisely on a par with the following: It is possible for a human being to be of the female sex; [but] I am a human thing; therefore, it is possible that I am of the female sex. The two premisses here are perfectly true, and yet obviously it does not follow from them that I do not know that I am not of the female sex. I do (in my view) happen to know this, in spite of the fact that the two premisses are both true; but whether I know it or not the two premisses certainly don't prove that I don't. The conclusion seems to follow from the premisses because the premiss "It is possible for a human being to be of the female sex" or "Human beings may be of the female sex" is so easily falsely taken to be of the same form as "Human beings are mortal," i.e., to mean "In the case of every human being, it is possible that the human being in question is of the female sex," or "Every human being may be of the female sex." If, and only if, it did mean this, then, from the combination of this with the minor premiss "I am a human being" would the conclusion follow: It is possible that I am of the female sex; or I may be of the female sex. But in fact the premiss "Human beings may be of the female sex" does not mean "Every human being may be" but only "Some humans are." "May" is being used in a totally different sense from any in which you could possibly assert of a particular human being "This human being may be so-and-so." And so soon as this is realized, it is surely quite plain that from this, together with the premiss, "I am a human being" there does not follow "I may be of the female sex." ("Four Forms of Scepticism," 219–221)

The argument obviously applies to the case we are discussing. Philosophers have argued, as we have seen, that if it is possible that you might be mistaken, then it follows that you can't know what you claim to know. Moore's point is that because of an equivocation upon "possible" the argument is fallacious. His reasoning is compact, but I think cogent. Let's briefly examine it to see why.

We can begin by distinguishing two senses of "possibility." There is, first, a sense we can call logical possibility. To say that it is possible that I am not a human being using this sense of "possible" is to say that the proposition "I am not a human being" is not self-contradictory. In short, it is to say that the proposition is contingent. But this use of "possible" does not exclude or imply that I know whether the proposition is true; that is, to assert it is logically possible that I am not a human being is consistent with saying either that I do know that I am a human being or that I do not know it. This sense of "possible" thus carries no epistemic import. But there is a different sense in which "possible" is used that does carry such epistemic import, and we can call this sense epistemic possibility. It can be explicated in terms of the words "may or may not." To say it is possible that it will rain today is equivalent to saying that it may (or may not) rain today. But in such a use, it is presupposed that in saying what I do, it is excluded that I know that it will rain or that I know it will not rain today. I can employ this sense of "possible" only if I do not know that p and do not know that not p. That is, if I know it will not rain today, I cannot sensibly say "it may rain today." Or to take Moore's own example, since he knows he is not female, he cannot sensibly say that he may be female. So epistemic possibility excludes or is inconsistent with the fact of one's knowing.

Moore's point is that the sceptic begins his argument using the sense of logical possibility, claiming in effect that with respect to a given p, it is logically possible that p is false. What he says is true but epistemically innocuous, for, in effect, he is saying p is contingent. But that sense of "possible" does not exclude one's knowing that p, for example, that one is male, as Moore points out. The rest of the sceptical argument then employs a premise that invokes the sense of epistemic possibility, and from that premise the sceptic is able to conclude that one cannot know that p (i.e., not know that one is male). But that shift from one sense of "possible" to another amounts to an equivocation on "possible." The argument is thus fallacious, and the sceptical conclusion does not follow. Moore claims, then, that the sceptic does not provide him with a cogent reason for abandoning his claim to know that he is a human being.

The preceding considerations, powerful as they are, amount only to a stand-off with the sceptic. They amount to saying that the sceptic has not made out his case but do not themselves establish that Moore knows that p. Therefore, we want some positive grounds for holding that Moore does know at least one primordial proposition with certainty. I shall now provide an argument to that effect.

The argument turns on a concept I call negational absurdity. This concept, in turn, is closely related to a notion that is an important element in Wittgenstein's defense of a version of the common sense view, namely, the distinction between a mistake and an aberration. Let me speak to the second notion briefly.

If one is counting a large number of chairs in an auditorium and arrives at the number 239 when the correct total would be 240, we can describe the result as a mistake. That person followed a normal counting procedure, but in carrying it out he went astray somewhere; but the result was close.

In contrast, we need a different way of characterizing the outcome of a deliberative process if it wildly misses the mark. A paranoid who believes that everything he eats has been poisoned by an unknown enemy has not made a mistake when he finds that his food is invariably safe: he is suffering from some sort of conceptual aberration. We might say he needs psychiatric treatment; we would not say that he should carry out his line of reasoning more attentively. The person who has made a mistake in counting chairs does not need a course in how to count—he simply has to be more careful. There is nothing psychologically wrong with him, nor is there anything wrong with the process he uses in order to arrive at the correct number of chairs. So given that he is all right and the process itself is all right, it makes sense to say that he made a mistake in his application of that process. But with our paranoid, his reasoning process is so deviant that we cannot urge him to be more meticulous in its application; some other way of dealing with him and his mode of reasoning is requisite. We can say, then, that the outcome of such a process is aberrant and not mistaken.

Now suppose that someone challenged Moore's remark that he knows the earth existed long before he was born. Clearly, Moore cannot know this proposition to be true on the basis of his own experience. How then does he know it? Moore, of course, refuses to say. So, in challenging Moore, this person—let us say Russell—might argue that for all he or Moore knows the earth came into existence one hundred years ago. There is nothing logically impossible about this conjecture, though it is false. Moore would agree that the assertion is not logically impossible, but he would add that it is "absurd." The suggestion, if taken seriously, that the earth could have come into existence only one hundred years ago is not a mistake, it is an aberration. One wishes to say that it runs counter to everything we know. If a person seriously proposed such an idea, we would not say he had made a mistake in his calculations but that his conception of reality was wildly deviant. In dealing with him we would treat him analogously to our way of dealing with a paranoid. We would not suggest he go over his calculations again; we might suggest that he see a therapist.

Now the notion of negational absurdity is a concept we can use in explicating what I noted above when I said that one way of characterizing an aberration is to say that it runs counter to what we all know. And to say it runs counter to what we all know is to say, in effect, that it runs counter to that set of primordial propositions we call the common sense view of the world. We can thus say that if any primordial proposition were false, the world as it now is would be incomprehensible to us. The denial of any primordial p thus has the property of being negationally absurd. I said earlier that there were characteristics other than being circumstance-independent that distinguished primordial propositions from other types of contingent statements, and this property of being negationally absurd is one of those features. I will illustrate what is intended here by comparing the proposition "The earth is 4.5 billion years old," taken from

Group A in List I, with the primordial proposition "The earth is very old," taken from Group B in List I. I shall show that the negation of the latter proposition is absurd in a way in which the negation of the former is not.

In order to see why this is so let us ask, Is it *sensible* to suppose that the world came into existence exactly one hundred years ago? One might think so, and one might support one's suggestion with this line of reasoning: let's assume, Russell might have said, that the earth is actually 6 billion years old rather than 4.5 billion years old, as scientists now believe. The conjecture that it is not 4.5 billion years old, which is the negation of the proposition taken from Group A, is perfectly conceivable and accordingly not absurd. The world as we now know it would be perfectly comprehensible to us if it were 6 billion rather than 4.5 billion years old. The error, which is admittedly large, is nontheless not to be described as an aberration, since it was the outcome of standard scientific reasoning based upon the evidence that was then available. But the important point is that our world picture would in no way be altered by this new finding. At most a scientific conjecture and a few theoretical implications following from it would have to be abandoned. But everything else would be the same—all of our institutions would be what they now are, our present practices, such as the study of history, would remain intact, and so on. There would thus be no discernible or practical difference in our attitude toward or comprehension of the world. And if that is so, there is nothing absurd about the hypothesis that the earth came into existence much earlier than we once believed it did.

Therefore, Russell might have asked, How does that hypothesis differ from the hypothesis that the world came into existence much later than we believed it did, say only one hundred years ago? The difference is, after all, merely one of degree—a difference between one hundred years and 6 billion years. What then is absurd about claiming that the earth came into existence only one hundred years ago? Or if one hundred years ago seems implausible, how about the contention that the earth was created in 4004 B.C., as Bishop Ussher argued? In 1650 many people believed this statement to be true. They went about their daily activities just as we do now: was their world picture really different from ours? And if it wasn't, then there was nothing absurd about their conception of reality. Admittedly, Ussher's assertion is false, but the issue is whether it is absurd, as you claim. Wouldn't our world outlook, and the everday activities predicated on it, be just the same as now? If so, the assertion is not absurd.

The answer is that the world as we now know it would not be the same. The difference between its being 6,000 years old, as Ussher claimed, or one hundred years old and the difference between its being 4.5 or 6 billion years old, as some scientists assert, is not merely a difference in "degree." It is a difference in order. The difference between the earth's being 6 billion or 4.5 billion years old has no effect upon our comprehension and understanding of the world in which we now live. But if the world were really only 6,000 or one hundred years old, that world would be incomprehensible to us: The claim would be absurd. The proposition is thus aberrant and not merely mistaken. Consider how we would react if we sent out a student accurately to count the approximately 250 seats that we knew a large lecture room contained and he returned with the answer that there were none, or with the answer that there were only five. If, puzzled by this finding, we then went to the room and found these sorts of answers to be wholly inconsonant with what we could immediately see to be the case, we would not say he had made a mistake in counting; we would realize that something had seriously gone wrong if he had indeed understood our request.

Well, perhaps the student had not understood our request—was that the reason for his peculiar finding? But if he had understood it, how could he possibly have come up with the answer he did? Clearly, his answer was not the result of miscounting. His finding is so peculiar it would have to be characterized in some other way—as aberrant, strange, incomprehensible. So it is with the claim, if seriously advanced, that the earth is only one hundred (or 6,000) years old. If someone *seriously* advanced such a claim, could we really understand it? Of course, there is a trivial sense in which it is understandable: the words are in English, and the syntax is in order. But in the sense in which our student's statement is absurd, so is this claim. For if it were true that the earth is only one hundred years old, none of our present rational practices would be comprehensible. If one is engaged in the study of papal politics in the twelfth century, a task requiring accumulating and dating documentary materials that are the basis of information we now possess about events that happened then, how would one continue to act if one were informed that the world had come into existence after the twelfth century? If the hypothesis were to be entertained seriously, the kind of investigation that one is conducting into medieval papal politics would be some kind of delusion or fantasy.

But now a sceptic like Russell might say, "Isn't it possible that all historians are deluded; perhaps what they regard as the past is just an illusion, a kind of dream they have created and that they think they are investigating." Wittgenstein answers this question in various ways, as we shall see in chapter 10. For the present let us reaffirm the distinction between a mistake and an aberration. History as a discipline is not aberrant; it is not a psychic fantasy but a rational activity that, tracing causal chains, carries present knowledge steadily backward in time with no serious lacunae. If this tracing of causal chains should be wholly wrong, our total comprehension of the world would be out of joint: there are no compelling accommodations we could make to explain the error. No rewriting of the facts, as Ussher tried to do, would work; in the end his attempted explanations would break down.

We know, therefore, that Russell's conjecture cannot be taken seriously. If it were it would be aberrant. In this sense, then, we can say that the negation of the proposition "The earth is very old" is absurd. If it were true the world as we now know it with all of its institutions, practices, and daily activities would make no sense whatsoever. We conclude, then, that Moore is correct in asserting that he knows with certainty that the proposition "The earth existed long before my birth" is true. Not only does he know this proposition to be true, so do you and I. It follows that some primordial propositions are certain.

Let us put all this in the form of an explicit argument. Human beings engage in various activities, among them history, geology, and anthropology, which are dedicated to exploring the past. Such explorations involve the detailed retrospective tracing of temporal causal sequences, for example, that A lived for a certain number of years, that A was the progeny of B, that B lived for a certain number of years, that B was the progeny of C. If the hypothesis that the earth was not very old were true, such explorations would not be rational but aberrant, chimerical, or delusive. But they are not aberrant, chimerical, or delusive. We can say—using Wittgenstein's parlance—that all the evidence speaks for them; or we could put the point negatively by saying that the opposite hypothesis has nothing on its side. The idea that a hypothesis is absurd *both* if nothing speaks for it and everything speaks against it is a notion that Wittgenstein returns to again and again. Here is a typical quotation: "What we call historical evidence points to the existence of the earth a long time before my birth;—the opposite hypothesis has *nothing* on its side" (*O.C.*, 190).

Therefore, both because the opposite hypothesis has nothing on its side and because history, geology, and anthropology have everything on their sides, it follows that the earth existed long before Moore was born. Moreover, because Moore and many others have engaged in such activities it follows that at least one primordial proposition ("The earth is very old") is known to be true by those engaging in such activities. Moore is thus correct in asserting that he knows this proposition to be true with certainty.

In the light of this result, we are now in a position to draw together a large number of threads woven in the previous chapters. We have seen that Moore believes he cannot *prove* that he knows such primordial propositions to be true and yet that he still insists he knows them to be true. His approach to scepticism is thus a curious mixture of boldness and caution. In effect, he is saying he cannot *prove* that scepticism is wrong while at the same time asserting he knows that it is wrong. Moore, no doubt, would say of the strong supporting argument we have just given, whose conclusion is that at least one primordial proposition is certain, that it is still not a proof, since we cannot prove that its premises are true, even though we know they are true.

Given Moore's assessment of the situation, he must adopt a wholly different strategy in meeting sceptical challenges. In concluding this chapter I shall explain what that is and, in particular, why Moore does not argue his case. I concede, of course, that what I am proposing here goes beyond what Moore actually says, since, in fact, he is silent on this point. Nevertheless, there is strong textual evidence in favor of this interpretation, as I shall indicate momentarily. Apart from this support, what I am suggesting is consistent with and, I believe, deepens our understanding of his mode of procedure. We are thus in the not unusual situation of a critic who interprets a literary text as conveying some sort of message, even though its author never makes that message explicit by a meta-discussion of it. The merit of such an approach thus ultimately turns on the degree of insight the interpretation provides, with the proviso, of course, that it is not inconsistent with whatever clues—textual or otherwise—may be available. So I will here speak of Moore's strategy, as if this were something Moore actually had in mind, while cautioning the reader that what is being presented is really my interpretation of a complex text.

As we have seen, Moore distinguishes two different kinds of claims. He is willing to assert that he knows certain propositions to be true with certainty. But he is unwilling to say how he knows these propositions to be true, or at most is willing to say he is less sure how he knows than that he does. Now are these simply naive pronouncements, as many commentators have contended? I do not think they are. Moore was an ingenious and profound thinker, so we shall assume these comments were not merely honest avowals but were also part of an underlying strategy in coping with the sceptic. But if so, what could Moore have had in mind?

In order to answer this question, we need to understand an essential feature of scepticism, which is especially prominent in its most radical or Pyrrhonic forms. In the hands of its cleverest proponents, such as Michel de Montaigne, Pyrrhonic scepticism is not a theory or a doctrine, and accordingly it is not composed of, nor does it put forth, any assertions. In particular, such radical sceptics do not assert that nothing can be known. To make such a claim would expose them to rebuttal, to the question, How do you know that nothing can be known? And this, of course, would be self-defeating, requiring just the sort of affirmation of knowledge that the sceptic cannot countenance. Instead, the clever sceptic is like a counter-puncher in boxing. He waits for his opponent to make a move, and then he exploits the opening.

In this form we might think of scepticism as an *attitude* rather than a theory, something like the mental set of a compulsive critic who has no views of his own but is always ready to find a counter-example to any assertion that another might make. It is important in understanding the radical sceptic's *modus operandi* that one realize that such sceptics also avoid generalization; they respond to the proposals of their opponents on a case-by-case basis. That is true even when an opponent proffers a generalization—for example, that one can know what the world is like on the basis of reason alone. The strategy is thus designed to avoid any initiative that equals or exceeds what an opponent has himself put on the table.

But if the sceptic is not putting forth any theory, then one cannot *prove* that his position is wrong because *there is no position to be confuted*. The sceptic is simply making hay with the views that his opponent, the so-called dogmatist, advances. Now I think that Moore (and Wittgenstein as well) realized this, though Moore, as I have indicated, never says so explicitly. What Moore realized subliminally or intuitively, as one might put it, was that sceptical challenges could not be met by conventional modes of argumentation, such as a proof, and accordingly that what was necessary in this situation was to develop a *non-argumentative counter-strategy*. The point of such a strategy would not be to *beat* the sceptic at the game of argumentation but to offer *resistance* to certain sorts of sceptical maneuvers and in this way to *blunt* their effects. To many commentators Moore has seemed incredibly obstinate, even simple-minded. In his *Philosophical Analysis*, Max Black said of Moore:

> One reason for Moore's great influence upon the younger philosophers may have been the refreshing contrast between his simplicity and clarity and the pretentious technicality of some of his predecessors. After the intoxication of metaphysics, it is good to look upon the world again as a child might—to be told "After all, this *is* a hand. I have a body, so have you, and there are many other people like both of us who can say the same." (7)

And though Black in all sorts of ways admired Moore, he added to the previous assessment the following:

> Yet there is a kind of dogmatism in his work which will continue to bother some of his readers. Careful examination of his essays shows again and again that he fails, or rather, does not try, to *argue*; on crucial issues, he seems to attack his opponents by vehement affirmation and reiteration. (8)

These characterizations represent Moore as naive, as just another Dr. Johnson who intends to refute Berkeley by kicking a stone. But such assessments miss the power and the point of what Moore was doing. In effect, he refused to play the sceptic's game and by this sort of obduracy prevented the sceptic from winning. The outcome of this sort of resistance was in boxing parlance a draw: Neither side could be said to have defeated the other. But from a certain standpoint one might give the verdict to Moore—on points, as it were. For the sceptic is a kind of parasite who lives off the views of others. To deny him sustenance is to diminish him, and that is what Moore did. From Moore's perspective, that is, from the perspective of one who believed that he knew certain sorts of propositions to be true with certainty, his non-defeat by the sceptic allowed him to carry on business as usual. And that is a kind of victory in a war of attrition.

What is the evidence that Moore thought the best he could obtain against the sceptic is a kind of draw? Part of the evidence is to be found in Moore's frequent affirmation in most of his epistemological papers that he cannot prove this or that, but knows this or that to be true. I take this sort of remark to indicate that he cannot prove that the sceptic is wrong, though he knows that he is. But in "Certainty" we find even stronger evidence that entails both that he realizes he cannot defeat the sceptic and yet that he can obtain at least a stand-off with him. These admissions occur in the penultimate paragraph of the paper and represent its climax. There Moore argues that because he knows he is standing up, he knows he is not dreaming. But he admits that the sceptic will reply by saying that because you cannot prove that you are not dreaming, you do not know that you are standing up. Moore concedes that he cannot prove that he is not dreaming, but he still insists he knows he is standing up. From this he concludes: "My argument, 'I know that I am standing up, and therefore I know that I am not dreaming' remains at least as good as his, 'You don't know that you are not dreaming, and therefore don't know that you are standing up'" (250).

As this passage indicates, nothing the sceptic has advanced has forced Moore to give ground or to abandon his claim to know certain propositions to be true. Even though this result falls short of complete victory it contains a kind of vindication. Moore has seen deeply into the kind of strategy invoked by his opponent and has to some degree neutralized its effects. This is an achievement few philosophers have surpassed.

We can now spell out how this works. The sceptic's strategy leads to a famous conceptual difficulty, a kind of infinite regress, that some writers, such as R.H. Popkin and Roderick Chisholm, have called the problem of the criterion. Here is how the strategy works: Suppose someone, Moore, for instance, asserts he knows there is a door in that wall (said while pointing to a specific area in a room). The sceptic asks, "How do you know that there is?" The question seems perfectly appropriate. If someone makes a claim, it is generally in order to ask that person for the reasons that support the claim. So the question, "How do you know that p?" is in order, and this is the first move that the sceptic makes in developing the regress. We thus have two elements in a conversational scenario: an initial assertion by someone and the query "How do you know?" The question will naturally elicit a response from the first speaker: he will give the reason that supports his claim and thus will take another step toward developing the regress. Suppose the response is: "Because I can see that there is a door in the wall." What has happened by this move is that the person who made the original assertion has been maneuvered by the sceptic into *proposing a criterion* that supports his statement. In effect, what he is saying is that "because I can *see* that that such and such is the case, I therefore *know* that such and such is the case." But now the sceptic can ask, "Is the appeal to sense experience a good reason for saying that you know?" He can offer, as counter-examples, the familiar arguments based upon perceptual illusion and the existence of dreams. The regress is now in full flow. The speaker has been put in a position where he is required to give another reason, a new criterion, for saying that having certain sorts of visual experiences is a good reason for claiming to know, and then it will become apparent that the latter reason, in turn, must have its reason, *und so weiter.*

The sceptic can move in for the kill once his dogmatic opponent proffers a criterion for supporting what he has asserted. The kill consists in making it plain to the opposing speaker that there is a logical gap between the criterion he has given and the claim that criterion supposedly supports. It is important to understand the power of the sceptic's move here. The sceptic does not have to argue that the speaker was *in fact* mistaken when he claimed to see the door—that would be to put forth an assertion himself. His point is that whether the speaker is right or not, the *criterion* he has employed fails to guarantee that he does indeed know what he claims to know. But why is that so?

The answer concerns the nature of the conception of knowledge we described earlier, which the dogmatist employs. This conception entails that if A knows that p, then A *cannot* be mistaken. The "cannot" is all important here. To say that one knows that p entails that it is impossible that A could be mistaken. But now if one gives as a reason for claiming there is a door in that wall that one can see that there is, then one is advancing a criterion such that the criterion can be satisfied and yet the speaker *might* be mistaken. All the skeptic has to do to make his point is to show that *it is possible* the criterion will be satisfied, whereas the assertion *might* be false. All the familiar sceptical arguments, developed since time immemorial, can now be brought to bear to demonstrate that there is a logical gap between supporting criterion and epistemic claim: arguments about brains in vats, the argument from illusion, and so forth. These arguments entail that all our experience can be exactly what it is and yet that it might not correspond to any external reality. So the appeal to any sort of experience, such as seeing or hearing something, does not guarantee that one cannot be mistaken. Thus one might have the experience of seeing a door in a place where in reality there is none. Accordingly, the criterion of seeing does not provide air-tight support for the claim to know that there is a door, and therefore it is not true that one *knows* that there is a door there.

Without putting forth any claim himself, but just by bringing it to the attention of the dogmatist that his reasoning is fallible, the sceptic has made it plain to his opponent that he does not know what he claims to know. What is particularly powerful and ironic about this result is that it is parasitic upon a conception of knowledge the dogmatist himself is espousing. The sceptic is not putting forth some other conception. If he did, his moves would lack real force; the argumentative situation would be like two ships passing in the dark and never meeting. So the sceptic is, in effect, saying: I accept the conception of knowledge you begin with, my friend, but now let us draw out some of the consequences of that conception. When we do, we can see that your claim to know is defective because it rests on criteria that are not logically conclusive. The scenario thus ends with the defeat of the dogmatist on turf he has himself selected.

Moore met this set of maneuvers by refusing to play the sceptic's game. He did this by refusing to explain *how* he knew what he claimed to know. That refusal blocked the sceptical regress at its source: it made it impossible for the sceptic's pattern of moves to get off the ground. He thus blocked at an initial stage the pressures that would have led to the sceptical regress. By resisting the request to explain how he knew, Moore avoided putting himself in a position in which he was forced to give a criterion in support of his claim to know. It was an extremely effective maneuver that created an impossible dilemma for the sceptic.

The sceptic could assert, in response to Moore's obduracy, that Moore didn't, in fact, know what he claimed to know—did not know, for instance, such propositions as that the earth exists and that the earth is very old. But to have adopted that horn of the dilemma would have exposed him to the very question he had so sedulously worked to avoid: How do you know that Moore is wrong? The answer to that query would have required that the sceptic leave the posture of *epoche* and make a positive claim. But that would have completely undermined his strategy. The alternative was to say nothing, but that amounted to leaving the field unopposed to Moore, also an unacceptable option. Thus neither choice was possible. Moore's tactics had cleverly shifted the onus onto the sceptic, and without leaving his opponent room for rebuttal or further maneuver. His refusal to carry on the traditional conversational scenario was thus the key to blunting the sceptical onslaught.

I have been arguing here that Moore's consistent refusal in various papers to explain *how* he knew that which he insisted he *did* know was not accidental, though it may well have been motivated by factors that were intuitive and subliminal, since he never gives a meta-justification or description of his mode of procedure. But the quotations from "Certainty" establish convincingly that he was fully aware of his tactics and that they enabled him to achieve at least a stand-off with an ingenious and slippery opponent. They also reveal that the results he obtained were of satisfaction to him.

Still, it must be emphasized, the outcome was something less than victory and something more than defeat, and hence was not from a perfectionist point of view ideal. Wittgenstein, in particular, believed it was not good enough and that a complete refutation of scepticism was possible. Why he thought so and how he proceeded in attempting to achieve this goal are matters we shall explore, beginning with chapter 6. But to set the stage for that inquiry it is necessary to understand his sweeping criticisms of Moore. They range from matters about what it is appropriate to say in certain circumstances to a wholesale condemnation. With respect to Moore's contention that he knew that p but didn't know how he knew, Wittgenstein writes:

> If someone believes something, we needn't always be able to answer the question 'why he believes it'; but if he knows something, then the question "how does he know?" must be capable of being answered. (*O.C.*, 550)

And:

> Moore's mistake lies in this—countering the assertion that one cannot know that, by saying "I do know it." (*O.C.*, 521)

Clearly, Wittgenstein holds that Moore's refusal to answer the question, How do you know? is not a legitimate move in the language game that defines human communication and therefore cannot be the basis for dealing with sceptical doubt. In chapters 6 and 10 we shall explore his grounds for this claim, and we shall also ask whether he is right or not. Wittgenstein believed, more generally, that Moore's attempt to meet the challenge that one cannot know by saying "I do know" showed that he misunderstood the nature of scepticism; and that in part—though only in part—is why Moore's strategy for dealing with scepticism is flawed.

As Wittgenstein read him, Moore saw radical scepticism as a possible position, or better, as a particular "outlook" that can be held by someone. Even if that "outlook" is not expressed as a formal argument, Moore thought that it can at least be exhibited in an attitude one could adopt when faced with knowledge claims. Thus, Moore is willing to take at face value the legitimacy of that outlook, namely, that there is a coherent position that must be combated. Being coherent, there is at least the possibility that scepticism is right. So it must, therefore, be resisted. But the belief that there is something called scepticism that is coherent is what Wittgenstein wishes to show is misguided. Thus, it is not so much a possible position that needs refutation but the supposition of its legitimacy. Moore did not see this in his struggle with the sceptic. Because he presupposes the coherence of an opposing position, he is even willing to try to develop a proof to the effect that the external world exists. But for Wittgenstein it is profoundly misguided to think one needs such a proof. But to show this requires a new method, a new way of conceiving the nature of a philosophical conundrum. In a passage turning on the metaphor of seeing a painted stage set, Wittgenstein states that it is as if Moore had put it all in the wrong light:

> When one hears Moore say "I know that that's a tree," one suddenly understands those who think that that has by no means been settled.
> The matter strikes one all at once as being unclear and blurred. It is as if Moore had put it in the wrong light.
> It is as if I were to see a painting (say a painted stage-set) and recognize what

it represents from a long way off at once and without the slightest doubt. But now I step nearer: and then I see a lot of patches of different colors, which are all highly ambiguous and do not provide any certainty whatever. (*O.C.*, 481)

Wittgenstein's metaphor intimates that it is as if Moore's understanding of scepticism came "from a long way off." In *On Certainty*, Wittgenstein is suggesting that he has brought us closer, and now we can see that our original view of the matter through Moore's eyes did not give us a perspicuous view of the nature of scepticism. But what is it, then, that Wittgenstein wishes to tell us? How shall we interpret the patches of color we see from closer up? And what is it that we shall eventually see if not patches of color?

We can begin the transition to his views, somewhat obliquely, by an exploration of Moore's "Proof of an External World." In that paper Moore accepts Kant's challenge to prove there is an external world. But though he develops such a proof, he admits he cannot prove that he knows its premises to be true. But even while admitting this, he asserts he does know them to be true. So the work is replete with moves that by now are familiar. Wittgenstein was fascinated by this paper. Of the 676 entries that comprise *On Certainty*, nearly half refer, in one way or another, to "Proof of an External World," and about 80 specifically refer to one sentence, "Here is one hand," that Moore uses as a premise in his proof. Indeed, the first comment we find in *On Certainty* is: "If you do know that *here is one hand* we'll grant you all the rest" (*O.C.*, 1).

To see what Wittgenstein meant by this comment and, of course, by the many others directed at Moore, I will devote the next two chapters to Moore's paper. In chapter 5 I will try to explain sympathetically what Moore is doing in "Proof of an External World," but at the end of the chapter I will advance some fundamental criticisms of his approach that are different from those Wittgenstein makes. In chapter 6, I will turn to Wittgenstein's complex treatment of the essay and to some of the reasons he gives for thinking both that Moore has misused the word "know" and that any attempt to prove the external world exists is nonsensical. In this way, I will lay the groundwork for coming to understand in later chapters Wittgenstein's rationale for driving a wedge between the concepts of knowledge and certainty, which is one of the deepest ideas of *On Certainty*. It is this point he wishes us to see instead of a patchwork of colors.

The wedge

5

Moore's Proof of an External World

What, then, was Moore trying to do in "Proof of an External World?" As he says explicitly, he is taking up a challenge laid down by Kant, who wrote: "It still remains a scandal to philosophy . . . that the existence of things outside of us . . . must be accepted merely on faith, and that, if anyone thinks good to doubt their existence, we are unable to counter his doubts by any satisfactory proof" (*Critique of Pure Reason*, N.K. Smith, trans., Bxxxix, note, p. 34).

At the very beginning of the paper Moore states that

> there seems to me to be no doubt whatever that it is a matter of some importance and also a matter which falls properly within the province of philosophy, to discuss the question what sort of proof, if any, can be given of "the existence of things outside of us." And to discuss this question was my object when I began to write the present lecture. (*P.E.W.*, 127)

But from a Wittgensteinian standpoint, for a philosopher—especially for a defender of common sense like Moore—to have taken on the task of proving there is an external world was ludicruous. As Austin once said, all the serious mistakes are made in the first five pages, and from a Wittgensteinian perspective, Moore's big mistake occurred on page one: to have thought there was a legitimate philosophical task here at all. But be that as it may, Moore saw himself as picking up the gauntlet thrown down by Kant, namely, to rid philosophy of a scandal by giving such a proof. And Moore thought he had met the challenge. Near the end of the essay he writes:

> It seems to me that, so far from its being true, as Kant declares to be his opinion, that there is only one possible proof of the existence of things outside of us, namely the one which he has given, I can now give a large number of different proofs, each of which is a perfectly rigorous proof; and that at many other times I have been in a position to give others. (*P.E.W.*, 145)

Moore's "large number of different proofs" are essentially variations of the first proof he presents, which is generally known as Moore's proof. Let us explore it a bit. As he initially formulates it, the argument consists of two premises and a conclusion:

55

(1) Here is one hand.

(2) Here is another (hand).

(3) Therefore two human hands exist.

But this turns out not to be an exact formulation. For example, Moore utters (1) while making a certain gesture with his right hand and (2) while making a certain gesture with his left hand, so it seems that the proof contains some non-linguistic components. Let us assume that these are not essential and that we can understand what he is referring to in uttering (1) and (2). But because he is waving his hands now, he does mean to imply that the hands he is referring to exist at this moment. Therefore, he himself later amplifies (3) so that it reads:

(4) Therefore two human hands exist at this moment.

Hence we are to understand that the conclusion he wishes to establish is (4) rather than (3). But if this is the final version of his proof, it clearly won't prove what needs to be proved if Kant's challenge is to be met, which is to establish that these two hands now exist "outside of us." All Moore has shown so far is that from the fact that this hand now exists and that hand now exists two hands now exist. But that is a simple numerical calculation, an application of the theorem that $1 + 1 = 2$. Having made the calculation, we have certainly not proved that some things exist "outside of us," as Kant requires. After all, an idealist, such as Bishop Berkeley, could admit that each of Moore's hands now exists, but could argue that a hand is simply a heap of ideas and that all ideas exist in the mind. According to this Berkeleyan analysis, to say that something exists in the mind is to deny it exists outside of us. So from the fact that two hands now exist it does not follow that anything now exists outside of us. It is clear that Moore's proof needs additional premises if it is to prove that two hands exist outside of us at this moment.

In fact, in formulating his argument Moore has covertly made use of two principles he believed he had, after extensive argumentation, shown to be true. He imported these, without acknowledgment, into his statement of the argument, so that in effect they function as enthymemes. What are these principles that he uses as submerged premises? On the basis of some distinctions (which I shall discuss in detail shortly) Moore had argued that a human hand is something whose existence does not depend upon our now, as he puts it, "having a certain sort of experience,"—that is, upon our being in a certain psychological state such as perceiving the hand in question. In a more familiar parlance he had argued that a hand is something that is mind-independent. And then, appealing to those as well as to certain other distinctions, he had argued that anything whose existence does not depend upon our being in such a psychological state exists outside of us. He also explained that he was interpreting Kant's phrase "x is outside of us" to mean "x is outside of the human mind" and that phrase in turn to mean "x is an external object." Thus, from his two premises, and assuming these additional principles and distinctions, he concluded that two things now exist outside of us. What is called Moore's proof, is, accordingly, a compressed argument whose actual premises are not fully spelled out. In order to reach his conclusion he was thus covertly buttressing his so-called proof with the following additional, unarticulated steps:

(5) The existence of any human hand does not depend upon our being in a certain psychological state.

(6) Anything whose existence does not depend upon our being in a certain psychological state exists outside of us.

Given these additional premises, Moore can deduce from (4), (5), and (6), the following proposition:

(7) Two human hands now exist "outside of us."

This revised argument is, strictly speaking, not what Moore has called his proof. But it is clear that what he does so characterize can be the sort of proof that will meet Kant's demands only if it is augmented in the way I have indicated. So let us call this rendering of what he does give us Moore's proof. I believe Moore would have accepted this reconstruction since the additional premises are embedded in his earlier discussion. Even as so expanded, he could still affirm that it is a rigorous proof, since it satisfies the three conditions every proof must satisfy, namely: (i) the premises must be different from the conclusion, (ii) the premises must be known to be true, and (iii) the conclusion must follow from the premises.

Let us focus for a moment on (1) and (2). As the reader will ascertain by reading the two quotations in chapter 2 from Moore's essay, Moore maintains that he knows that (1) and (2) are true, though he adds he cannot prove they are. The fact that he cannot prove (1) and (2) to be true does not affect the validity of his claim that he has given a rigorous proof, he stresses, since all the conditions for giving such a proof have been satisfied. It will also be recalled that Moore gives as a reason for not being able to prove these propositions that he would have to prove he was not now dreaming, and this he asserts he cannot do. Wittgenstein, reflecting on Moore's comment, remarked sarcastically: "The argument 'I may be dreaming' is senseless for this reason: if I am dreaming, this remark is being dreamed as well—and indeed it is also being dreamed that these words have any meaning" (*O.C.*, 383).

Let us set aside the question of whether it is necessary for Moore to prove that "here is one hand" is true as well as the question of whether it is nonsense to assert, as Moore does, that the reason he cannot do this is that he cannot prove he is not dreaming. As I will be arguing in what follows, these are not the only issues upon which the overall argument in the paper turns. Indeed, I will now argue that the central issues of the paper are to be located in the supporting reasons Moore gives for propositions (5) and (6). These, as I have just indicated, are essential if his proof is to have the import Moore takes it to have. I also believe that most commentators have not appreciated the centrality of these issues. Most of the vast critical literature on Moore's paper has focused on premises (1) and (2) and on Moore's meta-remarks, just quoted, about his not being able to prove these premises. We have already seen that this is true of *On Certainty* as well.

Because the proof is the climax of the paper, it is understandable, to be sure, that it should be in the fovea of the critical eye; but in a certain sense it is also peculiar. The so-called proof, with Moore's meta-commentary on it, occupies only the last five pages of a twenty-three–page paper. Most of the paper that precedes the proof is, in fact, taken up with a series of brilliant distinctions, for example, the difference between the concept of *to be met with in space* and the concept of *to be presented in space*. Moore maintains, correctly in my opinion, that Kant conflates these notions. Moore points out that what he calls *a negative after-image* is presented in space, but is not to be met with in space, so that the concepts are not equipollent, as Kant implies. Moreover, certain sorts of other visual images, for example, what Moore calls after-images, are not presented in space or to be met with in space. An example is the faint bulb-like glow one apprehends with one's eyes closed after one has, with one's eyes open, stared fixedly for some moments at a naked light bulb. This image is not presented in space in any straightforward sense because one's eyes are closed, and therefore one is not, as in the case of a negative after-image, apprehending any portion of physical space at all; and, of course, for reasons we shall discuss later, it is not to be met with in space either.

These distinctions (of which I have provided only a sample) turn out to play fundamental roles in the paper since they are part of the grounds Moore advances for believing that (5) and (6) are true. I thus find it surprising that so little attention has been paid to them. We shall also find that the reasons Moore gives for believing these principles to be true are compelling, and when they are fully appreciated his proof will come to seem more powerful and less quixotic than it has to most critics.

One who approaches the paper from this perspective will thus see something about it that is ordinarily missed or at least not emphasized by commentators. Moore's essay belongs to a long line of attempts by philosophers to do what might be called *drawing the line*. A famous instance of this procedure is in Mill's *On Liberty*. Mill tries to draw a defensible conceptual distinction between the private and public domains of human conduct. The line he draws is between those activities that concern only oneself and those that impinge upon others. (Whether he succeeds in drawing a useful distinction is not something I shall pursue here.) The purpose of drawing the line is to defend private, idiosyncratic behavior from state and government interference and from the pressures of public opinion. Once the distinction is clearly made, as he sees it, between the public and private domains, Mill will then go on to ask such questions as: Under what conditions does the government or state have the *legitimate* right to intervene in the private activities of its individual citizens?

Now Moore is doing much the same sort of thing. Kant has in his challenge presupposed a distinction between what exists external to the mind and what does not. Moore is puzzled by Kant's way of drawing the distinction, which tends, for instance, to conflate the notion of being presented in space with the notion of being met with in space. So what he wishes to do is redraw the distinction in the endeavor both to satisfy certain intuitions we have and to sharpen those intuitions. He is here thinking of a long philosophical tradition in which the notions of inner-outer, internal-external, private and public, *inter alia*, are appealed to both in formulating and in trying to solve the famous problem of our knowledge of the external world. The categories between which he wishes to draw such a line are the familiar ones of mind and matter. These are taken in the tradition to be both exclusive and exhaustive, so that if x is a mental entity, x cannot be a material or physical entity, and conversely. The purpose of drawing the line is to be able to assign items, if there are any, to the correct categories. Moore believes that once the line is drawn, that is, once we have a clear conception of what it is either to be internal or external to the mind, then it becomes an empirical question whether things exist that fit either characterization, and thus an empirical question whether, for instance, there are objects that exist outside of our minds. The distinctions I have alluded to and that we shall now discuss are thus designed to allow him to make these determinations. As Moore writes after having formulated the criteria he thinks will do the job, "and we can even say, I think, that just this and nothing more is what they have meant by these puzzling and misleading phrases 'in my mind' and 'external to my mind'" (*P.E.W.*, 143).

The intuition Moore wishes to capture by the distinctions we shall be considering is the following. It is widely believed that there is some fundamental difference among such things as aches, pains, headaches, certain sorts of visual experiences, thoughts, and desires on the one hand and such things as (to quote Moore's own list) "my body, the bodies of other men, the bodies of animals, plants of all sorts, stones, mountains, the sun, the moon, stars, and planets, houses and other buildings, manufactured articles of all sorts—chairs, tables, pieces of paper, etc." (*P.E.W.*, 130) on the other hand. Granted that the items comprising the first list differ from one another, it is nevertheless believed that all of them are mental; and however diverse those comprising the second group are, they are all thought to be physical or material.

Moore wishes to make this intuitive difference precise, and he will do so in terms of two criteria. For x to be material or physical (1) x must be publicly observable and (2) x must be mind-independent. Moore does not tell us whether each of these conditions is necessary or sufficient, but there is no doubt that taken in conjunction they are sufficient for x to be a material object. Without exploring these relationships and possible ambiguities further, we can state that for him anything which satisfies the conditions of being neither publicly observable nor mind-independent are mental. Or to put this last point positively, anything that is only privately observable and/or mind-dependent is a mental object. Much of "Proof of an External World" is directed toward making these two conditions precise. Moore develops two principles that I call the *Privacy Principle* (PP) and the *Dependence Principle* (DP), respectively, which will allow him to draw this line exactly.

Moore's method of doing this is a little more complicated than I have indicated. What he is trying to describe is what it is for x to exist in the human mind. His procedure is, once this has been done, to say that if some x does not exist in the human mind, in the sense he has specified, then it exists "outside of the human mind"—that is, is part of the external world. He uses this method of exclusion for a specific reason. Such things as the pains of animals, which exist in the animal mind and are thus mental in some sense, nonetheless exist outside of our minds. Thus, not every thing that exists outside of our minds is physical. More specifically, what he is doing then is to try to explain what it means to say of any *human mental x* that it is private or that it is mind-dependent. It is these two conditions that Moore focuses on. Let us see how he carries out this task.

We begin with the Privacy Principle (PP). It is contained in the last line of the following passage from "Proof of an External World":

> Upon reading these words recently, I took the trouble to cut out of a piece of white paper a four-pointed star, to place it on a black ground, to "look stead-fastly" at it, and then to turn my eyes to a white sheet of paper: and I did find that I saw a grey patch for some little time—I not only saw a grey patch, but I saw it on the white ground, and also this grey patch was of roughly the same shape as the white four-pointed star at which I had "looked steadfastly" just before—it also was a four-pointed star. I repeated this simple experiment successfully several times. Now each of those grey four-pointed stars, one of which I saw in each experiment, was what is called an "after-image" or "after-sensation"; and can anybody deny that each of these after-images can be quite properly said to have been "presented in space." I saw each of them on a real white background, and if so, each of them was "presented" on a real white background. But though they were "presented in space" everybody, I think, would feel that it was gravely mis-leading to say that they were "to be met with in space." The white star at which I "looked steadfastly," the black ground on which I saw it, and the white ground on which I saw the after-images were, of course, "to be met with in space": they were, in fact, "physical objects" or surfaces of physical objects. But one important difference between them, on the one hand, and the grey after-images, on the other, can be quite naturally expressed by saying that the latter were *not* "to be met with in space." And one reason why this is so is, I think, plain. To say that so and so was at a given time "to be met with in space" naturally suggests that there are conditions such that *anyone* who fulfilled them might, conceivably, have "per-ceived" the "thing" in question—might have seen it, if it was a visible object, have felt it, if it was a tangible one, have heard it, if it was a sound, have smelt it, if it was a smell. When I say that the white four-pointed paper star at which I looked steadfastly, was a "physical object" and was "to be met with in space," I am imply-ing that anyone, who had been in the room at the time and who had normal eye-sight and a normal sense of touch, might have seen and felt it. But, in the case of those grey after-images which I saw, it is not conceivable that anyone besides myself should have seen any one of them. It is, of course, quite conceivable that other people, if they had been in the room with me at the time, and had carried out the same experiment which I carried out, would have seen grey after-images very like one of those which I saw: there is no absurdity in supposing even that they might have seen after-images exactly like one of those which I saw. But there is an absurdity in supposing that anyone of the after-images which I saw could also have been seen by anyone else: in supposing that two different people can ever see the very same after-image. (*P.E.W.*, 131–132)

In this quotation Moore is distinguishing physical objects from non-physical objects, and one of the differences he is calling attention to is that a physical object, such as a star cut out of paper, can be seen at the same time by more than one person: This is what it means to say that the object is publicly observable. Note also that Moore says a physical object—depending on what it is—is the sort of thing that can be touched as well as be seen and, of course, in principle that can be touched at the same time by more than one person. Moore also states that one criterion for saying an object can "be met with in space" is not only that at a given time more than one person can see it but also that more than one person can touch it if it is the sort of object that can be touched at all. In contrast, an after-image cannot be touched, not even by its proprietor, but only "seen." Furthermore, it is not publicly observable. For these reasons, an after-image is not the sort of object that can be "met with in space." It is observable by one person only—the person who has it. As such it is a private entity.

We should also emphasize that Moore is drawing a distinction between x's being the sort of object that can be met with in space and being an external object. I earlier gave an example (the pains of animals) of the distinction. But he means it to apply not only to the pains of animals, mental entities that exist outside of us, but even to physical objects:

> Isn't it possible that a dog, though it certainly must be "to be met with in space" might not be an external object—an object external to our minds? . . . Of course, if you are using "external" as a mere synonym for "to be met with in space," no proof will be required that dogs are external objects. . . . But I find it difficult to believe that you, or anybody else, do really use "external" as a mere synonym for "to be met with in space." (*P.E.W.*, 138)

As the quotation illustrates, Moore is distinguishing among three concepts: to be presented in space, to be met with in space, and to be an external object, that is, to exist outside of us. On the basis of these distinctions, he is appealing to our intuitions that there is a difference between physical and mental existents. This is part of the process of drawing the line between these two different categories. But in order to do so he must become more specific, so at the end of this long passage he states the PP: "there is an absurdity . . . in supposing that two people can ever see the very same after-image."

In the discussion that follows, he makes similar comments about tooth-aches, certain sensations, double-images, after-images, negative after-images, and pains, and it is evident that he means to say the same thing about anything that could correctly be said to be in the mind of A, where A is a human being. It is, of course, important to emphasize that Moore is using "see" to cover cases in which we would normally say of the items being referred to (for example, pains and headaches) that we have rather than that we see or perceive them. Furthermore, he is stating in the Dependence Principle (DP) that none of these items exist at all unless they exist in some mind. With these stipulations, Moore is claiming it would be absurd to say of any given item that is in the mind of a particular person, A, that two or more persons can see or perceive it.

In the light of this preliminary discussion, we can generalize from the particular application of the PP, which occurs in the last sentence of the preceding quotation, and formulate the principle itself as follows:

(PP) *If x is in the mind of A, then it is absurd to suppose that anyone other than A perceives x.*

As so formulated, the PP presupposes that if x is in the mind of A, x exists and is perceived by A; and it explicitly affirms rather than merely presupposes that it would be absurd to suppose that anyone other than A perceives x. It is this claim that we shall examine in what follows.

Before turning to the DP, I wish to make explicit two propositions I believe Moore would agree are entailed by the PP:

(I)   If x is in the mind of A, x can be perceived only by A.

(II) If x is in the mind of A, x exists only in the mind of A. (I will shorten this latter phrase and say that in such a case x exists *da solo*.)

A main difference between (I) and (II) and the PP itself is that neither of the former makes any claim about what it would be sensible to say or suppose about the perception of x. (I) holds, for example, that x can be perceived only by A, but it does not hold that it would be absurd to suppose that x could be perceived by someone other than A—though, of course, it implies that any such supposition would be false. (II) is even weaker. It does not maintain that only A can perceive x, and it says nothing about the absurdity of such a claim. While maintaining that x exists da solo (i.e., only) in the mind of A, it would allow as true that x could be perceived by someone other than A, and in this respect affirms less even than (I).

Obviously, Moore assumes that the PP could not be true unless (I) and (II) were true. For it could not be absurd to suppose that anyone other than A perceives x unless only A can perceive x, and x exists da solo in the mind of A; moreover, Moore must require that (I) could not be true unless (II) were true. For if x did not exist da solo, as (II) avers, then x might exist (at the same time) in the minds of both A and B and, accordingly, might not be perceivable by A only.

It is thus clear that (II), that x exists da solo, is a critical assumption for Moore's believing that the PP is true. As we shall presently see, it is also a key assumption in the line of reasoning leading to the (DP) and thus in the whole argument leading to his proof. We shall want to return to (II) for a closer look in assessing Moore's argument, but let us digress for a moment to see what role it plays in his statement of the DP.

The DP is contained in the following passage:

If this explanation of this philosophic usage of "having an experience" is clear enough, then I think that what has been meant by saying that any pain which I feel or any after-image which I see with my eyes closed is "in my mind" can be explained by saying that what is meant is neither more nor less than that there would be a contradiction in supposing that very same pain or that very same after-image to have existed at a time at which I was having no experience; or, in other words, that from the proposition, with regard to any time, that that pain or that after-image existed at that time, it follows that I was having some experience at the time in question. And if so, then we can say that the felt difference between bodily pains which I feel and after-images which I see, on the one hand, and my body on the other, which has led philosophers to say that any such pain or after-image is "in my mind," whereas my body never is but is always "outside of" or "external to" my mind is just this, that whereas there is a contradiction in supposing a pain which I feel or an after-image which I see to exist at a time when I am having no experience, there is no contradiction in supposing my body to exist at a time when I am having no experience; and we can even say, I think, that just this and nothing more is what they have meant by these puzzling and misleading phrases "in my mind" and "external to my mind." (*P.E.W.*, 142–143)

It is clear from this quotation that Moore is asserting a very bold claim, namely, that it is (self)-contradictory to suppose that a particular after-image or pain that is in the mind of A can exist when A is not having what he calls "an experience." Moore's complex description of what it is to "have an experience" is too long to be quoted here and is admittedly vague. Let us simplify by saying that he means roughly by "having an experience" that the person in question was conscious or was dreaming or was having a visual image at that time. Thus Moore can be taken to be asserting in this passage that it is (self)-contradictory to suppose that a particular after-image or pain that is in the mind of A can exist when A is not conscious, dreaming, or having a certain sort of visual experience.

We can thus formulate the DP as follows:

(DP) *It is self-contradictory to suppose that if x is in the mind of A, x exists at a time when A is having no experience.*

This principle lays down a necessary condition for the existence of x and as such entails:

(III) x cannot exist independently of the mind of A (i.e., when A is having no experience).

But why should Moore think that the DP entails (III)? His reasoning seems to be that if x could exist independently of the mind of A, then x could exist in the mind of B when A is not having an experience. But if that were true, two statements entailed by the PP (I) and (II), would be false. It will be recalled that (I) states that if x is in the mind of A, x can be perceived only by A, and it will also be recalled that Moore believes (I) entails (II), namely, that if x is in the mind of A, x exists *da solo*. We have seen that Moore believes (II) follows from the PP on the ground that if x did not exist *da solo* in the mind of A, then x might exist (at the same time) in the minds of A and B and, accordingly, would not be perceivable by A alone. We thus see that the condition that x must exist *da solo* in the mind of A is entailed by the DP.

This line of reasoning shows that Moore in depending on the principle that each after-image, pain, and so on, exists only *da solo* comes dangerously close to conflating the DP with the PP. He could have made the distinction between them sharper without affecting his overall argument. For example, he could have treated the PP as maintaining that A's pains, after-images, and so on, are each perceivable only by A and the DP as holding that none could exist apart from A's having an experience. As so interpreted, only the PP would entail the *da solo* doctrine. On the other hand, the DP would simply state that unless A was having an experience, x would not exist. It would thus leave open the question whether someone other than A could perceive x, provided that his perceiving x occurred at the time A was having an experience. This distinction would interpret the PP as excluding the possibility of a given mental event's being publicly perceivable, whereas the DP would not. It, instead, would exclude the possibility that such an event could exist apart from a specific person's having a certain experience.

As indicated earlier, I interpret Moore as holding that the DP and PP together provide necessary and sufficient conditions for saying of x that it exists in the mind of A and, indeed, by a generalization of these principles to say what it is for something to exist "in our minds." By providing such a set of conditions, Moore is thus in a position to argue that if something exists which does not satisfy these conditions, then it will exist "external to our minds." As I have previously indicated, his proof thus crucially depends on where he draws the line between the internal world of the human mind and the world that is external to it. The DP and PP together enable him to draw this line exactly.

The resulting picture of the human mind is traditional; it comes close to the Cartesian and Berkeleyan conceptions—depending, of course, on how one interprets them. But if Descartes is interpreted as holding that ideas are modifications of thought, then in that sense of idea each idea will exist *da solo* in the mind of the person who has it. And if Berkeley is taken as holding that an idea or a set of ideas exists *da solo* and is dependent on the mind of the person perceiving it, then Moore's view in that respect is reminiscent of Berkeley's. Of course, Moore's general philosophical outlook differs from that of either Descartes or Berkeley, since he holds that there are physical objects that exist external to the mind and that we know with certainty that they do. Still, resonances of the Cartesian tradition are found in his work, for he also insists that such knowledge is not direct. See Part IV of a "Defense of Common Sense," for example, where this point is made explicitly.

So far, then, we have seen that Moore distinguishes two principles, the DP and PP, which in conjunction lay down necessary and sufficient conditions for x's being in the mind of A; that he interprets both principles to entail the *da solo* thesis; and that in the light of these principles he is now in a position to specify what it is for an object, if it can be found, to exist external to the mind of A—to "the minds of human beings living on the earth"—and, accordingly, to be part of the external world. We are now moving into a position where we can begin to understand why his proof is less peculiar than it might otherwise seem. For in saying "Here is one hand" and "Here is another" Moore claims to be exhibiting two objects that satisfy the criteria for existing external to our minds. To produce two such objects is thus to prove that there is an external world.

What is not yet clear is why Moore holds that it would be "absurd" or "self-contradictory" to suppose that after-images, pains, double-images, and the other pieces of furniture that belong to the mind do not exist *da solo*. That he does imply this is evident:

> It is, of course, quite conceivable that other people if they had been in the room with me at the time, and had carried out the same experiment which I carried out, would have seen grey after-images *very like* one of those which I saw; there is no absurdity in supposing even that they might have been *exactly like* one of those which I saw. But there is an absurdity in supposing that any one of the after-images which I saw could also have been seen by anyone else; in supposing that two different people can ever see the very same after-image. . . . It is quite conceivable that another person should feel a pain exactly like one which I feel, but there is an absurdity in supposing that he could feel *numerically the same pain* which I feel. (*P.E.W.*, 132–133)

In that passage Moore uses the term "absurdity" and in the passage to follow the term "contradiction," and I will assume in my interpretation of him that these are more or less interchangeable. Throughout the essay he does the same with "the very same" and "numerically the same," and I will also assume that these are interchangeable.

> . . . I think that what has been meant by saying that any pain which I feel or any after-image which I see with my eyes closed is "*in* my mind" can be explained by saying that what is meant is neither more nor less than that there would be a contradiction in supposing *that very same pain* or that *very same after-image* to have existed at a time at which I was having no experience. . . . (*P.E.W.*, 142–143)

In these passages, then, Moore is not only saying that two persons cannot, as a matter of empirical fact, see the same after-image or have numerically the same pain; he is saying something more—that it is logically impossible that they could. This is the message that his use of the epithets "inconceivable," "contradictory," and "absurd" is designed to convey. Yet though the text is clear that this is his position, it does not tell us why he thinks it absurd to suppose that two persons could, at the same time, see the same after-image or have the same headache. Moore, reverting to a technique we have seen exercised earlier, simply asserts that they can't and nowhere gives an argument to that effect. Yet the issue is critical. If he is wrong in thinking that it is impossible that you and I could have numerically the same pain or see numerically the same after-image, his effort to draw the line between that which exists in the mind and that which exists outside of it would collapse, and his proof would be no proof at all. It is thus important to try to understand why Moore assumes the posture he does.

Of course, since Moore remains silent on the matter, one could simply discontinue the exegesis we have been proffering here and allow the point to remain moot. But given its importance, I propose to explore the matter. My general assessment of what Moore is trying to do, and the insuperable difficulties that his approach encounters, will not be determined by the interpretation that follows. But I think it is consistent with this assessment and adds a deeper dimension to it. In particular, it illuminates our understanding of the covert principles that underlie Moore's philosophical practice, especially its Cartesian underpinnings.

Fortunately, we don't have to probe into Moore's subconscious for a plausible reconstruction of what he might have been thinking in this connection, for in "Proof of an External World" and in such essays as "Some Judgments of Perception," "Visual Sense-Data," and "A Defense of Common Sense" (Part IV) there are important clues. The most explicit of these is in the last three essays I have mentioned, in which Moore holds that various types of images, double-images, negative after-images, after-images, and so on, are *existent entities*.

According to Moore, such entities are things that are directly perceived, in contrast, say, to a hand, which is indirectly perceived. Why he draws this distinction is a complex question I discussed at length in my book *Surfaces* (1988) and therefore will not pursue here. More generally, Moore calls *whatever is directly perceived* a "sense-datum," and this term includes, *inter alia*, such things as visual images. There is no doubt on the basis of the textual evidence that he holds that visual sense-data are entities. It is this assumption that gives rise in the theory of perception to a profound difficulty for Moore, a perplexity that troubled him throughout his long career.

The puzzle arises when one reflects on the following perceptual situation. Suppose one is looking at a penny, an object that is known to be approximately circular. When one looks at the penny from an oblique angle the penny appears to be elliptical. According to Moore, in such a case one is directly aware of an elliptical visual entity that appears to be located exactly where the upper surface of the coin is located and whose shape exactly fits that surface. But according to Moore, since the surface of the coin is not elliptical, what the observer is directly perceiving, namely, the elliptical object that exists in his visual field, is an entity that cannot be identical to the surface of the coin. The observer is thus perceiving some sort of intermediary, a sense-datum, that stands, as it were, between him and the actual surface of the coin. But if the sense-datum cannot be identical to the surface of the coin and therefore cannot exist where the surface is really located, then where does it exist? And what is its relationship to the surface of the coin? This is the puzzle that confounded Moore.

Now note that this puzzle arises on the assumption that what exists in one's visual field under those conditions is an entity. This is why I said earlier that the Privacy Principle presupposes the existence of the sense-datum one is perceiving. Some of the deepest and most puzzling problems Moore confronted arose from this existence assumption, which he never abandoned despite severe criticisms by defenders of the so-called theory of appearing. I will therefore assume that the evidence for the statement that Moore holds that after-images are existent entities is beyond dispute. We thus have one piece of solid evidence to use in our reconstruction of his position that it is inconceivable that you and I could see the same after-image or have the same pain.

The second piece of evidence is more problematic. It is to be found in "Proof of an External World" itself. In explaining what it is, let's begin with something we know for sure. On the basis of previous passages I have quoted, we know that Moore distinguishes three notions from one another: (i) being presented in space, (ii) being met with in space, and (iii) being an external object.

I will now suggest that he is making unacknowledged use of a fourth concept, that *of existing in a place or existing in space* and that this notion is key to understanding the unarticulated thought process that leads to Moore's inconceivability thesis. That there is such a notion at the bottom of his thinking is, I acknowledge, a matter of conjecture. But I believe there is evidence for it and that it is embedded in the following passage. But we'll need some work to ferret it out. Here is what Moore says:

> And the second important example is this. Bodily pains can, in general, be quite properly said to be "presented in space." When I have a toothache, I feel it *in* a particular region of my jaw or *in* a particular tooth; when I make a cut on my finger smart by putting iodine on it, I feel the pain in a particular place in my finger; and a man whose leg has been amputated may feel a pain *in* a place where his foot might have been if he had not lost it. It is certainly perfectly natural to understand the phrase "presented in space" in such a way that if, in the sense illustrated, a pain is felt *in* a particular place, that pain is "presented in space." And yet of pains it would be quite unnatural to say that they are "to be met with in space," for the same reason as in the case of after-images or double images. (*P.E.W.*, 133)

In the opening sentences of this quotation, Moore identifies the concept of feeling a pain in a particular place, such as in one's jaw, with the concept of having that pain presented *in* space; then, later, he asserts that neither of these is to be identified with the concept of a pain's being met with *in* space. These remarks lead to a puzzle: How can a pain be felt in a jaw and yet not be met with *in* space, since a jaw can be met with *in* space? Of course, one might argue that the pain only appears to be felt in one's jaw but isn't really in the jaw. One would then support this contention by an appeal to the phantom leg phenomenon, where one can feel a pain in a leg that no longer exists. But even one who argues this case would find it hard to deny that at least the pain exists as distinct from merely appearing to exist. I take it that what the proponent of such a view would be urging as a minimum is that wherever the pain exists it can't be in the phantom limb. I think Moore would accept this caveat about the phantom limb but would insist, nevertheless, that the pain exists. If it is granted that the pain exists, even if it is not to be met with in space, we can continue with our reconstruction. What we now wish to show is that it is plausible to hold that the pain exists in space or in a place, even if it is not to be met with in space or in a place.

Moore is unquestionably correct in saying that we can often identify the place in which a pain is felt. I shall leave the sorts of complexities raised by the phantom leg phenomenon aside for our purposes here, for normally one's toothache is felt in an existing tooth and not in a phantom tooth. Moore would thus say that it normally makes sense to ask a person who is in agony, "Where are you feeling the pain?" Since this is patently a sensible question designed to *identify the locus of one's pain*, he would contend that it is hard to deny that in normal cases one's pain exists in the place in which it is felt, say in one's jaw. It is also hard to deny that one's jaw exists at some locus in the space-time continuum. So it is hard to deny that one's toothache exists in a place, that is, in the place where one's jaw is located.

But granting all this for the moment, Moore nonetheless insists that the pain could not be met with in space. What then is the difference between a pain's existing in one's jaw and and a pain's being met with in space? It seems that Moore believes, as our earlier quotations in this chapter establish, that for something to be met with in space it must be the kind of thing that at a given time more than one person can see, touch, hear, and so on (depending on the sort of thing it is). This, he affirms, is one difference between a pain and a dog. Only one person can have a specific pain, but more than one person can pet a dog at the same moment.

The important point that emerges for our reconstruction from this insight is that in order for two persons to pet a dog at the same time, the dog must exist at some place so that it can be encountered there. Dogs are thus the sorts of things that both exist in space and can be met with in space. But though a toothache exists in one's jaw it cannot be "encountered" there by more than one person at a given time and, therefore, in Moore's idiom cannot be met with in space. But that does not mean that the pain does not exist in one's jaw. It does and, accordingly, it is plausible to hold with respect to normal cases (as I think Moore does hold) that since one's pain can be felt in a place, it exists in that place.

Therefore, what I infer from the material I have quoted is that Moore is covertly appealing to another principle, that of existing in space or in a place that is designed to cover those normal cases in which a question arises about the location of a pain. This is a concept that is logically prior to the notion of "being presented with in space." That is, to say that something is presented in space implies that it exists in space no matter whether it is a physical object or a mental one. Accordingly, I am suggesting that in order to understand Moore's thought processes, we shall have to draw a distinction between the notion of existing in space and the related notions of being presented in space, being met with in space, and being an external object.

To be sure, Moore does not explicitly identify any such concept as that of existing in a place or existing in space. But I suggest he is presupposing this concept in making the distinctions he does make. Suppose the question is asked, Where are the pains of animals? Moore's answer is that they exist "outside of us." That answer implies not only that pains exist but that they exist somewhere. But where? An obvious response is that they exist in the bodies of the animals that have them, just as, according to Moore, our pains exist in various places in our bodies. They thus exist somewhere in space, within animal bodies to be specific, but nonetheless they are not to be met with in space. Since Moore states that the pains of animals are not presented in space, he has, in effect, identified a class of phenomena that have the characteristic of existing in space without either being presented in space or being met with in space.

Now I submit, on the basis of these textual clues, that Moore is thinking of certain sorts of after-images in much the same way he is thinking of the pains of animals. Indeed, in the last sentence of the quoted passage he says as much: "And yet of pains it would be quite unnatural to say that they are 'to be met with in space,' for the same reason as in the case of after-images or double images" (P.E.W., 133).

According to Moore, one can "see" an after-image, and if so, as he has asseverated in the essays dealing with perception that I mentioned above, that after-image exists. Some of these images are different from what Moore calls "negative after-images" in that they are neither presented in space nor are to be met with in space. But then where does an image of this sort exist? There is the strong implication in the text that the after-image you see, like the pain in your tooth, is not outside of your body, indeed in particular that it exists in your head. Similarly, there is the strong implication that the after-image I see exists in my head, but further it is implied that since our heads exist in different places in space, so must the after-images we see. And, accordingly, it is implied that if they are in different places at the same time, they cannot be the same object. I take it that some such pattern of implicit reasoning lies behind Moore's unsupported claim that you and I cannot sense the same after-image. But, of course, his claim is even stronger, for he states that it is not merely an empirical fact that we cannot be sensing the very same after-image: The impossibility is logical. Moore thus seems to be presupposing that it is a necessary truth that if x and y exist at different places at the same time, then x and y cannot be identical.

Generalizing from this example, one arrives at Moore's position. Moreover, one seems to have a good reason for it, for if x and y exist in different places at the same time, then we seem to be able to appeal to Leibniz's law to explain why x cannot be numerically identical with y. And if Moore is thinking of Leibniz's law as being applicable to these sorts of cases, then we can explain why he says that it is impossible or inconceivable that you and I could sense numerically the same pain or the same after-image. To assert the opposite would be to contravene a necessary truth. I do think, if I may pun, that something like this is what Moore had in mind in telling us what anyone had "in mind."

Unfortunately, there is an immediate difficulty in thinking that the principle that if x and y exist at different places, x is not identical with y is an application of Leibniz's law. Taken in this general way, the principle is not true. Clearly, the existence of universals, such as colors or certain types of disseminated substances, such as gold and water, would be counter-examples to it. The color red, for instance, can exist at more than one place in space without being two objects. So in order to defend the principle Moore would have to interpret it as applying only to particulars—that is, to items traditionally defined as existing at a definite place in the space-time order. This defense would then make such things as after-images particulars, which in turn would require that they exist at a place. So in order to make Moore's view plausible we have another reason for thinking we must require that after-images exist at a place. With that stipulation, it does seem as if Moore is thinking of Leibniz's law as applying to after-images and pains, and if so, we have an explanation for his contention that you and I cannot be sensing numerically the same after-image or the same pain.

The intuition that your after-image and mine are not numerically the same particular is a compelling one. In teaching "Proof of an External World" I have yet to find a student, graduate or undergraduate, who does not share that intuition. To be sure, some students have the notion that this is an empirical truth, that it is a matter of fact that your image and mine are distinct. They thus conceive of the situation as if the status of after-images were just like that of stars cut out of paper. Here you have one paper star and there you have another. And here you have an after-image and there you have another. It is just the way the world is that your image is located where you are and mine is located where I am; and since it is an undisputable fact that we are located in different places, it follows that our images are different from one another.

But Moore's position is that of the sophisticated theorist. He asserts that it is a necessary truth that we cannot sense the very same after-images and pains, that the necessary truth that no particular can be in two different places at the same time rules out that A and B could be identical. No matter what the empirical facts are, it is inconceivable, he affirms, that what each of us is apprehending could be numerically the same thing. Upon reflection, some students are eventually inclined to agree with Moore. But under either interpretation, they find it a highly attractive idea. And, of course, since this conception is at the basis of the line Moore wishes to draw between what exists in the mind and what exists outside of it, it tends to make that discrimination a compelling one as well.

Yet, I will now argue, the project Moore has embarked upon, resting as it does upon this principle and these distinctions, is fatally flawed. But in turning to such criticisms, I wish again to stress that some of the line of argumentation I have been expounding is not advanced in that form by Moore. It is an extension and reconstruction of the statements he makes in "Proof of an External World," so that there are risks in attributing views to him, however natural they may seem, that he, in fact, might not have accepted. But since I cannot think of any other plausible reconstruction of his reasoning—that is, why he holds that it is absurd to suppose the image you sense and the image I sense can be identical, except that these images exist in different places—I will go with the best we can do for him. Indeed, to a great extent the criticisms I make of Moore do not depend on conjecture but are based on what he actually says. I confine my discussion to his treatment of visual images, though my objections to his theory can also be applied, with minor modifications, to what he says about pains.

1. It will be noted that Moore emphasizes that whatever we know about images is based entirely upon what we can see. We cannot touch, feel, squeeze, or manipulate these images as we can, for instance, the stars we cut out of paper. Moore also claims that I cannot see your after-image and you cannot see mine because each image is private to its proprietor. From this supposed fact he argues that it is inconceivable that you and I could have numerically the same after-image. I shall now show that this account is subject to severe difficulties.

Moore is on safe ground in implying that a paper star I cut out and a paper star you cut out could be said to be very like one another or even exactly like another. One might say the latter if both cutouts were the same color, were composed of the same paper, and were exactly the same size, so that visually they could not be distinguished except in terms of their differing spatial locations. In such a case we have criteria for determining what it is correct to say about these two paper stars: for example, if they were exactly the same color, size, and shape, the expression "they are exactly alike" would be applicable to them. If they differed in certain respects but generally satisfied the above criteria, we might use the expression "they are very like one another." These criteria apply to such physical objects as paper stars in a straightforward way. Moreover, we can implement these criteria in practical ways. If two stars are stuck together, we can separate them manually. We can place one on top of the other to see if they are duplicates, and so forth.

Moore wishes to use such expressions as "very much alike" and "exactly alike" about the after-image I see and the after-image you see. But now we run into a difficulty. Since we cannot touch them, we cannot compare our after-images by setting them beside one another or by overlapping them, as we can with the paper stars, to see if they really are the same color and the same shape. But if we can't do this, then how can we know that they resemble one another in any respect, either exactly or roughly? Since I cannot see your after-image and you cannot see mine, there is no way—on the basis of what we each observe—of knowing that what you see and what I see resemble or don't resemble one another. Moore seems to have painted himself into a corner of the other minds problem. If his account were correct, we could never know on the basis of vision alone that we are sensing resembling visual images. The analysis rather than being helpful thus gives rise to one of the most troublesome problems in the philosophical arsenal.

Now Moore might try to respond to this difficulty. He might say that it is true that on the basis of vision alone we cannot compare after-images, but from that fact it does not follow that we have no way of making any comparisons.

Suppose, in support of that suggestion, he were to say that though I can't see your after-image and you can't see mine, we can surely talk about each of them. So imagine a case in which our descriptions of what we see are quite different. You say, for instance, that your after-image of a light bulb is grey, and I say that mine is red. We can stipulate that each of us is saying something that is true. Then we should be able to conclude that our after-images do not resemble one another. A comparison is thus possible after all. Hence, in the contrary case, where our verbal descriptions do coincide, why shouldn't we be able to say that the two after-images are exactly alike? And, of course, one could imagine intermediate cases in which our descriptions generally coincided but with some small differences. In the latter case would it not be reasonable to infer that the after-image I was seeing was very like the one you were seeing, though not exactly like it? So what is wrong with that response, Moore might ask?

There are several things wrong with it—the obvious one being that we cannot, in fact, superimpose our after-images upon one another as we could the paper stars. So despite similarities in verbal descriptions, we can't really be sure the after-images are the same shape or color. This is one of the difficulties that arises when all of the knowledge we have about after-images is based upon what we can see. But there are two other, more serious objections.

First, if sometimes we can sensibly claim on the basis of our verbal descriptions that our after-images are exactly alike, then it should also be the case that we could sometimes sensibly claim on the basis of our verbal descriptions that what we are both seeing is the very same after-image. According to this interpretation of Moore, it sometimes makes sense on the basis of our verbal reports to say that our two after-images are exactly alike. But if that is so, then when our verbal descriptions are identical it should make sense to say that we are seeing the very same after-image. The question is not whether this claim is true or not but whether it makes sense. Clearly, it makes sense if the basis of the claim lies in our giving identical verbal reports of what we each see. But if it does make sense, as I think it does, then Moore's inconceivability thesis is untenable.

The second difficulty with Moore's response is this. Presumably Moore would contend that if there is a difference in our verbal reports, it follows that we cannot be seeing the very same after-image. In short, according to our interpretation, he would aver that if you say your after-image is red and I say mine is grey, the contrast shows that we cannot be sensing the same after-image in the numerical sense of "same," since the same after-image cannot be both red and grey. I claim the conclusion does not follow and offer the following scenario as a counter-instance.

Suppose you and I are seeing a friend off at the airport. We wait to watch her plane depart and together we follow its flight. Obviously, we are both seeing the same physical object in the numerical sense of "same." But I am less far-sighted than you, so that at some point the object in my visual field begins to lose its outlines and becomes fuzzy. I say to you, "I can hardly make out the shape of the plane now." But you say, "I can still see it clearly." From the fact that we have given different descriptions of what we are seeing it does not follow that we are not seeing the same object: Indeed, we are—it is just that our powers of visual discrimination differ. Thus, even though our verbal descriptions of our after-images may differ, it does not follow that we are not seeing exactly the same image. It may well be that the differences we describe are due to our differing visual capacities rather than to the nature of the perceived object. It is thus fallacious to argue, as presumably Moore might, that from the fact that our descriptions of what we see differ, it follows that we are not seeing numerically the same after-image. It clearly doesn't follow. So Moore's inconceivability thesis cannot be sustained on the sorts of logical grounds to which he seems to be appealing.

2. The preceding comments lead me to a second major criticism of Moore, which is based on what he himself says, namely, that after-images cannot be touched or felt but only seen. The difficulty I am now about to describe applies to all mental phenomena and to certain physical phenomena as well. Consider the following cases.

Suppose the shadows cast by two people as they meet on a street corner meld indiscernibly into one another. Can one decide on the basis of what one sees whether there are two shadows there, one covering the other, or only one, as if one of them had been obliterated by their interdigitation? Obviously, what one would be inclined to say on the basis of what one can see is that there is only one shadow there. But can one be sure? Is the case like that of trying to decide whether two pieces of paper are stuck together? Not really, because one can't squeeze a shadow the way one can squeeze paper to see if it will separate into sheets. So when the two persons part and two shadows are visible again, shall we say there were two shadows there all along?

Moore claims that each of our after-images exists *da solo*. But since the basis for his claim is restricted to what he can see, how can he possibly know this? Suppose as I am observing an after-image of a light bulb with my eyes closed "it" begins to bifurcate and that two similar bulb-like images slowly form and drift apart, coming to rest in discernibly different places in my visual field. In such a case, would I say that there had been two after-images there all along and that for some unknown reason they had suddenly drifted apart, like two tectonic continental plates? Or should I withold judgment, for how do I know that each of them is not superimposed upon another and that if I continue to observe them they will not split again, so that I might have four images in my visual field? Or shall I say that there is only one complicated after-image there? There are grave objections to any way of describing the situation that I finally choose.

The moral to draw from these cases, which include both physical and mental phenomena, is not that we are seeing one and the same after-image after all or the opposite conclusion, that we can't be, but that we either lack or cannot apply the criteria we normally use for making these kinds of determinations. This is one difference, though not the only difference, between mental and physical phenomena. With respect to physical objects (i.e., three-dimensional entities) we invariably have such criteria and can apply them to resolve problematic situations, say whether I am holding twelve or thirteen playing cards in my hand.

The situation, as we have seen, is different with respect to certain physical phenomena. And with respect to mental phenomena such undecidability is the rule. We do not in general have criteria for deciding whether I am suffering numerically the same pain or seeing numerically the same after-image. Even if we did, we could not apply them in the way we can apply criteria in order to decide whether two playing cards are stuck together. That is, we cannot manipulate after-images; we can only see them. Moore's notion that each of us is experiencing exactly one after-image or pain is thus an undecidable contention. And if so, his further claim that you and I cannot sense numerically the same after-image is also undecidable. The criterion he is thus invoking for drawing an exact line between the categories of the mental and the physical is infeasible. Because that is so his proof based upon his ability to draw such a line will not go through.

A final note in this connection: we cannot argue that the distinguishing characteristic of mental phenomena is that criteria for individuation are not applicable to them. That may well be true of mental phenomena, but, as we have seen, it is also true of such physical phenomena as shadows, rainbows, and flashes of lightning, so undecidability as a criterion will not allow us to draw the line in the way Moore proposes. And if not, we have no way of deciding what it means to say that something exists "outside of us."

3. My next criticism is based upon Moore's use of the concept of numerical identity. This notion is normally contrasted with the concept of qualitative identity, and Moore unquestionably has that contrast in mind when he asseverates that your after-image and my after-image can be exactly alike without being numerically identical. In this context he is employing "exactly alike" as a

synonym for "qualitatively identical." What is the distinction, and why is it important in this context? Norman Malcolm provides a standard description of the contrast:

> If it were said that after dinner Petersen and Hansen smoked the same cigar, the remark could be ambiguous. It could mean that the cigar Hansen smoked was not distinguishable in respect to size, shape, color, or brand from the cigar Petersen smoked. We could express this, in ordinary speech, by saying that they smoked "the identical cigar." We say for example that "Six ladies at the ball were wearing the identical dress." What these remarks tend to mean is that two cigars were being smoked by Petersen and Hansen, and that neither cigar had any feature that distinguished it from the other; and among the dresses at the ball there were six that were indistinguishable—"You could not tell them apart."
>
> But one could mean something different by saying that the two men smoked the same ("the identical") cigar; namely, that altogether only one cigar was being smoked by them (they passed it back and forth like a peace pipe). The expression "numerical identity" is supposed to take care of this case. We are to say that the two men smoked "numerically the same" cigar. . . . If you have told me that A and B are smoking the same cigar at the dinner table, and I ask "Numerically the same?" you could understand me to be asking how many cigars, altogether, are being smoked by A and B. (*Thought and Knowledge*, 115–116, Cornell, 1977)

The important point that emerges from Malcolm's account for the objection we shall be developing is that the distinction between numerical and qualitative identity depends on the assumption that if two objects are qualitatively identical they cannot be in the same place at the same time, and that if x is numerically the same object, it cannot be in two places at the same time. This is why when A and B smoked numerically the same cigar they had to pass it back and forth like a peace pipe. But when they were smoking the identical cigar in the qualitative sense, each was smoking a cigar that was located in a different place.

Moore is palpably using these terms in a standard way. Therefore, we can say that his statement that your after-image and mine are not numerically identical, though they can be qualitatively identical, entails that if these notions are indeed applicable to after-images, each such image must be an entity that exists in a place. We also saw earlier that the notion that after-images are particulars also entailed that they must exist in a place. Now we have another reason for thinking that each such image must exist in a place.

Moreover, as the text establishes, Moore believes that the distinction between numerical and qualitative identity is applicable to after-images and pains. I shall challenge this assumption in the next and final section of this chapter, but before turning to that matter, I shall briefly describe a kind of conceptual incoherence that Moore's whole argument embodies. This incoherence derives from the idea, just mentioned, that after-images can be said to be in a place.

As we have seen, throughout "Proof of an External World" Moore is working with two metaphysical categories, the mental and the physical, and is trying to draw an exact line between them. But to say, generally, that something is physical is to say as a minimum that it is localizable. That is so whether one is speaking about physical phenomena, such as shadows, or physical objects, such as rocks. One difference here, of course, is that philosophers normally think of a physical object as being three-dimensional, as having bulk, and, accordingly, as displacing or occupying a certain portion of space at a given time. But because that is so, not more than one such object can occupy the same place at the same time. In contrast, physical phenomena can be located in a place without displacing or occupying any portion of the space in which they are located. A shadow that is two-dimensional can therefore be located in the same portion of space that, say, a stretch of road is occupying. So shadows have an existence in space without displacing space.

But now if one wishes to claim that an image or a thought occurs in a place, one would be committed to the paradoxical notion that the image or the thought satisfies one of the necessary conditions for being physical. In effect, then, one would be trying to define the mental in terms of the physical. But this effort would be incoherent, since these categories are supposedly both exclusive and exhaustive. Moore's whole program is thus set up to do the impossible: to define the mental by means of the physical by giving mental phenomena a place in the space-time order. But, of course, any attempt to define the mental in terms of the physical destroys the presumed distinction between these notions. If that is so, Moore's proof, which depends upon his ability to draw an exact line between the mental and the physical, is ultimately abortive.

One might think that Moore has an alternative, that is, to abandon the notion that an after-image must exist in a place. But if he were to do so, he could no longer apply the concept of numerical identity to that image; nor could he think of it as a particular. Accordingly, the *da solo* doctrine upon which his inconceivability thesis depends would have to be given up. Thus, neither alternative will enable him to save the program designed to show that objects exist "outside of us."

4. I will now turn to my final criticism of Moore's view. This is again based on his use of the distinction between numerical and qualitative identity. What I shall be denying is that we can always sensibly apply this distinction in every case in which we can sensibly use the terms "the same" or "the very same." That is, I will be denying that we can always sensibly say of some x that it is numerically the same or of some x and y that they are qualitatively the same, thus making it more precise, as it were, what we intended in saying what we did. Let's consider a series of examples in support of this contention.

Suppose we are looking at two cigars that are identical in the qualitative sense mentioned by Malcolm. They can, by stipulation, be said to have exactly the same color: a specific shade of brown, say. So we can sensibly say the cigars are the same color or are identical in color. We could vary the idiom. We could say there is exactly one color they both share, and so on. Now, can we sensibly say of that color that it is numerically the same color or that it is qualitatively the same color? One might argue either case. The case for saying the color is qualitatively though not numerically the same is that there are two places where it exists (i.e., where each of the cigars is located) and that the colors we see at those places are indistinguishable from one another. There seems to be a perfect analogy here with the case in which we say Petersen and Hansen have smoked the same cigar, meaning they smoked two different cigars. But note: by stipulation, we agreed that the two cigars exhibited only one color, not two. Clearly, the analogy with the cigars should lead to the conclusion that they contain two colors, indistinguishable from one another. But it doesn't. The "colors" are indistinguishable because they are the same color: one color, not two.

Shall we then say that the color is numerically the same color? This also seems plausible. By analogy with the case in which Petersen and Hansen smoked the same cigar—but meaning that they smoked one cigar which they passed back and forth—the color the cigars have is one color. Of course, we can't pass the color back and forth like a cigar, but that is not relevant here. What is relevant and what defeats the analogy are that the color exists at the same time in two places. There is no way that the single cigar Petersen and Hansen jointly smoked could have existed at the same time in two places.

The upshot is that though we can describe both cigars as being exactly the same color, even as being the very same color, the color they have cannot correctly be described as being numerically or qualitatively the same.

In order to avoid the impression that the preceding objection somehow turns on some specific feature unique to colors, I will vary the example. Consider this scenario.

After a considerable amount of work, I have composed a final examination that my class will take. I've had thirty copies run off, and I give one to each student who enters the room. It's true to say that all of the students are taking the same examination. Can I clear up any putative ambiguity by adding, "They are taking numerically the same examination" or by adding, "They are taking qualitatively the same examination"? Would either epithet add clarity to what I've said?

What I originally said—"they are all taking exactly the same examination"— is perfectly in order. I might have given four or five different examinations to the class to minimize cheating. But I didn't. I gave them all the same exam. Was it qualitatively or numerically the same?

Again one might try to argue either case. The argument for the former position might go as follows. Each student has a copy of the examination. Each student (and hence each copy) is situated at a different place in the room. Each copy is, except for location, indistinguishable from any other. So we have an exact analogy with the case in which Petersen and Hansen smoked the same cigar in the qualitative sense; that is, they each smoked at the same time and in a different place a different cigar. Therefore, it makes sense to say that the students are taking the same examination in the qualitative sense of "same." But does it? Remember that this idiom entails that there are two different cigars; accordingly, it would entail that I have given two different examinations (or in this case thirty), which the students take. But we agreed at the outset that it was the very same examination they were taking, that is, one and not more than one examination. The analogy collapses.

But if they were taking exactly one examination, then can't we sensibly say that they are taking "numerically the same examination?" Well, we can't. There is, of course, a peculiarity in even speaking, as we did, of the examination as existing in different places in the room. But this kind of talk is presupposed by anyone who wishes to use such locutions as "numerically" and "qualitatively" to modify "the same." So playing that game, we can say that the examination existed at more than one place at the same time and therefore that it could not be the same examination in the numerical sense of identity. Again the analogy fails. I submit that the distinction does not apply to the examination the students are taking.

Similar comments apply to ideas, thoughts, intentions, and desires. One can say, "We suddenly both hit on exactly the same idea." Can I now add that my idea is numerically distinct from hers? Or can I say the ideas are qualitatively the same? We lack the criteria for adjudicating the issue. Similar remarks apply to pains and after-images. We saw in (2) above that because we cannot see each other's after-images, and because our descriptions of our after-images are indecisive, the question of whether you and I are having numerically distinct after-images or qualitatively the same after-images is not resolvable even in principle. Yet we can and do use such expressions as "I have had exactly the same pain in my shoulder that you have now; it's really excruciating."

We can now generalize. We can see a pattern in Moore's approach to mental phenomena. He wishes to apply distinctions to them that can be applied only to certain sorts of physical objects in certain circumstances. But, as the preceding considerations show, the numerical-qualitative distinction cannot sensibly be applied to everything, though it can sensibly be applied in certain circumstances to such physical objects as cigars or dresses. In particular, it does not sensibly apply to after-images, pains, double-images, dreams, intentions, desires—not to any of the items comprising the furniture of "our minds" in Moore's sense of that term.

In effect, then, Moore has taken a distinction that one can sensibly apply to a limited range of things in limited circumstances and extended it in such a way that it seems to apply universally and in all circumstances. But this very stretching of the distinction robs it of sense. His whole argument in "Proof of an External World" thus rests upon a mistake that arises from giving physical objects and the criteria that apply to them priority over the whole range of describable phenomena. One might call this the fallacy of physical object primacy. The fallacy is manifested in his thinking that because it makes sense on a given occasion to assert that you and I are seeing numerically the same physical object, say a particular light bulb, it also makes sense to apply the adjective "numerically the same" to the after-image I have of that light bulb. It is this mistake in reasoning that allows Moore ultimately to infer that the after-image I am seeing on that occasion is numerically distinct from the after-image you are seeing on that occasion. But the cases of the light bulb and the after-image cannot be assimilated to one another. We do have criteria for ascertaining whether we are seeing numerically the same light bulb, but none for whether we are seeing numerically the same after-image.

I submit, then, that Moore has not succeeded in giving us workable criteria for determining what it is for an object to exist in our minds. Moore's strategy in developing his famous proof thus fails for want of a sensible contrast between what is in the human mind and what is external to it.

Our approach in this chapter has been different from anything we shall find in *On Certainty*. Our concentration has not been on Moore's proof per se. We have not addressed Moore's contention that his argument is indeed a proof or that he knows its premises to be true with certainty or the matter of whether Moore is misusing "know" in this particular context. Nor have we looked into certain deeper perplexities, such as the relationships that hold between believing x and knowing x.

In contrast, these and many others are the kinds of issues with which Wittgenstein is concerned in *On Certainty*. As I mentioned at the end of chapter 4, his way of treating such matters will put them in a new light and will raise for him the central question of *On Certainty:* what is the difference between knowledge and certitude? Wittgenstein's attempt to grapple with this issue follows a complex dynamic that unfolds in two stages: first, the growing recognition that a sharp conceptual wedge must be driven between the notions of knowledge and certainty; and, second, the deepening insight that certainty itself must be understood in non-propositional ways. As we shall now see, it is this second development, in particular, that will differentiate his treatment of scepticism from Moore's.

6

Finding the Beginning

After months of thinking and writing about Moore, and only twenty-five days before his death on April 29, 1951, Wittgenstein confessed that he was dissatisfied with what he had achieved so far in *On Certainty* or what he was likely to achieve in his rapidly constricting future. Putting this avowal in brackets, almost as if he were admonishing himself, he wrote, "[Here there is still a big gap in my thinking. And I doubt whether it will be filled now]" (*O.C.*, 470). His next entry is equally pessimistic: "It is so difficult to find the *beginning*. Or, better: it is difficult to begin at the beginning. And not try to go further back" (*O.C.*, 471).

Wittgenstein, of course, knew that he was dying and that his death was not far off. Over and over again in those final days, writing obsessively, he returned to the themes in Moore's three famous papers: Moore's proof of an external world, Moore's claim to know various propositions to be true with certainty, and Moore's treatment of scepticism. But he was characteristically disssatisfied with his struggles to bring out what was wrong with Moore's approach to these matters and, more important, what it was right to say about them himself. At various times he chided himself for putting something in the wrong way. In 358, for example, he said: "Now I would like to regard this certainty, not as something akin to hastiness or superficiality, but as a form of life. (That is very badly expressed and probably badly thought as well)."

These sorts of comments echo those in the Preface to *Philosophical Investigations*. There, it will be recalled, Wittgenstein wrote: "After several unsuccessful attempts to weld my results together into such a whole, I realized that I should never succeed." A paragraph later he said: "The same or almost the same points were always being approached afresh from different directions, and new sketches made. Very many of these were badly drawn or uncharacteristic, marked by all the defects of a weak draughtsman."

What was especially bothering Wittgenstein in 1951? The answer—or better, at least part of the answer—is a combination of his own unrealizable standards of perfection, his profound awareness of just how complex those epistemological problems were, and his frustrating attempts to make clear to others what he was driving at. If, as indeed it eventually turned out, Wittgenstein was never content with what he had achieved, how much more daunting must it be to the philosopher-critic who wishes to explain what he is attempting to do. Our aim in this book is not only to bring out the nature of his criticisms of Moore but, more important, to follow his intellectual struggle to advance those same topics in new and fruitful ways. But for numerous reasons any interpretation of what Wittgenstein was trying to do and what he actually accomplished is inordinately difficult.

Prominent among such reasons are Wittgenstein's awareness that philosophical problems resist theoretical simplification, generalized solutions, or easy explanation and that they therefore require a special sensitivity both to understand why they arise in the labyrynthian forms that they do and how, if at all, they are to be "resolved." That special sensitivity is crystallized into what Wittgenstein calls a method, and that method itself gives rise to further complications for the interpreter. Wittgenstein never explains exactly what it is or indeed exactly what it is supposed to accomplish. He tells us in the *Investigations* that it will issue in "sketches of landscapes," and by this locution he seems to be implying that it will not take the form of explicit argumentation leading to the sorts of definitive conclusions that traditional philosophy has aimed at.

That method is evinced in an aphoristic style, marked especially in *On Certainty* by the quasi-Socratic device of posing questions and often leaving them hanging and unanswered. These questions are sometimes addressed to an unnamed auditor or reader, sometimes to himself, and sometimes it would seem to no one at all. Even some of the aphorisms that take the form of assertions can be thought of as implicit queries, as if they should finish with a question mark. The same topics are discussed over and over again, looked at from this perspective and from that. But this kaleidoscopic process is never brought to closure. Thus there is never a summary of earlier sections or a signpost as to where one stands at that moment in the text or any indication that these aphorisms are gradually unraveling the threads of a submerged argument. The method will not allow one to write Q.E.D. at the end of the investigative process. In fact, it is dubious that the investigative process has anything that could be called an end. Perhaps it can and should just go on and on.

Compounding the exegetical challenge, *On Certainty* consists of a series of notes in first draft form. With his life ebbing, Wittgenstein never had a chance to polish these notes. In this respect his jottings form a marked contrast to those comprising the *Investigations*. As Ray Monk has pointed out (see pp. 319ff. of his biography of Wittgenstein), for many years Wittgenstein worked, reworked, polished, and edited the materials that finally were published as the *Investigations*. That work, though not wholly formed as one unit, is thus a product of Wittgenstein's most sophisticated ruminations on the topics he discusses. But the situation was entirely different with respect to *On Certainty*. Many of the entries have the status of first thoughts, something to be put down on paper for further reflection or reconsideration. It is not clear to what degree Wittgenstein was committed to many of these comments. They often strike the reader as tentative efforts to express an idea, and, indeed, other remarks are often at odds with them. Perhaps the greatest danger is applying some traditional theory to this diffuse collection and then foisting it off on Wittgenstein. It has been asserted that Wittgenstein is a relativist, naturalist, pragmatist, behaviorist, conventionalist, and so on. These sorts of assessments assimilate his work to familiar philosophical categories. (Kripke has even spoken of Wittgenstein as if his philosophy were a variation of Hume's or even of Berkeley's.) To settle for this sort of understanding is to give up the exegetical ghost and minimize Wittgenstein's originality and importance. Accordingly, all such construals are to be rejected. We need to discover the categories he is working with rather than importing them and assuming that they fit.

So, then, where does one begin in attempting to understand what Wittgenstein is getting at in *On Certainty?* Can any pattern be found in this collection of fractals? I believe that one can. There is, I suggest, a kind of dynamic structure to the work. It begins with a set of comments about his proof of an external world and about Moore's claims to know, with certainty, the premises of his proof. From this beginning the investigation branches in various directions, but it is impossible to find a straight or continuing line through any of them. Wittgenstein comes back again and again to older comments, sometimes repeating them, sometimes varying them. But interspersed in these are sudden, nodal moments: flashes of insight that show a deepening grasp of the issues. These nodal moments carry the reader forward; in a way that chaos theorists would enjoy, there is a kind of stepwise, progressive movement in this apparent randomness. The work gradually shifts its focus from Moore to the actual roles played in "the language game" by such "practices" as doubting, asserting, claiming to know, and so on, and from these considerations a new understanding of the nature of certainty slowly emerges. Knowledge and certainty are revealed to be independent concepts that play related but different roles in communication and other forms of human interaction. Eventually Wittgenstein's focus is turned upon certainty itself, and this notion is explored relentlessly in a series of brilliant metaphors.

All of this eventually leads to a way of thinking about scepticism that is partly directed to those attracted to it, partly to those, like Moore, who wish to reject it. What is the upshot of this elaborate exercise, given that it does not issue in "results"? The answer is that one's perspective on what is wrong with scepticism and how it can be defeated has shifted dramatically. One now has a different orientation toward or understanding of a network of facts that most of us, in some sense, were always aware of. The outcome is thus philosophical wisdom, a kind of deeper insight than we possessed before. But, of course, none of this is articulated in any perspicuous way by Wittgenstein. So for the interpreter it is a matter of collecting quotations, following their progress insofar as any such can be discerned, and then trying to articulate what Wittgenstein has left inexplicit. In the rest of this book, we shall roughly follow this dynamic pattern, beginning in the next chapter with Wittgenstein's discussion of Moore's proof and Moore's claim to know certain propositions with certainty and ending in the last chapter with Wittgenstein's treatment of scepticism.

I have emphasized here the obstacles that any interpreter of this subtle and difficult text must face. Still, there is room for optimism, even if it must be guarded. Despite the pessimistic thrust of certain remarks in Wittgenstein's later writings about the possibility of expressing himself correctly and thus of being understood by others, there are occasional suggestions that some comprehension of what he is attempting to achieve and indeed what he has achieved may be possible. It may be possible by those philosophers who can "think for themselves," he says. As he puts it in a somewhat self-deprecating aside, "[I believe it might interest a philosopher, one who can think himself, to read my notes. For even if I have hit the mark only rarely, he would recognize what targets I had been ceaselessly aiming at]" (O.C., 387).

Yet even following this clue, the matter of interpreting Wittgenstein correctly is not all that simple. What is clear is this. In order to see what targets he had been "ceaselessly aiming at" and what he hoped to achieve by hitting them, one cannot start with his treatments of scepticism, doubt, knowledge, certainty, and proof but instead one must go further back—back to the beginning, back to the source or sources of the conceptual models, the intuitions, the basic principles he is working with in grappling with these matters. But, as he tells us, "It is so difficult to find the *beginning.*" Nonetheless, let us try.

As I have said, one thing seems clear. The beginning is not to be found in the targets Wittgenstein had been ceaselessly aiming at. Obviously, Moore was one of those targets, but Moore was a transparent mark. What Wittgenstein wished to hit were philosophical and not personal targets. These, as I have been stressing, were those concentric rings defining the epistemological discipline itself: whether there is a common sense view of the world, whether this view is propositional in character, and if so, what it is; and if not, what its relationships to certainty, knowledge, belief, doubt, community judgment, and scepticism are. These targets are interconnected. To hit one of them is to raise a blinding dust of others, and each of those, when struck, will further splinter into a network of perplexities and conundra: when it is true and/or appropriate to say one knows, why doubting must come to an end, what counts as a proof, when the adducing of evidence is relevant, and even what it is to look for a lost button. It is this vast range of subjects that are his targets. But they are so numerous and so interconnected that they cannot be located at the beginning of his investigation; instead they belong to its mature or even senescent phases. So we shall have to look elsewhere.

I submit that a good place to start is with what Wittgenstein calls his method. To begin with it will allow us to see what basic conceptual models Wittgenstein is invoking in his understanding of the nature of philosophy; what sorts of problems philosophical activity, as so construed, generates; and, finally, given the "peculiar nature" of philosophical problems as he interprets them, how they can best be dealt with. As I mentioned earlier, Wittgenstein stated that his greatest achievement was to have contributed a new method for dealing with philosophical problems. In a key passage he writes: "Instead, we now demonstrate a method, by examples; and the series of examples can be broken off.— Problems are solved (difficulties eliminated), not a *single* problem" (P.I., 133).

This is a method not yet developed in the *Tractatus* or even in the *Philosophische Bemerkungen* of 1930, though there are stylistic and conceptual anticipations of it in both cases. By the time of the *Brown Book* (1934–1935) it has reached an explicit literary form. It is then applied without much change or development in the *Investigations* and in the notebooks that follow. We can pretty well locate its genesis in the transition period of 1930–1933. Moore, who attended Wittgenstein's lectures during those three years, reports Wittgenstein as saying the following:

> He said that what he was doing was a "new subject," and not merely a stage in a "continuous development"; that there was now, in philosophy, a "kink" in the "development of human thought" comparable to that which occurred when Galileo and his contemporaries invented dynamics; that a "new method" had been discovered, as had happened when "chemistry was developed out of alchemy"; and that it was now possible for the first time that there should be "skilful" philosophers, though of course there had in the past been "great" philosophers.
>
> He went to say that, though philosophy had now been "reduced to a matter of skill," yet this skill, like other skills, is very difficult to acquire. One difficulty is that it required a "sort of thinking" to which we are not accustomed and to which we have not been trained—a sort of thinking very different from what is required in the sciences. And he said that the required skill could not be acquired merely by hearing lectures: discussion was essential. As regards his own work, he said it did not matter whether his results were true or not; what mattered was that "a method had been found." ("Wittgenstein's Lectures in 1930–33," 322)

In bringing out the fundamental importance of Wittgenstein's method, I shall concentrate on three of its features: first, its intimate connection with his conception of the nature of philosophy; second, its manifestation in a special literary style that I shall call "the broken text"; and, finally, its purpose or aim, that is, what Wittgenstein hopes to accomplish by its use. From these topics we can move on to Wittgenstein's discussion of Moore's proof and the use of "I know." Let us begin with his conception of philosophy.

Wittgenstein's most sustained meta-discussion of the nature of philosophy and its problems is found in the *Investigations*, from approximately entry 89 to 133—that is, in about nine pages of text. Those nine pages are extremely concentrated, and one could easily devote a book to them. We shall restrict our discussion to a few salient points.

In these pages Wittgenstein uses the term "philosophy" in two different ways. In one use he is referring to what might be called traditional philosophy. Philosophy on this interpretation is a conceptual activity that attempts in non-scientific, non-empirical ways to understand the nature of the world and the beings that inhabit it. It attempts to facilitate such an understanding by finding coherent patterns in what seems to be a confusing flux of events and happenings. These patterns are not to be found in surface phenomena; if they were they could be discerned by anyone. Rather, they are deep-lying, hidden beneath the buzzing, blooming confusion that we all confront. So traditional philosophy becomes a quest to uncover the hidden, the essences of things, the covert principles that will allow us to make sense of the world as we find it. "We feel,"

Wittgenstein writes, "as if we had to *penetrate* phenomena," and about the philosopher's quest for the essence and the hidden he says:

> For they see in the essence, not something that already lies open to view and that becomes surveyable by a rearrangement, but something that lies *beneath* the surface. Something that lies within, which we see when we look *into* the thing, and which an analysis digs out.
> *"The essence is hidden from us"*; this is the form our problem now assumes. (*P.I.*, 92)

Philosophy when done in this way has the character of depth. It is profound in its attempt to discover the basic principles of reality. And the problems themselves are profound. As Wittgenstein puts it, this is an activity that gives rise to "deep disquietudes." Its problems have roots "as deep in us as the forms of our language and their significance is as great as the importance of our language." As can be seen from the attitudes he is expressing here, Wittgenstein does not disparage traditional philosophy. He respects it and the intractable problems it is attempting to solve. His attitude is thus completely different from that of such logical positivists as A.J. Ayer, who asserted that "The traditional disputes of philosophers are, for the most part, as unwarranted as they are unfruitful" (*Language, Truth, and Logic*, ch. I).

Wittgenstein's main criticism of traditional philosophy is that it does not so much discover patterns in reality as to impose them on reality and that this process leads to misunderstanding, misdescription, and paradox. Philosophy is not a fact-finding activity—even though it thinks of itself in this way.

> Logic lay, it seemed, at the bottom of all of the sciences. For logical investigation explores the nature of all things. It seeks to see to the bottom of things and is not meant to concern itself whether what actually happens is this or that. It takes its rise, not from an interest in the facts of nature, nor from a need to grasp causal connections; but from an urge to understand the basis, or essence, of everything empirical. Not, however, as if to this end we had to hunt out new facts; it is, rather, of the essence of our investigation that we do not seek to learn anything *new* by it. We want to *understand* something that is already in plain view. For *this* is what we seem in some sense not to understand. (*P.I.*, 89)

What is it that is in plain sight and yet that we do not understand? Take the notion of time, for instance—a philosophical subject if there ever was one. What is in plain sight are references we make to time in our everyday activities. In those references we show our mastery of the notion. And yet when we come to reflect on the concept itself our grip suddenly becomes insecure. We no longer know our way about. In chapters 14–16 of the *Confessions* Augustine soliloquizes about time, asking:

> What is time? Who can easily and briefly explain this? Who can comprehend this even in thought, so as to express it in a word? Yet what do we discuss more familiarly and knowingly in conversation than time? Surely we understand it when we talk about it, and also understand it when we hear others talk about it. What, then, is time? If no one asks me, I know; if I want to explain it to someone who does ask me, I do not know. . . .

We term ten days ago, let us say, a short time past, and ten days to come, a brief future time. But in what sense is something non-existent either long or short? The past no longer exists, and the future is not yet in being. Therefore we should not say "it is long," but we should say of the past, "it was long," and of the future "it will be long." . . . That past time which was so long, was it long when it was already past, or before that, when it was still present? It could be long at the time when that existed which could be long. Once past, it did not exist, hence it could not be long, since it in no wise existed. . . . See how the present time, which alone we found worthy to be called long, is contracted to hardly the space of a single day. . . . one hour itself goes on in fleeting moments; whatever part of it has flown away is past, whatever remains is future. If any point of time is conceived that can no longer be divided into even the most minute parts of a moment, that alone it is which may be called the present. It flies with such speed from the future into the past that it cannot be extended by even a trifling amount. For if it is extended, it is divided into past and future. The present has no space. Where then is the time that we may call long? Is it to come? We do not say of it that it is long, because it does not yet exist, so as to be long. We say that it will be long. When, therefore, will it be? Even then, if it will be to come, it will not be long, since that which will be long does not yet be. . . . Still, O Lord, we perceive intervals of time. We compare them to one another and say that some are longer and some shorter. But it is passing times that we measure, and we make these measurements in perceiving them. Therefore, as long as time is passing by, it can be perceived and measured, but when it has passed by, it cannot be measured since it does not exist.

Is there some fact or set of facts about the nature of time that Augustine lacks? Wittgenstein would say no. Augustine concedes that he is not at a loss when it comes to the use of temporal terms in his everyday life. It is when he theorizes about the nature of time that it seems incredibly puzzling to him. But why should this be so? Wittgenstein's diagnosis in the *Brown Book* (107–108) is that a philosopher like Augustine is importing a certain conception or "picture" of time in trying to understand what it is. That "picture" seems to be that time is a kind of river, flowing by a fixed observer ("as long as time is passing by, it can be perceived and measured," Augustine says). This vision carries with it certain implications: just as the river is extended in space, so time, it would seem, is extended in space, having forward and backward parts. This "picture" seems intuitively plausible and, moreover, to fit the facts, for it does seem as if time flows, moving, as it were, past a motionless percipient.

Yet for Augustine this conception gives rise to deep perplexities: if the past and future do not exist and the present—the so-called now—is contracted into an indiscernibly short span, then what has happened to the river of time? A river always remains extended, having parts that have not yet reached an observer and parts that have passed the observer. We can speak of the reach of the river that has not yet arrived as being of a certain length, and similarly of the part that has passed and is on its way to the sea. But if one holds that neither the past nor the future now exists, the river model of time does not help us explain what we ordinarily mean when we speak of the distant past or of a long prospective future. And even worse, if the present "now" is instantaneously disappearing into the past and being replaced by an ever-intruding future, at what time has the river passed our "fixed observer"? And does "fixed" mean that the observer is some-how not in time? But surely that is impossible. Yet what other conception of time might one have except as something that flows? The picture seems unavoidable to the reflective person.

Wittgenstein generalizes from the case of Augustine. All powerful philo-sophical insights will issue in pictures or conceptual models of this sort, models that are unremitting in their hold on the reflective individual. We say of the world "this is how it has to be." As Wittgenstein puts it, "a picture held us cap-tive. And we could not get outside of it, for it lay in our language and language seemed to repeat it to us inexorably." These pictures force themselves upon us; they seem unavoidable and to be great philosophical discoveries. They help make sense of our ambience by illuminating it like flashlights that cast spears of light into the dark. Another example of such a model would be the notion that human beings are nothing but machines—the kind of model we find in Hobbes, who asks, "What is the heart but a spring; what are the nerves but so many strings?" This is a picture that is today accepted, even fanatically, by many elimi-native materialists. Such a picture does provide an ordering scheme for compre-hending the world. But just as Augustine's conception of time leads to paradox so does this conception. It does so by obliterating the differences between such things as computers and human beings, subsuming both under the category of *machine*. It is this obliteration of distinctions we ordinarily make that is a mark of paradox; traditional philosophy in its quest to order reality via some simple but powerful conceptual model will inevitably issue in paradox, that is, in a con-stricted and distorted picture of the world. One cannot therefore do philosophy in that way; some alternative to it is needed. But what could it be? This is what Wittgenstein's new method is designed to provide.

There is thus a second conception of philosophy referred to in Wittgen-stein's later works, one designed to give us a better understanding of the world than traditional philosophy and, in particular, one designed to avoid paradox. The two conceptions are contrasted in this passage: "The real discovery is the one that makes me capable of stopping doing philosophy when I want to. The one that gives philosophy peace, so that it is no longer tormented by questions which bring *itself* in question" (*P.I.*, 133).

The first occurrence of "philosophy" in this passage refers to the traditional way of doing philosophy, one that issues in paradox and in self-torment. But, as the second occurrence indicates, this older way can be avoided or suppressed and can be replaced by a new way of doing philosophy—one that "gives philoso-phy peace"—which Wittgenstein describes in a series of striking apothegms:

> The work of the philosopher consists in assembling reminders for a particu-lar purpose. (*P.I.*, 127)

> Philosophy simply puts everything before us, and neither explains nor deduces anything. . . . One might also give the name "philosophy" to what is pos-sible *before* all new discoveries and inventions. (*P.I.,*, 126)

> We must do away with all *explanation*, and description alone must take its place. (*P.I.*, 109)

These comments about *reminders* and *description* are crucial to understanding the new way of doing philosophy. Wittgenstein agrees with the traditional philosopher that the facts are complex. Our ordinary ways of characterizing time are enormously complicated: these characterizations are embedded in a multiplicity of idioms in which the notion of time plays a role. The philosopher looking carefully at this multifarious array of idioms wishes to discover a comprehensible order in it and does so by trying to look deeper—to find the essence or real meaning of time itself.

What Wittgenstein says in opposition to this highly intuitive philosophical move is, "Don't do it." Do not attempt to look more deeply. Your everyday practice reveals that you know what time is, that you have a mastery of the concept. As we have seen, Augustine has admitted that he has no problems in everyday life in employing this notion. What he fails to understand is that his everyday employment of the concept *is* a mastery. And he also fails to understand that because that is so there are no residual problems about time to be solved. Thus, Wittgenstein emphasizes that Augustine's problems are of his own making. He wishes to impose a model that will simplify and order a seemingly chaotic set of uses of the concept of time. But this is both unnecessary and confusing. As Bishop Berkeley was later to say, "We first cast up a dust and then complain we cannot see."

So Wittgenstein's first step in developing an alternative philosophy to this older way is to say that no real facts about time are at issue. No facts are missing, and there is nothing left to be explained. Virtually everyone knows how to use the concept in his or her daily life, and so everyone knows what time is. What is strongly suggested here—I say "suggested" because it doesn't strictly follow, though it is the point Wittgenstein is urging us to see—is that there is no *theoretically* adequate description of time because "time" is used in many ad hoc ways. What is true of the concept of time is true of *all* the concepts philosophers have traditionally analyzed: knowledge, truth, certainty, name, object, and so on. It will be a function of the new philosophy to *remind* traditional philosophers that in every case they possess such knowledge. One can do this by "bringing words back from their metaphysical to their everyday uses." As Wittgenstein writes:

> When philosophers use a word—"knowledge," "being," "object," "I," "proposition," "name"—and try to grasp the *essence* of the thing, one must always ask oneself: is the word ever actually used in this way in the language-game which is its original home?
> What *we* do is to bring words back from their metaphysical to their everyday use. (*P.I.*, 116).

It is difficult to overestimate the originality and historical importance of Wittgenstein's assessment of traditional philosophy and the alternative he is proposing to it. In effect, he is standing on its head the received view about the nature of philosophy. Since the time of the Greeks the commonly accepted view of the philosopher contrasts him with the ordinary person. It is the ordinary person who is not reflective, who lives the unexamined life, who follows conventions and authority (especially political authority) blindly. It is thus the ordinary person who lives at the surface, in the world of appearance, to use Plato's phrase, and thus cut off from reality. By contrast, it is the philosopher probing beneath the surface who discovers (or at least tries to discover) reality. It is the philosopher who exposes the shallowness of the everyday conventions we all follow and who, by such probing, discovers the true nature of things. Socrates is the model of the exemplary philosopher, ultimately condemned to death by plain men, terrified by his obsessive search for truth. That the philosopher holds the key to wisdom, knowledge, and truth has been the accepted picture since time immemorial—accepted by nearly all intellectuals as well as by most common persons—and it is part and parcel of this view to denigrate the plain man.

But Wittgenstein's originality consists in turning this picture on its head. It is the plain man who is all right, who is not troubled by mental cramps, and who does not cast up a dust that prevents him from seeing things as they are. It is, rather, the traditional philosopher who does these things, who cannot see what is in front of his face and who in looking for the hidden is only chasing chimeras. In Wittgenstein we thus find the deepest challenge to the widely espoused picture of traditional philosophy. But that does not mean that Wittgenstein rejects philosophy entirely; instead he wishes to replace the older conception, with its vision of the invidious relationship between the philosopher and the ordinary person, by an entirely different one.

When he says, "what *we* do is to bring words back" the "we" is referring to himself and to a new way of doing philosophy; a way that will give us an accurate picture of the world. It will be non-distorting because it will flatly describe what is there "on the surface." It will not attempt to explain the world's surface features by looking for what lies beneath them, for such an explanation is at least redundant and at worst misleading. This careful description will thus function as a set of reminders of what each of us has always known, including those persons who do traditional philosophy. But unlike the ordinary person, traditional philosophers set aside what they have known because they are under the grip of a powerful conceptual model. In their search for a deeper explanation (normally a theory) they suppress the facts (say about time) that are available to everyone. Nothing beyond those facts is needed to understand the temporal aspects of the world. To remind oneself of those facts is thus to understand some particular aspect of reality as it is. I will continue this discussion of Wittgenstein's new way of doing philosophy below, but now let us turn to his use of the "broken text" as a seminal element in the method that the new philosophy should employ.

By "broken text" (a term suggested to me by Pellegrino D'Acierno) I mean a literary style of writing that is non-systematic, rambling, digressive, discontinuous, interrupted thematically, and marked by rapid transitions from one subject to another. The broken text typically takes the form of pithy remarks, such as maxims, apothegms, aphorisms, short paragraphs, or other sorts of scattered fragments. These short sayings function as the basic units by which the author wishes to communicate his or her thoughts. In that sense the broken text is distinguished from more standard, discursive forms of writing in which ideas are coherently organized and disseminated in larger units: sections, chapters, or

even whole books. One might briefly characterize any such broken text as a collection of snippings. No wonder Wittgenstein called one of his bundles of notes,
mostly composed between 1945–1948, *Zettel*. This literary style has ancient
antecedents, in Hippocrates and Heraclitus, for example; it is also found in in
such later authors as Leonardo, Bacon, Pascal, Vico, Kierkegaard, Nietzsche,
Karl Kraus, Gramsci, Heidegger, N.O. Brown, Barthes, and Derrida. And as
this list indicates, it can be used for both philosophical and non-philosophical
purposes. Wittgenstein is, of course, the consummate master of this mode of
writing in philosophy.

The use of the broken text is generally not accidental but purposive, and it is
commonly used in an adversarial or even subversive way. In such cases it is used
to challenge standard or received ways of representing various features of the
world, such as those expressed in the "spare, pure, transparent language" of traditional philosophy, as Professor D'Acierno puts it. Wittgenstein's use of it is
characteristic. He is reacting against *any* attempt by philosophers to understand
the world in neat, sharp categories. His invocation of the method thus rests on a
number of presuppositions: (i) the world is complex; (ii) no simple conceptual
model of the sort traditional philosophy imposes on those facts will accommodate their variety, and, accordingly, all forms of reductionism will eventually fail;
(iii) a discursive, organized, argumentative literary style is part and parcel of
reductionist model building; and (iv) the new mode of doing philosophy, in
which description replaces explanation, requires a different literary style. As
Wittgenstein puts it succinctly in the preface to the *Investigations* his use of that
style is "connected with the very nature of the investigation. For this compels us
to travel over a wide field of thought criss-cross in every direction."

Three further comments should be made in discussing this topic. First, the
frequent appearance of aphorisms and apothegms does not entail that a text is
broken. Historically, there have been many documents replete with aphorisms,
among them the *Tractatus*, which lack the characteristic features of broken texts.
Even in texts like the *Investigations* and *On Certainty*, in which aphorisms and a
broken text are present and almost inextricably intertwined, it is important that
this discrimination be made. Second, the notion of the broken text should not
itself be identified with any particular method, though once again in the case of
Wittgenstein his method and the use of a broken text are interdigitated. In this
instance one might think of the broken text as a special device or technique used
to enhance the effectiveness of a certain method. Third, Wittgenstein's method,
using the technique of the broken text, is designed for certain specific purposes,
mainly to break the hold that conceptual models exercise on philosophers,
including those attracted to scepticism. I will now speak briefly to each of these
points.

As I mentioned above, Wittgenstein uses apothegms and aphorisms in the
Tractatus, but it would be a mistake to infer from this practice that we are dealing with an exemplar of the broken text. The broken text, as defined above, is
non-systematic, digressive, and not marked by a tight logical structure. The text
of the *Tractatus*, in contrast, exhibits just such features. It is highly organized,
with major sections being defined by single natural numbers from 1 through 7.

Subsections are organized in progressively narrowing numbers according to topic and the thrust of the argument. We thus have a schema that, say, starts with a major section, such as 3, and moves to subordinate sections, such as 3.01, 3.03, 3.031, 3.1432, and so on. As distinct from the use of aphorisms in the later writings, there is a coherent, tightly knit pattern of ratiocination in the *Tractatus*. The aphorism is used there as a summary of lengthy reflections engaged in elsewhere and not recorded in the text. Rather than trying to accommodate all the complexities those reflections uncovered, Wittgenstein's method in the *Tractatus* is to extract an essential point from them and to incorporate it into a maxim (e.g., "Roughly speaking, objects are colorless."). As Wittgenstein was to say later (and in a different context), he was condensing a "whole cloud of philosophy into a drop of grammar." The effort to distill philosophical reflection into such a small compass is precisely the opposite technique exhibited by the kaleidoscopic ramification of apothegms in his later work.

Further, it is necessary to distinguish the broken text as a literary style or as a technical device from its philosophical purpose. A new philosophical method, such as Wittgenstein developed, is connected with its aim, with what it hopes to achieve in the understanding or resolution of philosophical problems. It is thus possible for a philosopher to use the technique of the broken text but to use it for familiar or conventional philosophical purposes. We can illustrate the point with reference to Pascal's *Pensées*. Pascal's purpose in using the device of the broken text was completely different from Wittgenstein's. His aim was to convert free thinkers (*libertins*) to Christianity. His literary style took the form of fragments, often aphoristic in nature, describing in multifarious idioms what is wrong with those whose lives are devoted to the pursuit of pleasure and the gratification of their egos and whose intellectual stance is an agnosticism derived from Montaigne. But that technique was put to a classical and familiar philosophical use: to defend a traditional religious view which held that faith was the result of God's inclining the human heart rather than convincing the mind, and doing so solely through Christ, without whom he avers it is not possible to know God at all. The broken text of the *Pensées* was thus not mustered in the service of a special method for rethinking the nature of the problems its author wished to grapple with so much as to defend a particular and familiar solution to them.

This brings us then to Wittgenstein's method per se, what he was trying to achieve by using the various literary devices he employs. As we have seen, Wittgenstein believes that traditional philosophers are gripped by pictures that "bewitch the intelligence." These pictures are designed to give human beings a deeper, more penetrating understanding of the world and certain of its features. But the application of these pictures gives rise to perplexity, puzzlement, and anomaly. These difficulties, he contends, are not empirical and therefore cannot be solved by an appeal to the facts. As he says, "The problems are solved, not by giving new information, but by arranging what we have always known" (*P.I.*, 109). The new method is devoted to helping philosophers rearrange what they have always known. One of the most powerful applications of the method is to scepticism. Like Moore, Wittgenstein does not believe that the sceptic is putting forth any thesis. But if that is so, then how does a Wittgensteinian treatment apply to the sceptic? The response, which we shall work out in detail in our final chapter, is that scepticism is parasitic upon a conceptual model developed by its dogmatic opponents. In effect, the sceptic is buying into the model and is committed to some of its basic suppositions. To show how and why the model fails is thus to remove the ground upon which sceptics take their stance. Once that "ground of language is cleared," as Wittgenstein puts it, nothing will be left standing in its place. The Wittgensteinian point of view is perspicuously captured in the following entry:

> Where does our investigation get its importance from, since it seems only to destroy everything interesting, that is, all that is great and important? (As it were all the buildings, leaving behind only bits of stone and rubble.) What we are destroying is nothing but houses of cards and we are clearing up the ground of language on which they stand. (*P.I.*, 118)

I pointed out at the beginning of this chapter that Wittgenstein never explicitly describes what his method is and what it is supposed to achieve. One must put together a range of more or less exiguous hints in arriving at an interpretation of what he believes he is doing. With respect to what the method is supposed to accomplish, I submit that it is designed to do two things: first, to loosen or eliminate the grip that certain conceptual models exercise upon philosophers and, second, to make explicit, through a set of reminders, the actual roles various notions play in our everyday lives.

With respect to the first point, we can say that the Wittgensteinian diagnosis of what is wrong with traditional philosophy resembles (as John Wisdom has emphasized) the diagnosis that a psychoanalyst might make of a neurotic patient. Let us say that the patient is suffering from a form of paranoia. He believes that some unknown person is trying to poison him. Suppose the analyst tries to explain to his client that there is no evidential basis for his belief. As the history of psychoanalysis makes abundantly clear, that approach would be unsuccessful. An appeal to the facts will not ultimately influence the patient; on the contrary he will absorb them into his model and thus neutralize their impact. The patient's problem is thus not resolvable by bringing more information to his attention. The analyst must instead somehow develop a method that will alter the patient's conceptual set. In effect, the analyst is trying to replace one (a misleading) world view by another (the view that the analyst represents and that most normal persons hold). The latter, the "correct" view, is in opposition to the one the patient holds. The change would consist in bringing the patient back to "normality," to possessing an outlook that will allow the facts to play their normal roles in his life.

A wonderful example in *On Certainty* illustrates these points. I will quote the whole passage, which stresses that when differing conceptual models are in opposition an appeal to the facts will not typically resolve the conflict between them:

> However, we can ask: May someone have telling grounds for believing that the earth has only existed for a short time, say since his own birth?—Suppose he had always been told that,—would he have any good reason to doubt it? Men have believed that they could make rain; why should not a king be brought up in the belief that the world began with him? And if Moore and this king were to meet and discuss, could Moore really prove his belief to be the right one? I do

not say that Moore could not convert the king to his view, but it would be a conversion of a special kind; the king would be brought to look at the world in a different way.

Remember that one is sometimes convinced of the *correctness* of a view by its
simplicity or *symmetry*, i.e., these are what induce one to go over to this point of
view. One then simply says something like: "*That's* how it must be." (*O.C.*, 92)

When Wittgenstein says that if Moore could convert the king to his point of
view it would be a *conversion of a special kind*, he is emphasizing that an appeal to
the facts will not in general change one's deepest picture of the world; that picture is too firmly embedded for the facts to do their normal work. Some other
way needs to be pursued to effect such a conversion.

I am not here asserting that Wittgenstein was intentionally aping the meth-
ods of psychoanalysis but merely that there are striking similarities. But there is,
in addition, at least one important difference, and this is to be found in the second point I mentioned above. Wittgenstein wishes the philosopher to learn
something by reading a book like *On Certainty*. He does not merely wish to dis-
solve the hold that a certain picture exercises but to give the philosopher an
appreciation for a set of facts that person has overlooked or minimized. This, in
the case of *On Certainty*, will consist in a detailed and positive account of the
roles played in "the language game" (i.e., in everyday life) by certain important
notions: knowledge, certainty, doubt, proof, evidence, and so forth. I take it that
the psychoanalytic process does not issue in positive learning of this sort.
Wittgenstein's main problem, which the methodology is dedicated to resolving,
is how to bring about the kind of attitude in a philosopher that will allow him to
learn positive things of this sort. In facing this kind of difficulty he is con-
fronting a problem not unlike the one the analyst faces, and that is why he feels
it important to weaken the hold that a picture exercises.

Unless one starts in this way the philosopher will be resistant to Wittgenstein's reminders. As we have seen, Augustine knows all the facts there are to
know about time and yet remains puzzled. Therefore, he must somehow be
maneuvered or manipulated into the position of giving up the model that time is
a river. When that has been achieved he can reach a state of mind in which he
will recognize and acknowledge his actual command of the ordinary temporal
idioms. But before one can cross that bridge there is a first step to take: how can
one get a philosopher to abandon a picture whose hold seems to be inexorable?
Wittgenstein's method was designed to meet that challenge.

In explaining this first step, the first element in Wittgenstein's method, one
finds the psychoanalytic analogy helpful to some extent. The basic technique of
Freudian analysis is the method of free association. The patient's associations,
embedded in talk, gradually reveal to the analyst where a particular model is
exercising its grip. But more important, of course, those associations freely
expressed will begin to reveal this to the patient himself. That person will eventually come to understand that his neurosis is based upon an incorrect assessment of certain aspects of reality, that his behavior and attitudes are driven by a
false picture. In cases in which a cure is effected the patient will come to an
assessment of his situation the way any non-neurotic person would. He will then
be free of an incubus, of the picture that held him captive. A philosopher read-

ing *On Certainty* will find in the play of aphorisms something like free association. That play of ideas, apparently unstructured and returning again and again to certain basic themes, will do for the philosopher who is willing to tolerate this "criss-cross" movement of ideas something comparable to what free association will do for the neurotic patient. It is to be hoped that it will liberate him from the conceptual set in which he is embedded and which forces upon him a certain way of looking at the world.

I said that *something like* free association is going on here. But we must not exaggerate the psychoanalytic analogy. Wittgenstein is not a psychoanalyst. There is no particular patient he is trying to treat, and there is no one in his "office" who is freely associating. Nor is Wittgenstein freely associating in his notebooks. He may not know in advance what the best formulation of a point is, but his approach is not random. He has a definite purpose in mind. Rather than freely associating he is in control. One might say, as he does, that he wishes to strike a number of specific targets. But even the archer analogy is not quite right, for the archer has no problem that corresponds to the best way of formulating a point. Let us therefore move away from such metaphors and describe the method in its own terms.

In a passage I cited earlier, Wittgenstein speaks about "demonstrating a method, by examples." I shall vary his terminology slightly; instead of speaking of "demonstrating a method by examples," I shall characterize what he is describing as a "method of cases." This method often relies on appeals to ordinary language, but such appeals should be distinguished from the method itself. For example, the language games that begin the *Investigations* describe a number of different situations (cases) involving a pair of builders, but the points Wittgenstein wishes to make in describing those situations do not depend on distinctions drawn from ordinary language. However, let's look at a pair of passages that exhibit Wittgenstein's typical use of the method in *On Certainty* (i.e., where infusions from ordinary language do play important roles).

> I go to the doctor, shew him my hand and say "This is a hand, not. . . ; I've injured it, etc., etc." Am I only giving him a piece of superfluous information? For example, mightn't one say: supposing the words "This is a hand" *were* a piece of information—how could you bank on his understanding this information? Indeed, if it is open to doubt "whether that is a hand," why isn't it also open to doubt whether I am a human being who is informing the doctor of this? But on the other hand one can imagine cases—even if they are very rare ones—where this declaration is not superfluous, or is only superfluous but not absurd. (*O.C.*, 460)

> Suppose that I were the doctor and a patient came to me, showed me his hand and said: "This thing that looks like a hand isn't just a superb imitation—it really is a hand" and went on to talk about his injury—should I really take this as a piece of information, even though a superflous one? Shouldn't I be more likely to consider it nonsense, which admittedly did have the form of a piece of information? For, I should say, if this information really were meaningful, how can he be certain of what he says? The background is lacking for it to be information. (*O.C.*, 461)

Note that in the first passage Wittgenstein says "one can imagine cases—even if they are very rare ones—where this declaration is not superfluous, or is only superfluous but not absurd." This sentence not only uses the term "cases" to describe Wittgenstein's method (and it is partly for that reason that I have so labeled it) but it also illustrates the method: what it is and what it is trying to accomplish. Wittgenstein is asking his reader—a philosopher like Moore, in this instance—to consider a number of different situations in which a sentence like "This is a hand" might be used.

Let's begin with a straightforward, standard use of the term. For such a case we need a particular background. Suppose there has been a massive earthquake in Sicily and that a large number of persons and animals have been trapped beneath collapsed stone structures. Rescuers might find whole (or even parts of) persons buried underneath the debris. Suppose after removing some fallen material they suddenly see something exposed, but not enough of it to identify it. As they continue digging more of the object is uncovered. Suddenly one of the rescue party might say, "This is a hand." In the scenario just described, the remark is not superfluous. Because he has suddenly identified the object, it is also informative for him to say to his companions, "This is a hand." We can call this whole scenario, which includes the description of a certain situation and certain things said in it, a case.

Wittgenstein would now ask us to alter the scenario slightly, and if we do we shall have a different case. What sort of alteration would allow us to say that the remark was superfluous? Suppose the members of the rescue party, working inward from the periphery, had come upon a hand sticking out of the rubble. All of them simultaneously notice the hand. Let's assume that they gather around the hand, look at it, look at one another, but say nothing. Still, there is a common understanding, as revealed by their actions, that they all know that what they are seeing is a hand. Now if one of them, after a pause, were to say, "This is a hand," the remark would be superfluous. It would be superfluous because the rescuer's saying those words in that circumstance would entail that he supposed his colleagues had not noticed and therefore had not identified the object as a hand. But since they had all seen the object at the same time, clearly recognized it as a hand, and each knew all the others knew it was a hand, the remark is superfluous. Thus, it requires only a small change in the description of the scene to produce a different case.

Let us move on to a third case. Here the issue is whether "This is a hand" is superfluous or whether it is nonsense, despite its grammatical form. Suppose someone suffering from an injury to her hand went to a doctor and said, "This thing that looks like a hand isn't just a superb imitation—it is a hand" and then went on to talk about the injury. How would we characterize what the person had said? Was what she said superfluous? One might argue affirmatively as follows: What the patient was showing the doctor was a hand, and the doctor knew that it was. So the doctor was being told something he already knew, and the patient knew the doctor already knew; therefore the remark was superfluous. One who argued in that way would be assimilating this case to the one we have just considered. But another person might argue the contrary case, contending it would be a mistake to assimilate this scenario to the previous one. Why is that so?

The sentence the patient is uttering would normally suggest to the doctor that there is something about the object being shown to him that might mislead him into thinking that it is *not* a hand. But to convey that impression is not to say something superfluous. It is to say something misleading—just as if I had said, "All my dogs are corgis" when I do not have any dogs. In the previous scenario the rescuer who said, "This is a hand" was not misleading anyone. What he said was superfluous for the reasons given. But in this last scenario the remark is being used as if it were designed to forestall a certain assumption, an assumption nobody in normal circumstances would make, namely, that there is something unusual about the object the speaker is showing to the physician.

Now if the patient did not mean to suggest that there was something unusual about her hand and yet uttered those words, what would she be trying to communicate? If there is nothing unusual about her hand and she made the remark she did, her words would lack any conversational point. Wittgenstein's scenario is designed to make the philosopher see that how a person is able to understand an utterance depends at least in part on the contextual background in which it is uttered. The normal idiom, as he makes plain, would be "I have injured my hand; here is what I have done to it, etc." That idiom is normal because it presupposes a standard conversational scenario in which the speaker is taking it for granted that the doctor is in no doubt that what he is being asked to examine is a human hand. But if the patient began by saying, "This thing that looks like a hand," he would be presupposing that the doctor was or might be in some doubt about the nature of what he was being shown. In raising the specter of such a doubt the utterance—though taking the form of a piece of information—is not a piece of information because it lacks the requisite background for such a doubt to make sense. Instead, *in that context* it is, as Wittgenstein says, a piece of nonsense.

We stressed in the previous chapter that the sentence "Here is one hand" is a critical premise in Moore's proof of an external world. Moore never doubts that his uttering this sentence produces a genuine statement or proposition; he simply assumes it to be significant and therefore assumes it can function as a premise in his argument. But as we have just seen from the preceding examples, this assumption may be mistaken. Though the sentence is well formed and satisfies the rules of English grammar, those factors taken by themselves do not allow us to understand it. Its status will depend on the kinds of contextual factors we have just been describing. It is also clear that whether Moore's so-called proof, which incorporates this sentence, is a proof or not will turn on such matters. These are among the issues we shall consider in chapter 7. What should by now be palpable is that Wittgenstein's approach to the traditional moves that philosophers make is highly original and is obviously apposite in the case of Moore.

One could go on elaborating a spectrum of differing cases, beginning with those in which what is said is sensible and straightforward and continuing with those in which what is said is not. That is precisely what Wittgenstein does in *On Certainty*. That work contains a panoply of cases, resembling and differing from one another and ranging over an array of topics. The "criss-cross" technique of coming back to a case, showing how it resembles and differs from others, is what we mean by the method of cases.

The use of the broken text in Wittgenstein's later writings is intimately connected with the method of cases. It allows him great flexibility in describing and then discussing a wide variety of cases without being tied to a conventional organizational schema. It is the perfect literary mechanism for the use of the criss-cross technique. And in aphorism after aphorism, building upon example piled upon example, it allows the method to have its maximum effect.

The point of the method should now be apparent. It is designed to sensitize the philosopher to the complex ways in which various cases resemble and differ from one another. The message Wittgenstein wishes to communicate is that how we speak about, understand, and assess various features of the world and its inhabitants will depend on the subtle discriminations we make between resembling and yet differing cases. The philosophical significance of the method is that no overarching, synoptic theory or conceptual model will do justice to this variety of cases. The import of this method is thus twofold: first, to assist the philosopher in freeing himself from the compulsion to make such generalizations and, second, to make him realize that there is much to be learned about the world and its diverse features by comparing and discriminating these cases from one another. I submit that in his method we have found the beginning we were looking for. This will enable us, then, to appreciate Wittgenstein's profound and unique understanding of the nature of philosophical problems and, in particular, why their resolution requires a new methodology. We are now in a position to grapple with his treatment of Moore's proof of an external world and with Moore's claim to know the premises of that proof to be true with certainty.

7

The Oddity of Moore's Proof

From Wittgenstein's perspective Moore's two papers "A Defense of Common Sense" (1925) and "Proof of an External World" (1939) exhibited a profound difference in philosophical insight. We know that Wittgenstein greatly admired the first of these papers and did not think much of the second. He may well have wondered as he began to write *On Certainty* whether Moore's sensitivity to the nature of a philosophical problem had deteriorated in those fourteen years. In "A Defense" Moore had made no effort to prove that the common sense view was true; he merely asserted that he knew it was. The power of Moore's approach at that time lay in vigorous assertions that had the effect of making others agree that they indeed knew what he knew, including that "external objects" existed. But there was a feature of this paper that particularly impressed Wittgenstein, namely, Moore's insistence that radical deviations from the common sense view—such as the claims that time does not exist or that all objects are mind-dependent—had paradoxical implications. This insight represented an advance of historic proportions in understanding the nature of philosophical practice.

Moore, of course, did not think that paradox was a feature of *all* philosophical activity; in this paper he had only certain forms of idealism and scepticism in mind. But Wittgenstein seized on the concept of philosophical paradox and generalized it, so that, as we have just seen, the notion that all traditional philosophical views are paradoxical became an essential element in his treatment of philosophical problems from the early 1930s on. Moore had averred that if idealists were correct, it would follow that nobody had ever been on time or late for an appointment and that the wheels on the train carrying somebody to Cambridge from London did not exist when they were not being perceived. To draw such absurd implications from claims that contravened common sense thus bolstered the position that Moore, without direct argumentation, was advancing.

Moore was perspicacious in not attempting to prove that the common sense view was true. Since the propositions comprising that view were "obvious truisms," it was *obvious* that every normal mature adult knew that they were true; so a proof would have been otiose. Moreover, as we have also seen, Moore sedulously refused to say how he knew these propositions to be true, a refusal that struck many of his critics as sheer obduracy. But what seemed like obduracy had a deeper significance. In effect, Moore was refusing to participate in a familiar philosophical dialogue that demanded such a proof. This refusal, as I pointed out in earlier chapters, was an effective device in blunting the radical sceptic's tactics.

But then why did Moore in 1939 offer a proof whose conclusion was that the external world existed? One answer—and it is probably the answer Wittgenstein originally entertained—was that Moore had become co-opted by the traditional philosophical game. As Moore explicitly says in "Proof of an External World," he was accepting a challenge laid down by Kant, and Kant was, of course, standing at the terminus of a lengthy epistemological tradition from Descartes through Hume in which that challenge had been taken with the deepest seriousness. So as an initial response to the question, a plausible answer is that Wittgenstein might well have thought that Moore's philosophical nose had suddenly lost its sensitivity. We find the opening seven or eight pages of *On Certainty* to reflect this kind of judgment. Wittgenstein's remarks about Moore's proof range from condescension to sarcasm. The very first entry in *On Certainty* is, "If you do know that *here is one hand*, we'll grant you all the rest." And a comment like the following is equally indicative of his attitude: "It would surely be remarkable if we had to believe the reliable person who says 'I can't be wrong' or who says 'I am not wrong.' (*O.C.*, 22)

But as his understanding of Moore deepened, Wittgenstein came to realize that Moore's earlier paper embodied much the same philosophical outlook— though in a less explicit form—as was embedded in "Proof of an External World." As he reflected on the matter, it became clear to him that Moore, like most traditional epistemologists, was working under the spell of a powerful philosophical model deriving from Descartes. This model made the need to give a proof of the external world virtually irresistible. The model critically turned on an inner-outer distinction. It identified what was "inner" with the mental, the mental with what was private (accessible to one only), and the private with what was hidden from others. The model thus gave rise to the notion that each human being is encapsulated within the circle of his or her own ideas. Two "big" questions then followed: what reason does anyone have to suppose that there is a reality external to those ideas? And even if there is such a reality, what reason do we have to suppose that we have knowledge of it?

Those philosophers who emphasized the mental aspect of the model were led to idealism, the doctrine that all reality is mental, that is, to the thesis that there is no reality outside of our ideas and, accordingly, that the question of our knowledge of such a supposititious reality does not arise. Berkeley's immaterialism is the prime historical example of this position. Those philosophers who emphasized the privacy feature of the model were led to scepticism. We see the beginnings of such an outlook in Locke, who while not espousing scepticism nonetheless supposed there was an external reality underlying and giving rise to our ideas that was unknowable—a "*je ne sais qua*," as he put it. From Locke it is but a short step to Hume. Hume begins with the notion that nothing is ever present to the mind but perceptions and, accordingly, that it is impossible for us to conceive or form an idea of anything different from our ideas and impressions. He also admits that as an ordinary human being he is of the firm conviction that there are objects external to our ideas. But given his commitment to the principle that we cannot transcend the circle of our ideas, Hume concedes that no rational justification of this conviction is possible.

These two positions are logically independent; one could be an idealist without being a sceptic, and conversely. But Moore tended to conflate them for his particular argumentative purposes, so that "A Defense" and "Proof" are directed against both positions. He probably did so because in the epistemological tradition of the first half of the twentieth century, these two forms of Cartesianism were combined in complex ways in the work of Russell, Broad, Price, and Ayer. For these writers, knowledge, belief, and doubt were mental states; one could distinguish between such states only by looking inward, as it were, checking to see whether with respect to a particular proposition one knew or only believed that proposition. They also, generally speaking, believed in a world that existed outside of the human mind, so their puzzle was like that found in earlier writers, namely, what reason do we have to believe that these mental states correspond to such posited external factors. Moore, of course, asserted unequivocally in "A Defense of Common Sense" that he knew that such external objects as tables, chairs, other persons, planets, and so on, existed.

Yet when he enumerated his long list of propositions, his comments about them suggested that he had personally checked each to see if he knew or only believed it. He thus seemed to Wittgenstein to be espousing a main feature of the Cartesian model—that knowledge is a mental state. And this is what Wittgenstein in particular wished to deny. He says explicitly in *On Certainty* (308) that knowledge and certainty are not mental states like surmising and being sure. It was, of course, another great achievement of Moore's not to have identified inner states with those entities that could be known with certainty. And because he insisted that one could have knowledge about objects "*ausser uns,*" his critics did not see that at the deepest level he was buying into the traditional model. But Wittgenstein realized this. As he diagnosed the situation, Moore's claim to know with certainty that external objects exist involved only a partial rejection of the model. The disposition to look inward for confirmation or assurance indicated that the model was still playing its fundamental role in his thought, and for Wittgenstein Moore's peculiar use of "I know" confirmed this judgment. Putting the point at first rhetorically, he asks: "But now, isn't it correct to describe my present state as follows: I *know* what this color is called in English? And if that is correct, why then should I not describe my state with the corresponding words 'I know, etc.'?" (*O.C.*, 531). And then he says, this time assertively: "So when Moore sat in front of a tree and said 'I know that that's a tree,' he was simply stating the truth about his state at the time" (*O.C.*, 532).

Wittgenstein, of course, had no objection to the use of the term "mental state" per se. It was the identification of knowledge as a mental state that he rejected. Using "mental state" in one of its common employments, he makes the following remark about Moore's use of "I know": "Now can one enumerate what one knows (like Moore)? Straight off like that, I believe not.—For otherwise the expression 'I know' gets misused. And through this misuse a queer and extremely important mental state seems to be revealed" (*O.C.*, 6).

The "queer and extremely important mental state" that he is alluding to is the Cartesian model, and much of what follows in *On Certainty* is addressed to showing what is wrong with this conception. We thus find at the beginning of *On Certainty* an exegetical tie Wittgenstein made between the oddness of Moore's proof and Moore's particular use of "I know." Both are products of that queer mental state that distorts the philosopher's view of reality. It is the hold this model exercises that must be exorcised; and it takes a particularly subtle and sophisticated form in Moore's work, since, as we have seen, he does not espouse the standard version of this model, which insists that certitude is to be found only in the direct awareness of private mental entities

Thus, the major oddity that struck Wittgenstein when he reflected on the relationship between "A Defense of Common Sense" and "Proof of an External World" is that in 1939 Moore should have given a proof at all. Here, after all, was the philosopher par excellence of common sense asserting in one paper that it was obvious there was an external world, and yet feeling the need in another paper to prove the obvious. All of Moore's intuitions and his best philosophical judgment should have militated against such a move—a move that by Moore's own criteria is at best unnecessary and at worst absurd. Many of the comments in *On Certainty* are directed at trying to understand what could have motivated Moore in this way. The answer, put broadly, is that it was the Cartesian model, working its magic on Moore, that ultimately convinced him of the need to prove we could get outside the circle of our own ideas.

What is especially interesting to the exegete is what Wittgenstein thinks is wrong with the proof per se, that is, in what particular form or forms the model is expressing itself. That is, setting aside the genetic question of why Moore offered such a proof, one can find the proof worth discussing for a variety of reasons. In particular, Wittgenstein thought it of the highest philosophical interest to see how and why it fails. His deliberations about the proof fall into three classes: first, a set of difficulties he poses about the argument itself—that is, difficulties that apply to a range of sentences, organized in the form of an argument; and, second, an array of difficulties that concern the components of such an argument, namely, some of its premises and its conclusion. Wittgenstein concentrates upon the premise "Here is one hand," but he has important things to say about the conclusion, "There are physical objects." The third class of difficulties turn on meta-claims Moore made about the argument and/or some of its premises. The most important of such meta-claims are Moore's assertions that the argument is a legitimate proof, that he knows its premises to be true, and that he cannot prove they are true. The last statement is supported by the further assertions that in order to prove he knows these premises to be true, he would have to prove he is not now dreaming, and he cannot prove this. Wittgenstein discusses each of these three classes of difficulties in great detail. To attempt to treat each of them in similar detail would take us beyond the scope of a single chapter. Instead in this chapter we shall concentrate on the proof itself. In the course of doing so we shall touch on some of the items Wittgenstein treats in the other classes of difficulties. But we shall leave a sustained discussion of "I know" to chapter 8, where we shall tie his treatment of that topic to his discussion of doubting. Let us turn to his treatment of Moore's proof.

The point of giving such a proof would be to set to rest doubts that some philosophers have expressed about the existence of the external world. Once expressed, these doubts are transmitted through an historical, literary chain to later philosophers, who see them as a challenge that must be met for themselves and for their contemporaries. Locke and Hume stood in that historical relationship to Kant, so that Kant's aim in developing his proof was to dispel for himself and his coevals those doubts. As I have indicated, this sort of scepticism, cum idealism, was also widespread among epistemologists in the first part of the twentieth century, for example, in Russell, Broad, and Price. Moore's proof presumably would have been directed to restoring some degree of confidence in these writers about the existence of external things. The question Wittgenstein raises at the beginning of *On Certainty* is, What sorts of doubts are these? Are they the kinds of doubts Moore's proof will allay? I will have more to say about the nature of such doubts in the next chapter, showing again how they derive from the Cartesian model, so my comments here will be brief. But at least it is worth emphasizing that a profound question Wittgenstein is raising about Moore's proof is whether it meets the sorts of doubts that philosophers of a sceptical/idealist persuasion have evinced. Hence, some reference to that topic is necessary here. As we shall now see, Wittgenstein believes that Moore's proof is misguided in this respect, that it misses the so-called idealist/sceptic's point. He begins to develop his criticism with the following remark:

> "Doubting the existence of the external world," does not mean for example doubting the existence of a planet, which later observations proved to exist.—Or does Moore want to say that knowing that here is his hand is different from knowing the existence of the planet Saturn? Otherwise it would be possible to point out the discovery of the planet Saturn to the doubters and say that its existence has been proved, and hence the existence of the external world as well. (*O.C.*, 20)

With this example we see the method of cases beginning to do its work. Wittgenstein is asking us to compare three cases with one another: (i) doubts about whether a certain planet exists, (ii) doubts about whether one's hand exists, and (iii) doubts about whether the external world exists. Moore does not see that (i) and (ii) should be distinguished. His focus is, rather, on (ii) and (iii), and his aim is to persuade sceptics to blur any supposed differences between them. In effect, he is trying to persuade the sceptic that there is no difference between doubting the existence of a human hand and doubting the existence of the external world. Therefore, assimilating (iii) to (ii), he argues roughly as follows: "Here is one hand, so that one hand exists. But the existence of my hand does not depend upon my 'having a certain sort of experience,' and if not, then at least one material object exists. Therefore, the external world exists. Q.E.D."

But according to Wittgenstein, Moore's argumentative style raises the possibility that he is, in fact, assimilating (ii) to (i). That is, the power of Moore's argument seems covertly to rest on the notion that he has made an important discovery about his hand, namely, that it exists, a discovery similar to the one astronomers made about Saturn. In the passage I quoted, Wittgenstein wishes to make the point that if (ii) is assimilated to (i) rather than to (iii), Moore's proof not only would strike us as odd but it would also be deficient in meeting idealist and sceptical challenges. And why would that be so? If this is what Moore was really doing, his argument would look something like this:

> At one time, there was some doubt whether a planet existed in a certain por-
> tion of space-time. Astronomical investigation established that one did, and this
> planet was later named "Saturn." To have proved that there was such a planet
> shows that Saturn's existence did not depend on anyone's "having a certain sort
> of experience," from which it follows that Saturn is a material object. Therefore,
> the external world exists. Q.E.D.

What could be simpler or more effective? And this surely seems like a plausible interpretation of Moore's procedure. But, Wittgenstein asks, is Moore's proof really like that? If it is, then it is very peculiar indeed, for it presupposes that at some previous time there were doubts about the existence of Moore's hand. Was there ever any time after Moore was born that various persons, including Moore himself, doubted that Moore's hand exists?

If that were the situation, then Moore's proof presumably would be something like the proof that Saturn exists: it would provide evidence, new reasons for believing that such and such had been discovered to be the case. But the two situations are palpably different. Unlike the situation with respect to Saturn, there was never any time after he was born when anyone doubted that Moore's hand exists. From the time of his birth that hand was visible to anyone who cared to look at it. There was never any doubt about its existence before Moore gave his proof, nor was there any doubt about its existence when he gave it. So the difference between the two cases is enormous.

Wittgenstein's finding begins to explain one of the oddities of Moore's proof. Since no adducing of evidence occurred—and indeed since none would have been relevant because it was obvious that his hand exists—Moore's proof does not issue in a discovery that removes anybody's existing doubts about the external world, including those that Russell, Broad, and Price presumably had. Their question about the existence of the external world is not like the question about the existence of Saturn. It is indeed a very peculiar question, typically philosophical, in that it cannot be resolved by a factual discovery. As Wittgenstein says: "This situation is thus not the same for a proposition like 'At this distance from the sun there is a planet,' and 'Here is a hand' (namely, my own hand). The second can't be called a hypothesis. But there isn't a sharp boundary line between them" (O.C., 52).

Perhaps because "there isn't a sharp line" between (i) and (ii), Moore has failed to see how peculiar are the doubts of the traditional epistemologist. As Malcolm has pointed out, Moore does not take an ordinary case, the hypothesized existence of a planet, where doubt is apposite. Instead he chooses a case, the existence of his hand, about which nobody, including the idealist/sceptic, has any doubt. An idealist, like Berkeley, would agree that the object Moore is holding up is a human hand; about that he has no doubt. What he questions is that it is a material object. But what sort of a doubt is that? The answer is not obvious. But whatever sort of doubt it is, it is not one that belongs to the language game, since it cannot be allayed by the adducing of evidence. This is why Moore's attempted proof does not even address, let alone meet, the concerns of his opponent. As Wittgenstein puts it:

> The idealist's question would be something like: "What right have I not to doubt the existence of my hands?" (And to that the answer can't be: I *know* that they exist.) But someone who asks such a question is overlooking the fact that a doubt about existence only works in a language-game. Hence, that we should first have to ask: what would such a doubt be like? and don't understand this straight off. (*O.C.*, 24).

Thus, Wittgenstein's criticism is that Moore has failed to ask the right question, namely, what sorts of doubts are these? And because that is so his proof has not succeeded in meeting the objections to realism that his opponents have advanced. This is thus a case of the archer shooting at the wrong target.

This is only one of several criticisms Wittgenstein directs at Moore's proof. Again putting his point in the form of a question, he asks: "But can't it be imagined that there should be no physical objects?" (*O.C.*, 35). Well, what would it be like to imagine that? Let us try to provide an example. We would, of course, have to know what sorts of things count as physical objects. Let us say that among these are such things as tables, chairs, planets, and the earth. Could we form a picture of the resulting "world" if none of these things existed? Wittgenstein says, "Well, I don't know" (*O.C.*, 35). Let us pursue the question a little further. Suppose the earth did not exist: how would we discover the mistake? (see *O.C.*, 301, where the question arises in a slightly different form). It is obvious that if there were no physical objects, no astral bodies, including the earth, would exist. In that case whether human beings are considered to be physical objects or not, it is clear no human beings would exist either, since they depend for their existence on such bodies. So what would it mean to ask how *we* could discover the mistake? Given the suppositions that these "physical objects" do not exist and that we don't, the question would make no sense. It would be equivalent to asking, If we did not exist, how would we find that out? How can anything nonexistent find anything out? Suppose nothing at all existed; how could we find that out? When questions like this are formulated, language has indeed gone on a holiday, and nothing is really being asked.

The inference Wittgenstein expects the reader to draw from the question about the earth's possible non-existence is that there is no possible way one could be mistaken about the matter. With respect to the earth's existence Wittgenstein says we have reached bedrock. Since a mistake about the existence of the earth is not possible, the hypothesis that we could discover we were mistaken about its existence is not a sensible conjecture; it is conceptually vacuous. But in giving his proof, Moore is assuming that he is meeting a cognitively significant objection, the sceptical/idealist supposition, formulated as a "possibility," to the effect that no physical objects, including the sun, earth, moon, and so on, exist. But that so-called conjecture or possibility is vacuous, and, accordingly, Moore's proof to the contrary is also vacuous. As Wittgenstein says in

O.C. (35), Moore's statement "There are physical objects" is nonsense. The supposed proof, which derives this proposition as its conclusion, is thus not only pointless but empty of cognitive content.

I shall now turn to a third and (for our purposes in this chapter) final criticism of Moore's proof. There are, of course, other objections mentioned in the text, but the range is well exhibited by the three I will have surfaced here. This last objection is complicated and difficult to formulate explicitly. One can think of it as a submerged argument, something like an iceberg the top one ninth of which is visible. As usual, Wittgenstein's employment of the broken text does not issue in an overt argumentative structure. Instead of a string of connected assertions we are sometimes offered questions. These have to be transformed into declarative sentences if one is to bring the objection to explicit argumentative form, so a considerable amount of reconstruction is involved in setting forth his view. There are, in addition, gaps in the reasoning sometimes connected by a phrase like "of course," but the gaps are often enthymemes. These I will articulate. Finally, the objection does not occur in a consecutive set of passages but is interrupted by other materials, so some pasting together of passages is needed. These tortuous complications are worth following in detail because some of the notions on which the objection (let us now call it an argument) turns are both deep and original.

The argument is mostly, but not entirely, found in two places. It begins with passages 35–37, and picking up from those it is further elaborated in six entries, 54–59. Here I shall discuss its bearing only on the theses of realism and idealism, but in the final chapter I shall come back to one of its seminal ideas to show how Wittgenstein employs the objection against scepticism as well. Let us start with the first set of passages, 35–37. In 35 Wittgenstein asserts that Moore's sentence "There are physical objects" is nonsense. (Here, as I mentioned in chapter 1, we have resonances of the view expressed in the *Tractatus*, 4.1272; but as we shall see, the supportive grounds he now gives for this assertion differ from those in the earlier work.) In advancing his proof, Moore is presupposing that he is providing reasons in support of a certain conclusion that he expresses in various formulas, such as "There are external objects," "There is an external world," and "There are material (physical) objects." One such reason is expressed by the affirmation "I know that here is my hand." In entry 57 Wittgenstein implies "There are physical objects" is a logical consequence of "I know that here is my hand." He seems to be suggesting that if "There are physical objects" is nonsense and follows from "I know that here is my hand," that must be nonsense, too. This assumption is confirmed in 58, where Wittgenstein writes

> "The expression 'I do not know' makes no sense in this case." And of course it follows from this that 'I know' makes no sense either.

But then how these propositions are related is puzzling, since normally we would assume that B can be said to follow from A only if A and B are significant. There are also other difficulties. The kind of contrastive argument Wittgenstein is using here is subject to counter-examples. The words "true" and "false" used in a sentential context are often taken to express an exclusive contrast, so that if p is true, not-p is false, and conversely. This inference holds in certain regimented logical systems. In a two-valued logic if p and q are genuine statements, and if p is true, then q is false, and vice versa. But English is not constrained in this way. So some uses of "true" and "false" may not follow these rules. What is called a true corgi is determined by the criteria laid down at Crofts. But a dog of the same breed that fails to satisfy those criteria is not a false corgi, it is just a corgi. The opposition one wishes to make here does not use the term "false." We can formulate a similar counter-case using "I know." A teenager comes home at 2 A.M. The parent says, "You're late." The youth replies, "I know." The reply makes sense even though "I don't know" wouldn't. In what follows Wittgenstein uses such contrastive arguments against Moore, including versions of what were later to be called paradigm-case arguments. I believe the power of the point he wishes to make can be expressed without relying on these arguments, or where one must, by giving them an interpretation that preserves cogency. We shall address these and related exegetical difficulties in the course of the discussion.

Here is how Wittgenstein's train of reasoning begins:

> But can't it be imagined that there should be no physical objects? I don't know. And yet "There are physical objects" is nonsense. Is it supposed to be an empirical proposition?
>
> And is *this* an empirical proposition: "There seem to be physical objects"? (*O.C.*, 35)

Here we encounter our first exegetical hurdle. There is a difficulty in interpreting this entry. Does Wittgenstein mean that because "There are physical objects" is not an empirical proposition it is nonsense? Or does he mean that because it is nonsense it is not an empirical proposition? The former option suggests a verificationist approach whereas the latter does not. Evidence within the text, especially in entries 36 and 54–59, indicates that no is the answer to the first question and yes to the second, so that verificationism is not at issue. In a moment I shall cite the evidence based on entry 36. But we can set that issue aside here as it is not fundamental to the objection Wittgenstein is developing. What is clear is that he holds that the sentence is not an empirical proposition (this is "clear" on the assumption that one can convert his rhetorical questions into positive assertions). What he will argue instead in 36 is that sentences making a reference to physical objects are pieces of instruction in the use of the term "physical object." "And that," he will add, "is why no such proposition as 'There are physical objects,' can be formulated." As he says in *On Certainty:*

> "A is a physical object," is a piece of instruction which we give only to someone who doesn't yet understand either what "A" means, or what "physical object" means. Thus it is instruction about the use of words, and "physical object" is a logical concept. (Like colour, quantity, . . .) And that is why no such proposition as "There are physical objects" can be formulated.
>
> Yet we encounter such unsuccessful shots at every turn. (*O.C.*, 36)

The idea that "no such proposition as 'There are physical objects' can be formulated" gives us additional evidence in support of my suggestion that

Wittgenstein is answering no to the first question mentioned above. For to say that no such proposition can be formulated is to say something stronger than that it is not an empirical proposition. But as I have indicated, we shall not pursue the issue here for there is an immediate, more important exegetical complication that arises in the entry that follows 36:

> But is it an adequate answer to the scepticism of the idealist, or the assurances of the realist, to say that "There are physical objects," is nonsense? For them after all it is not nonsense. It would, however, be an answer to say: this assertion, or its opposite, is a misfiring attempt to express what can't be expressed like that. And that it does misfire can be shewn; but that isn't the end of the matter. We need to realize that what presents itself to us as the first expression of a difficulty, or of its solution, may as yet not be correctly expressed at all. (*O.C.*, 37)

The problem this passage raises is this. If "There are physical objects," said by a realist like Moore, or "There are no physical objects," said by an idealist like Berkeley, are nonsense and cannot even be formulated as propositions, how can Wittgenstein state that they are not nonsense for them? Is Wittgenstein implying that there is something meaningful they wish to say, though it cannot be expressed by the words they use? How shall we understand him here?

Let us develop three scenarios in an effort to grasp his thought, all of which take place in a restaurant. Here is the first one. Suppose I wish to say in a language I do not know very well, for example, Italian, that I would like the waiter to bring me a plate (*"Mi porti un piatto"*), but that the words I use tell him that I want him to bring me a flat-chested woman (*"Mi porti una piatta"*). Have I uttered a nonsensical sentence? What I say is certainly misleading, for it does not say what I wish to say; but is it therefore nonsense? Clearly, it is not nonsense because the waiter understood it; he understood me to mean that I want him to bring me a flat-chested woman. Perhaps one of the cooks fits the description, so it is a request he can even carry out if he wishes to. Is Wittgenstein saying that despite the misleading form of Moore's utterance it ultimately expresses a significant proposition, just as my misleading locution did, and that what Moore understood is a proposition analogous to what the waiter understood? The answer is surely no, since, according to Wittgenstein, there is no formulable proposition it expresses. Perhaps, then, the next example will come closer to capturing what Wittgenstein has in mind.

Suppose, instead, I had said to the waiter in perfect Italian, "Bring me some bits of green duration that are immersed in transcendental harmony." What sort of thing would he have brought me? Surely nothing that he could have found in the kitchen. We can say that in contrast to the previous case he would not have understood the sentence; that, furthermore, nobody would have understood it, and therefore that no one could have carried out my presumed request. With respect to this situation and with respect to that sentence, we can indeed say that what I uttered is nonsense. This scenario comes closer to satisfying the description Wittgenstein has provided. Moore's utterance is nonsense, and there is no coherent proposition it expresses. But this is too strong a scenario, for if it is correct, there is nothing expressed that anyone—Moore included—could have understood either. So there is nothing coherent being expressed in a misleading way.

Let us move to a third scenario. Here we replace the cast of characters. Let Moore be the person ordering, our waiter the classic "plain man," and Wittgenstein, standing behind the scenes, the cook. Once again (for whatever reason) Moore utters the words "Bring me bits of green duration that are immersed in transcendental harmony." The waiter does not understand this remark. On Wittgenstein's analysis, Moore actually wishes some bits of green duration brought to him. What he says is therefore nonsense. For the waiter the comment is also nonsense. But our waiter has just been hired. Unknown to him and to Moore, Wittgenstein, the cook, has just prepared a new dessert, a kind of cake that he calls green duration and a sauce for it that he calls transcendental harmony. Wittgenstein, of course, knows that neither Moore nor the waiter knows that such a dish exists. So when he hears the order, he realizes that though Moore is speaking nonsense, Wittgenstein could have used Moore's words to express a meaningful thought: that a particular dish be brought to him. This scenario comes very close to what Wittgenstein has in mind. He believes there is a correct and important idea that, as it were, lies behind the verbal façade that Moore has constructed. Wittgenstein thinks he knows what this notion is and that he will take great pains to formulate and then explain as *On Certainty* develops. Wittgenstein's idea about Moore's misleading way of expressing something that another (meaning himself) can articulate in a different way is put succinctly in *On Certainty* (116): "Instead of 'I know . . . ,' couldn't Moore have said: 'It stands fast for me that . . .'? And further: 'It stands fast for me and many others. . . .'"

We shall describe in the final chapter what Wittgenstein means by the phrase "It stands fast for me that." This concept makes an appearance for the first time in entry 116 of *On Certainty*. But in the section we are dealing with here the idea in that form has not yet appeared. Instead, there is a related notion that is, as it were, preliminary to it, namely, that, as Wittgenstein will say in entry 57, Moore's remark is a "grammatical proposition." We shall see as the discussion proceeds what Wittgenstein intends by this notion.

For the moment, working with this concept, we can see how Wittgenstein dissolves any suggestion of inconsistency when he says that Moore's utterances "I know that here is a hand" and "There are physical objects" are nonsense and yet that they can be taken to say something sensible in their peculiar, misleading ways. But it must be stressed that it is Wittgenstein who will give these words an interpretation that makes sense. Whatever that interpretation is, it is not what Moore had in mind or thought he was saying. It is something instead that Moore should have said. What Moore actually said is, in fact, nonsense, and because the sentences that Moore uttered occur essentially in his so-called proof, that proof is therefore also nonsense. Wittgenstein would reject any interpretation of Moore's proof that allows Moore's words to be making a sensible point about the existence of external objects. The alternative he is suggesting is that insofar as Moore's remark can be taken seriously at all, it must be interpreted in a completely different way: as a grammatical proposition or as conveying a logical insight. But such a grammatical proposition is *not* an empirical proposition; it is not about matters of fact or about the world. Moore, of course, does not think he is uttering a grammatical proposition at all. He intends his locutions to be empirical propositions that carry existential import and therefore intends his proof, containing those sentences, to establish that material objects exist. But taken in that way the proof crucially turns on locutions that are non-sensical and accordingly, fails.

In order fully to appreciate what Wittgenstein is getting at here we should separate the questions (i) Why are these locutions nonsense and misleading ways of expressing something that cannot be expressed like that? and (ii) What is it that they are trying to express in a misleading way?

The answers to these questions are found mainly in entries 35 and 36 and in six consecutive entries, beginning with 54, in *On Certainty*. The conceptual content of the last group of passages is especially compact; therefore, because of the difficulties of interpretation I mentioned earlier, I will quote them in their entirety here. Readers can decide for themselves whether with the additions of 35 and 36 they contain an argument at all, as I have been urging, and if so whether my construal of the argument captures Wittgenstein's intentions. Note also that in entry 58 a dubious contrastive, argumentative move occurs; we shall later show why this does not undermine Wittgenstein's reasoning or the conclusion he reaches. Here are the six entries:

> For it is not true that a mistake merely gets more and more improbable as we pass from the planet to my own hand. No: at some point it has ceased to be conceivable.
>
> This is already suggested by the following: if it were not so, it would also be conceivable that we should be wrong in *every* statement about physical objects; that any we ever make are mistaken. (*O.C.*, 54)

> So is the *hypothesis* possible, that all things around us don't exist? Would that not be like the hypothesis of our having miscalculated in all our calculations? (*O.C.*, 55)

> When one says: "Perhaps this planet doesn't exist and the light-phenomenon arises in some other way," then after all one needs an example of an object which does exist. This doesn't exist,—as *for example* does. . . .
>
> Or are we to say that *certainty* is merely a constructed point to which some things approximate more, some less closely? No. Doubt gradually loses its sense. This language-game just *is* like that. And everything descriptive of a language-game is part of logic. (*O.C.*, 56)

> Now might not "I *know*, I am not just surmising, that here is my hand," be conceived as a proposition of grammar? Hence *not* temporally.
>
> But in that case isn't it like this one: "I know, I am not just surmising, that I am seeing red"? And isn't the consequence, "So there are physical objects" like: "So there are colours?" (*O.C.*, 57)

> If "I know etc." is conceived as a grammatical proposition, of course the "I" cannot be important. And it properly means "There is no such thing as a doubt in this case," or "The expression 'I do not know' makes no sense in this case." And of course it follows from this that "I know" makes no sense either. (*O.C.*, 58)

> "I know" is here a logical insight. Only realism can't be proved by means of it. (*O.C.*, 59)

For the sake of perspicuity, I shall try to set out in a quasi-formal way the argument embedded in these passages. But remember, as I emphasized earlier, the reconstructed argument I shall present now cannot be found in that explicit form in the quoted materials. To illustrate the point consider Wittgenstein's comment in entry 55: "So is the *hypothesis* possible, that all the things around us don't exist? Would that not be like the hypothesis of our having miscalculated in all our calculations?"

This passage consists of two sentences, both interrogative. In my reconstruction of the argument the sentences are converted into declarative sentences and become premises (2) and (3). This is how they read:

> 2. The hypothesis that all things around us don't exist entails that we are wholly wrong about every statement we make about physical objects.
>
> 3. That hypothesis is similar to the hypothesis that we have miscalculated in all our calculations.

These premises, in this assertive form, cannot be found in passage 55 in the text. Accordingly, the sentences of my reconstructed argument, in two parts, that follows are not identical to those in Wittgenstein's text. There are also places where there is a greater deviation between the text and the reconstructed argument. But I submit that all these modifications allow us to capture Wittgenstein's intentions. My reason for reformulating what I take to be his argument and putting it in this explicit form is that when it is laid out in this way we shall be in a better position to understand it and the answers to the two questions I formulated a moment ago. I will divide the argument into two parts and will discuss the first part before stating and discussing the second. Part I is devoted to showing that sentences like "There are physical objects" and "There are no physical objects" are nonsense. It is thus dedicated to answering the first of our two questions. That part of the argument is to be found in passages 35–37 and 54–56. Part II is dedicated to explaining what idea Moore's misleading words should have expressed and thus will answer the second question. It is mostly contained in passages 57–59. The conclusion Wittgenstein draws from the two parts is that neither realism nor idealism can be derived from such locutions and, accordingly, that Moore's proof, which is designed to support one of these options and refute the other, is nugatory.

PART I

1. As we pass from the planet case to that of our own hand, a mistake becomes more and more improbable. At some point in this process a mistake has become inconceivable.
2. The hypothesis that all things around us don't exist entails that we are wholly wrong about every statement we make about physical objects.
3. That hypothesis is similar to the hypothesis that we have miscalculated in all our calculations.
4. But this is not a conceivable hypothesis; for in order to say that such and such is a miscalculation, we must be in a position to say that this (giving an example) is a case of a correct calculation.
5. But if all calculations are mistaken, then we could never be in that position.

6. Therefore, the hypothesis that we should be wrong in all our calculations is nonsense; and on similar grounds, the statement that we could be mistaken in all our statements about physical objects is nonsense.
7. Therefore, the statement that no physical objects exist is nonsense, and idealism cannot be derived from it.
8. The negation of "No physical objects exist" is "There are physical objects." But if p is nonsensical, then not-p is nonsensical, so that "There are physical objects" is nonsensical.
9. If p occurs essentially in R and R is "I know that physical objects exist," then because p is nonsensical, R is nonsensical. Therefore, realism cannot be derived from R.

I said above that in arguing that Moore's proposition "There are physical objects" is nonsense, Wittgenstein provides reasons that are both deep and original and that later such reasons are used against the sceptic as well as against the realist and idealist, as they are here. The first of these reasons is found in entry 54, which refers to the planet example we discussed earlier. Wittgenstein begins by saying that the case of the planet and the case of my hand differ not in degree but in kind. This is a deep and original insight, one that runs counter to our ordinary intuitions. We are inclined to think that the case of our hand is like the planet case: Both are susceptible to doubt. It is just that the planet case is less familiar, so doubt seems more apposite there. In principle it would seem that there is no great difference between them. But Wittgenstein says the opposite. As he puts it, it is not true that a mistake merely gets more and more improbable as we pass from the case of the planet to that of our hand. At some point there is a jump in incredibility. At that point a mistake has ceased to be conceivable. This is a profound insight, and we shall show later how it is connected with the basic notion of *On Certainty* that there is something that stands fast for all of us, something that is not open to doubt or to revision and therefore is something about which one cannot be mistaken. The concept of a mistake is a key concept in explicating why doubting must come to an end and how the latter conceit in turn is related to the correct use of "I know."

But why should we believe that at a certain point in the transition from the planet case to that of our hand a mistake has ceased to be conceivable? Wittgenstein answers this question in 54–56. His response rests upon an analogy. To ask whether it is possible that all things around us do not exist is like asking whether we have miscalculated in *all* of our calculations. But is that a sensible conjecture? Wittgenstein says no. The response, at this stage, makes use of what looks like a paradigm-case argument. In 56 he writes: "When one says: 'Perhaps this planet doesn't exist and the light-phenomenon arises in some other way' then after all one needs an example of an object which does exist. This doesn't exist,—as *for example* does. . . ."

This passage applies to the calculation case. In order to say sensibly that a mistake in any given calculation has been made, we have to know what it would be like to perform a calculation correctly. But in order to know that we need to point to a case—this one, for instance—in which no mistake has been made. With this sort of contrast in hand, the notion that we have miscalculated in this or that case makes sense. If we press our doubts and ask, "Isn't it possible that we have always miscalculated—that we have on every occasion been in error?" the argument indicates that the question cannot have a sensible positive answer.

But why can't it? the sceptic will persist in asking. The fact that the sceptic can continue to ask this question indicates that the paradigm-case argument lacks force. As I indicated above, there are other reasons for accepting this conclusion. Such moves work only in regimented cases, but may fail in open-textured languages like English. In this case, as the sceptic implies, the argument seems to beg the question. For how do we know that in *this* particular case our calculations are correct? Isn't it possible we are mistaken about it? The sceptic's point is well taken. But it does not undermine Wittgenstein's overall argument, which goes through independently of the paradigm-case move.

That argument, answering the sceptic's query, is contained in a difficult, compressed passage, entry 56. Let us try to articulate it. In everyday human practice, Wittgenstein asserts, "doubt gradually loses its sense," and he adds, "This language game just *is* like that. And everything descriptive of a language game is part of logic." I interpret him to be saying that what we call "the language game" consists (*inter alia*) of linguistic practices giving rise to instructional rules that define certain concepts. Among these would be the concept of doubt. According to the logic of the language game, the sensible employment of doubt entails that in principle all doubts are resolvable; they cannot sensibly be expressed ad infinitum. (This, of course, does not mean that, in fact, all are resolved.) Thus, to raise a so-called doubt that in principle cannot be resolved is senseless. We are no longer playing according to the rules of the language game that define the concept of doubting. Accordingly, to ask whether all of our calculations might have been mistaken and, by analogy, whether we might be wrong in every statement about physical objects is not to ask a sensible question at all. One is not playing the right game, namely, the "doubting game." A way of bringing out this point is to say that what the sceptic is calling "doubt" is not doubt at all. It is an activity related to and imitative of doubting but different from it in an important way. The difference between ordinary doubt and this sort of "philosophical doubt" is thus not one of degree; instead, we are speaking about things that differ in kind. To have seen this is a stroke of genius on Wittgenstein's part. It is, as I said earlier, a highly original contribution to our understanding of the nature of philosophy. In contrast, Moore's proof assumes that the question about our being wrong about the existence of "all things about us" is sensible and that he is providing an answer to it. But his response is then just as pointless as the putative conjecture it seeks to put to rest.

Wittgenstein's insight here that it is nonsense to raise certain sorts of synoptic doubts about various human practices occurs frequently in different forms in *On Certainty*. In 496, for instance, he changes the example but uses it to make the same point: "This is a similar case to that of shewing that it has no meaning to say that a game has always been played wrong."

Once again, with this analogy Wittgenstein is asking us to imagine whether it is possible that a given game, say chess, has always been played incorrectly. Chess has been played for centuries now, and an incalculable number of games have been played in that time. It is a reasonable assumption that books containing the formal rules for playing the game have been consulted again and again by players. What would it mean therefore to say that all such games had been played incorrectly? Would it mean that the persons consulting these books did not know how to read? Clearly, that is not a persuasive hypothesis. Suppose that a scholar had recently discovered in the first book describing the game of chess, written by the inventor of the game, a footnote saying the author had never played it. Suppose further that the scholar had discovered one of the rules in the book contained a misprint that affected the meaning of the rule and that the mistake had been replicated in all subsequent works on the subject. This scholar might then contend that there is at least one rule of chess that has never been followed and, accordingly, that every game of chess has been played incorrectly.

Would these comments be taken seriously by chess players? Clearly, they would not. Why should they accept this particular book or that particular rule as canonical—given the long history of their consensual conformity to a given practice. The issue would not even be open to argument. They would simply reject the contentions made by this person as irrelevant. Their point would be Wittgenstein's, namely, that our historical practice, even if fixed by an original misprint, defines what counts as playing chess. So anyone who follows present rules and present practice is playing chess correctly. It is thus not possible that chess has always been played incorrectly. Therefore when one asks, "Is it possible that we could be wrong in *every* statement about physical objects, including that no such things exist?" Wittgenstein says that would be tantamount to asking, "Is it possible we have always played chess incorrectly?" or "Is it possible that all of our calculations have been wrong?" The answers to these questions, for the reasons cited, are no. The sceptic's question is senseless, for it tries to question the historical practices that *define* game playing, the traditional procedures that *define* calculating, and our communal linguistic rules that *define* what it is to refer to such things as tables and chairs. This is what Wittgenstein means when he says that "at some point in our everyday practices, a mistake about such matters is no longer conceivable."

Wittgenstein's objection, in Part I of his argument, does not depend on a paradigm-case argument. Instead, it can be summarized as follows. It is not sensible, for the reasons just given, to suppose that no physical objects exist. For Moore to offer a proof that physical objects do exist fails to recognize this point. His proof is therefore misguided and unnecessary. From the outset he has been barking up the wrong tree.

Let us now try to formulate the second half of Wittgenstein's argument, which, as I have indicated, begins with entry 57. His thought here is extremely compressed. We cannot expatiate on each move he makes, but will confine ourselves to the main line of argumentation. Let us start with the step that precedes 57, which will help us tie the two parts of the argument together. That entry contains the notion that doubt gradually loses its sense. Here is how this part of the argument goes:

PART II

10. In the language game doubt gradually loses its sense (i.e., such doubts can be resolved in principle and therefore cannot go on indefinitely). The language game is just like that.
11. A description of the language game includes an account of how doubt gradually loses it sense; to give such a description is to describe the logic (or grammar) of the term "doubt."
12. "I know that here is my hand" is taken by Moore to be an empirical statement. But as we have seen in entry 55, this locution entails "There are physical objects." Since the latter, as we have seen in Part I, is nonsense, so is the former.
13. But to say it is nonsense leaves open the possibility that it is a grammatical proposition, used to describe the logic of "doubt" and thus to make a logical point. Hence it should not be taken *temporally* (i.e., as an empirical proposition, as Moore thinks). (*O.C.*, 57)
14. But in that case it is like "I *know*, I am not just surmising, that I am seeing red." From this proposition it follows "There are colors." "There are physical objects" is then like "There are colors." It follows from "I know that here is my hand." (*O.C.*, 57)
15. But if "I know that here is my hand" is a grammatical proposition, the "I" cannot be important. ("I" does not have its usual indexical function, making an ineliminable reference to the speaker.) The proposition instead means "There is no such thing as doubt in this case" or, alternatively, "'I don't know, etc.' makes no sense in this case." (*O.C.*, 58)
16. But if "I don't know, etc." makes no sense in this case, then "I know, etc." makes no sense either. (*O.C.*, 58)
17. "I know, etc." thus makes a logical point, that is, it serves as a grammatical proposition about the use of certain words. (*O.C.*, 59)
18. Such grammatical propositions have no existential import. Nothing follows from them about the nature of the world.
19. Therefore, realism cannot be proved by means of "I know that here is my hand." (*O.C.*, 59)

In this part of the argument Wittgenstein is answering the question, What are these locutions trying to express? His response must satisfy the criteria he laid down earlier, namely, (i) that Moore's remark "There are physical objects" is nonsense; (ii) that the remark is in some way misleading, because Moore is trying to express "something" that cannot be expressed in those words; and (iii) that the "something" to be expressed is indeed a coherent thought and philosophically important. Wittgenstein's initial answer, which attempts to satisfy these conditions, is that the something to be expressed is a piece of instruction for the use of such terms as "physical object," "doubt," and "I know." As a piece of instruction it says something coherent and in this case something important. But if it is a piece of instruction it is not an empirical proposition; and, if so, it cannot be used to prove that physical objects exist. This is why Moore's proof misfires.

But more generally, what does Wittgenstein mean by saying that such philosophical utterances are to be construed as "pieces of instruction"? And if they are, how can he also describe them as "nonsense"? Finally, how can they be nonsense and yet be understood? We shall now answer these questions.

Wittgenstein, unfortunately, never explains in *On Certainty* what he means by "a piece of instruction," "a grammatical proposition," "a logical insight," or "nonsense." Still, if we leave *On Certainty* and return to his earlier writings we can arrive at a plausible interpretation of what he intended here. To engage in a full study of these earlier works, with respect to this interpretation, would require at least a separate chapter. There is also a vast exegetical literature that addresses these matters, beginning with Moore's "Wittgenstein's Lectures in 1930–33" and coming down to the present. Our discussion cannot possibly rehearse the ingenious construals this literature contains. We will thus have to be summary if we are not to lose the thread of the present exposition. Within such contraints I will try to express the salient points in a paragraph or two.

As I explained in chapter 1, Wittgenstein held in the *Tractatus* that the only "significant statements" about the world are those belonging to the sciences. Let us call these (using a neutral terminology) empirical statements. The theorems of logic and mathematics, on his analysis, are not empirical statements but *tautologies*. Being tautologies they say nothing about the world. For example, one who knows that it will either rain or not rain knows nothing at all about the weather. Yet, being tautologies, they are necessarily true. And their negations, being contradictions, are necessarily false. Wittgenstein also held a pair of views that seem inconsistent with this analysis. He asserted, both in the *Tractatus* and in his lectures in the 1930s, that such locutions "say nothing" and also held that "they all say the same thing." Moore argued that it was obvious that such propositions as "It will either snow or not" and "It will either rain or not" are about snow and rain, respectively, and therefore say different things; and that because they do, they at least say something. Moreover, as Moore pointed out, how they could say nothing and yet be either true or false was inexplicable. Wittgenstein never succeeded in answering Moore's objections, but he was aware of them and grappled with them in his lectures in the 1930s.

In the lectures, as a way of resolving these difficulties, Wittgenstein explored the possibility that such "necessary propositions" can be construed as grammatical rules. In the *Tractatus* he had called such propositions "pseudo-propositions." From their surface forms, he said, one might suppose them to be real propositions, but since they did not speak about the world, they lacked sense. It also seemed to Wittgenstein that typical philosophical pronouncements could be assimilated to these "necessary propositions" and thus could also be described as "pseudo-propositions." In this connection he drew a distinction between propositions that were *senseless* (*Sinnlos*) and those that were nonsense (*Unsinn*). The propositions of mathematics and logic were senseless (*Sinnlos*), but those of philosophy suffered from more severe defects and were nonsense (*Unsinn*). In *On Certainty* (for example, in 35) he continued to use the term "nonsense" (*Unsinn*) for the kinds of "philosophical propositions" uttered by Moore.

Thus, from the *Tractatus* period through *On Certainty* Wittgenstein was using the term "to have sense" (*Sinnvoll*) consistently. It was only what I have called empirical.propositions that have sense in his view. He was thus using the notion of an "empirical statement" to define what counts as a significant utterance. Linguistic utterances that have the form of empirical propositions, but function differently, do not have sense. But they may lack sense in two different ways: they can either be *Sinnlos* or *Unsinn*. Grammatical rules are clearly not empirical statements. So they lack sense, but they are not nonsense. They are proposals to use linguistic terms in specific ways. If such proposals satisfy the lexical rules that govern grammatical coherence, they are comprehensible even though they lack sense. They are *Sinnlos* but not *Unsinnig*, to revert to the terminology of the *Tractatus*. With this distinction in hand we are in a position to understand how Wittgenstein can say that Moore's locutions are nonsense (*Unsinn*) when interpreted as Moore intended them, but not as nonsense when they are interpreted as Wittgenstein is suggesting. They lack sense (are *Sinnlos*) in the latter case. They are nonsense if construed as empirical propositions, but not nonsense when interpreted as grammatical rules.

According to this interpretation, a sentence like "I know that here is my hand" should be thought of as laying down a rule for the use of "I know" with respect to certain cases or in certain contexts. The rule says, in effect, that the term "I know" and its polar term "I do not know" cannot sensibly be used with respect to those cases or in those contexts. The strong evidence for this interpretation is; found in entry 58 of *On Certainty*. There Wittgenstein uses the term *keinen Sinn* rather than *Unsinn* to describe the lack of sense of grammatical propositions:

> If "I know etc." is conceived as a grammatical proposition of course the "I" cannot be important. And it properly means "There is no such thing as doubt in this case," or "The expression 'I do not know' makes no sense in this case" (. . . *hat in diesem Falle keinen Sinn.)* And of course it follows from this that "I know" makes no sense either.

Let us now return to the main line of argumentation. Earlier we saw that Wittgenstein's remark in entry 58 can be interpreted as a contrastive argument. In my reconstruction it appears in premises 12 and 16. We previously asked, How is it possible, as Wittgenstein asserts, for one proposition to follow from another if both are nonsense? Here we have an answer deriving from the nature of rules. Logical entailments can hold between differing formulations of rules even if the rules are neither true nor false. In Wittgenstein's interpretation such rules govern,for example, the use of physical object terms. They do not make empirical assertions and thus lack sense. Nonetheless, one may imply another. In this particular case he is speaking about the rules in English that govern such expressions as "I know" and "I do not know" *when those terms are used with respect to certain kinds of cases.* The important question to be addressed, then, given this suggested interpretation, is, What are the cases or the contexts to which Wittgenstein is alluding?

The answer I propose—an answer that if correct will bring us to the heart of Wittgenstein's objection to Moore's proof—is that these are cases and contexts that underlie "the language game." They relate to the language game in a very special way. They are those things, situations, and practices that "stand fast for us." As such they are not open to revision and therefore not open to doubt either. This is why Wittgenstein says, "There can be no such thing as doubt in this case." And if they are not "up for grabs" in these ways, the adducing of evidence, the process of justification or various affirmations of knowledge are likewise inapposite in our relationships to them. It is this that Wittgenstein means when he says: "The expression 'I do not know' makes no sense in this case. And, then, of course it follows from this that '*I know*' makes no sense either." Because Moore failed to see that whatever stands fast in this way is beyond the sensible predication of knowledge, his proof, resting on the affirmation that he knows such things, again misses the point. Realism, Wittgenstein concludes, cannot be proved in this way. "Moore's mistake," he writes, "lies in this—countering the assertion that one cannot know that, by saying 'I do know it'" (*O.C.*, 521). Moore's proof is thus abortive. It amounts to mischaracterizing or misdescribing something worth describing in the right way. But to give a correct characterization of that something—that which stands fast for all of us—is difficult. Wittgenstein struggled with this task throughout the later sections of *On Certainty*.

This concludes our exposition of the third objection. Unlike the two we discussed earlier in this chapter, which were simple and straightforward, this last we have found to be labyrynthian and complex. Any such complicated structure is likely to have some weak links. Is that the case here? Is it therefore as powerful and compelling as the others? How shall we evaluate it? Does it really destroy or undermine what Moore was trying to do in offering his proof? My assessment of it is that it is a very deep objection that sees profoundly into the nature of traditional philosophizing, as represented in a sophisticated form by Moore. I will conclude this chapter by explaining why I think so and, in effect, why Wittgenstein's understanding of the nature of philosophy has carried us well beyond Moore's and into a deeper understanding of what is wrong with Moore's proof. The insights conveyed by Wittgenstein transcend mere technical deficiencies with the supposititious proof: they show how *any* such endeavor is misguided.

According to Wittgenstein, Moore is not describing our actual practice because in the language game we play in everyday life doubting must come to an end. To urge the opposite, to advocate the kind of non-terminating doubt that the idealist/sceptic purports to practice, is to indulge in nonsense. Moore does not understand this. As he sees it there is no reason why doubting cannot or should not go on indefinitely. It is a telling point against Moore that in none of his epistemological writings did he ever arrive at the insight that doubting gradually loses its sense. On the contrary, his approach, as I have stressed in earlier chapters, was to block the seemingly endless regress that sceptical doubt entailed; but such an approach presupposed that doubting in that way makes sense. In effect, then, Moore supposed that philosophical doubt is just a species of ordinary doubt, though carried on more intensively, even obsessively. From his perspective there was nothing untoward in this philosophical practice, so he tried to meet such doubts by stating clearly and aggressively that he knew for sure those things the sceptic purported to doubt. But if saying "I know, etc." did not allay the sceptic's doubts, then one could also do something stronger; one could *prove* that there are external objects. But his assertion that he knew such and such, and his proof designed to lay such doubts to rest once and for all, implied that he took the sceptical position to be a meaningful one.

But this assumption, as Wittgenstein has just shown, is mistaken. From Wittgenstein's perspective both Moore and his opponents are playing a special, philosophical game in which at least one of the key concepts they employ is nonsense. One cannot play that game without giving away the show; for what is really at stake is whether the purported practice of doubt makes any sense at all. For Wittgenstein it doesn't, and this is an insight Moore never achieved. So Moore's way of dealing with his opponents shows a misunderstanding of the nature of philosophical practice and thus a profound misunderstanding of how to deal with the idealist and the sceptic.

Yet while giving us this assessment Wittgenstein thinks there is something right in Moore's approach. In using a term like "nonsense" to describe Moore's words, Wittgenstein is not being wholly negative in the way that a positivist might be. As we have seen, his characteristic posture in dealing with traditional philosophers is to acknowledge that in their search for the essence of things, and for deeper explanations, they are bringing important insights to our understanding of the world and its inhabitants. But these insights when pushed obsessively and expanded into models that incorporate and eventually co-opt obvious counter-examples lead to paradox and thus ultimately to a false picture of reality. So I believe that in this part of *On Certainty* Wittgenstein thinks that behind the nonsensical formulations that Moore gives in his proof there is something of importance that Moore is trying to get at, only he cannot articulate it. What Moore is trying to say, in his misleading way, that is correct is that the term "doubt" does not apply universally. He is trying to say that there are certain cases which arise in our lives with respect to which this term must be withheld.

But instead of putting the point in this way, he attempts to do it via assertions about what he knows to be true. In other words, his way of formulating this point is to say assertively, "I know that here is my hand." He thus thinks that in such a case, where he is looking at his own hand and saying what is true, doubt is no longer applicable: it is excluded by his knowing with certainty that his hand exists and by his assuring the sceptic that he does know. Wittgenstein believes there is considerable insight in Moore's assessment of the situation. That doubt is excluded in this case is something Wittgenstein agrees with and goes on to affirm in his own way. But he differs from Moore in how to express the point. He says instead that neither the locution "I know that" nor its polar correlative "I doubt that" *makes sense* in the situation Moore is depicting. To deny that these epithets can be used sensibly is to make a much more powerful point than Moore did. What supports Wittgenstein's approach and militates against Moore's is the insight that it is the language game we all play in our everyday lives that confers such restrictions on our use of these locutions. This is Wittgenstein's great achievement, and much of what follows in *On Certainty* is dedicated to showing why this is so.

At the beginning of this chapter I mentioned that Wittgenstein's objections to Moore's proof fall into three classes: a set of deliberations about the argument per se; a set of difficulties that concern the components of the argument, such as the premise "Here is one hand" and its conclusion, "There are physical objects"; and finally a set of meta-comments about the proof, for example, that Moore knows its premises to be true, but that he cannot prove them to be true. With respect to this last remark, he claims that in order to prove the premises to be true he would have to prove he is not dreaming, and this he cannot do. In this chapter our focus has been on Wittgenstein's main objections to the proof per se, but, of course, in order to explain these we have had to discuss some of the other matters falling into these three categories, such as Wittgenstein's claim that "There are physical objects" is nonsensical. We have not discussed some of the other important features of Wittgenstein's objections to Moore, such as whether Moore's remark that he cannot prove he is not dreaming makes sense at all; nor have we pursued in depth Wittgenstein's brilliant treatment of the term "I know that" This treatment illustrates both the correct use of this locution and the sorts of misuses that Moore has made of it—misuses that differ from those we have discussed here. And, of course, our discussion of the concept of doubt has only been extensive enough to illustrate its role in Wittgenstein's objections to Moore's attempted proof. All of these matters are important, and all of them exhibit Wittgenstein's genius at its most impressive. We shall turn to them now.

8

Dreaming, Knowing, Doubting

As I indicated earlier, Moore claimed that the argument he advanced in "Proof of an External World" was indeed a proof and that most of his critics were mistaken in asserting that it was not. He stated, correctly in my opinion, that a proof must satisfy three criteria: it must be a valid argument; its premise or premises must be true; and it or they must be known to be true. He also stated that his argument satisfied these conditions and therefore that he had proved there are physical objects. He thought his critics had confused the question of whether a certain set of sentences amounted to a proof with a different question, namely, whether he could prove that one of those sentences, functioning as a premise, was true. That sentence was "Here is one hand," and with respect to it he granted, as we have also seen, that he could not prove it. In order to do that, he said, he would have to prove that at the time he was speaking he was not dreaming, and this was something he could not do. Moreover, though he did not state this, he implied that he thought nobody could at any time prove he or she was not dreaming.

Two years later in his paper "Certainty" Moore made a similar admission in his discussion of scepticism. He again stated that he could not at the moment he was speaking prove he was not dreaming. He also said he agreed with the sceptic's argument that if he were dreaming he could not know he was standing up. Yet he went on to assert that he knew that he was standing up at that moment and therefore *knew* then that he was not dreaming, and he claimed that this argument was at least as good as the sceptic's. His one concession in the debate was his admission he could not prove that he was not dreaming. So though by making this concession he in effect was admitting that he could not positively defeat the sceptic, he felt he had at least earned a draw in the contest. This outcome, as I emphasized in previous chapters, was a considerable philosophical achievement, deserving of more recognition than it has received. In both papers, then, Moore adopted a similar strategy: affirming that he knew that p and also conceding that he could not prove that p. What is important for our purposes in this chapter is to recognize that in both papers Moore assumed it was a sensible demand on the part of the sceptic to ask for a proof of "Here is one hand." And

119

he also assumed that it was sensible for him to respond to the request by stating both that he could not develop such a proof and yet that he knew the proposition to be true.

It never occurred to Moore that a completely different sort of objection would be leveled at his so-called proof, namely, that certain of its crucial elements, for instance, its conclusion "There are physical objects," did not encode propositions at all but instead were specimens of nonsense. Moore was correct in asserting that one of the conditions a proof must satisy is that its premises and its conclusion must be true, but that condition presupposes that those sentences are significant. Therefore, if, for example, the final sentence of his argument were in fact nonsense—as Wittgenstein ingeniously argued—it could not be true. And further, if that sentence occurred "essentially" in the argument, the so-called argument was not a proof either but a complicated form of nonsense mimicking a proof. Wittgenstein's approach, highly original and different from anything that had previously been directed at the so-called proof, thus blind-sided Moore with a kind of criticism that he never anticipated. It never occurred to Moore that some of the sentences that comprised his proof were nonsensical—or at least that a powerful argument to that effect could be generated. But that was the thrust of Wittgenstein's approach. And if that objection was sound, then Moore's entire endeavor—his effort to prove there are external objects—rested on sand and could not be sustained. We saw in chapter 7 just how Wittgenstein's strategy played out.

In this chapter I will describe a different, though similar, move that Wittgenstein makes against Moore, once again hitting him from an unexpected direction. This time his target was not the proof per se, but the set of *meta*-remarks that Moore makes about it. Among those meta-remarks are the comments that he could not prove he was not dreaming and yet knew he was not. Moore once again assumed unquestioningly that the sceptic's remark "I may be dreaming" is a *sensible* thing to say and, accordingly, that what he (Moore) was saying *about* his proof, in responding to the sceptic, was also a *sensible* thing to say. It does not seem nonsensical for someone to say "I may be dreaming," and, therefore, it does not seem nonsensical for another to respond to this remark by asserting "I know I am not dreaming though I cannot prove it." Yet these are just the assumptions that Wittgenstein challenged. In this chapter we shall indicate how Wittgenstein's approach cuts the ground from under Moore's feet by powerful arguments which demonstrate that Moore's meta-remarks about dreaming and about "I know" are senseless. Wittgenstein's overall strategy here is to show, first, that the sceptic/idealist position is senseless and, second that Moore's attempt to confute it is also senseless. This is a very strong result. If we take Moore and his sceptical/idealist opponents to be representative of the Western philosophical tradition, Wittgenstein can be interpreted as arguing that the standard treatments of dreaming, knowing, and doubting in that tradition are senseless. As he says in 383, "The argument 'I may be dreaming' is senseless for this reason: if I am dreaming, this remark is being dreamed as well—and indeed it is also being dreamed that these words have any meaning."

This quotation is the first of the two most important passages in which

Wittgenstein challenges the assumption upon which the Cartesian dream hypothesis and Moore's rebuttal of it rest, namely, that "I may be dreaming" is a sensible thing to say. It provides two reasons in support of the thesis that "I may be dreaming" is senseless. Of course, Wittgenstein is here assuming—correctly—that Moore means these words to be taken literally. These words may be used in a variety of sensible ways to mean something other than what they literally express. So the considerations Wittgenstein is offering apply only to their literal employment. The first is that if I am dreaming, this remark is being dreamed as well, and the second is that it is also being dreamed that these words have any meaning. But just how these supposed reasons support the claim that "I may be dreaming" is senseless is not very clear. Why, if the remark is being dreamed, should that show that the remark is senseless? Suppose a person who is awake and knows himself to be awake should say, "I may be dreaming." Even if he knows the statement to be false, the fact that it is false shows that it is a genuine assertion and therefore not senseless. This seems to have been Moore's point. Why, then, if that person is dreaming and utters those words should that show that they lack sense?

If one's interpretation were confined to this passage alone Wittgenstein's reasoning would remain opaque and unconvincing. Fortunately, the second quotation, which is the last entry in *On Certainty*, provides additional reasons that are clear and compelling; and it indicates clearly what Wittgenstein means by saying that the utterance is "senseless." As he says in this second passage, "I cannot seriously suppose in such a case that I am dreaming," or again, "that one who says this is no more right . . . etc." The idioms "cannot seriously suppose" and "is no more right" seem to be interchangeable with "senseless." If we tie the two passages together we find ourselves in a better position to appreciate Wittgenstein's thinking. Here is the second quotation:

> "But even if in such cases I can't be mistaken, isn't it possible that I am drugged?" If I am and if the drug has taken away my consciousness, then I am not now really talking and thinking. I cannot seriously suppose that I am at this moment dreaming. Someone, who dreaming, says "I am dreaming" even if he speaks audibly in doing so, is no more right than if he said in his dream "it is raining," while it was in fact raining. Even if his dream were actually connected with the noise of the rain. (*O.C.*, 676)

The important point Wittgenstein is making in this quotation is that if "I am dreaming" is said by a person who is dreaming, that person is not really "talking and thinking" and therefore is making no genuine statement in uttering these words. The notion that a person who is not really talking and thinking is making no statement rests upon a familiar thesis in all of Wittgenstein's later writings, that certain background and contextual conditions have to be satisfied if an utterance is to count as a statement. The same words said in certain circumstances are sensible but said in others are not. So the words "I may be dreaming," uttered by someone who is awake and knows that he is, may have a sensible use in certain situations.

Suppose someone has just won a lottery. That person might use those words to express his astonishment at his good fortune. That he has used those words to say something significant entails he was awake when he uttered them. Now, are there circumstances in which he could use the words literally, to mean that at the moment of speaking he might be dreaming? Wittgenstein would say no. For if he did mean them in that way his utterance would be self-defeating, since it would entail that he was awake at the time he spoke. This is thus a case in which the necessary contextual conditions for significance would have been absent, and nothing sensible would have been said. Perhaps the most brilliant illustration of this thesis in the entire Wittgensteinian corpus is found in the following passage:

> "I know that that's a tree" is something a philosopher might say to demon-strate to himself or to someone else that he knows something that is not a mathe-matical or logical truth. Similarly, someone who was entertaining the idea that he was no use any more might keep repeating to himself "I can still do this and this and this." If such thoughts often possessed him one would not be surprised if he, apparently out of all context, spoke such a sentence out loud. (But here I have already sketched a background, a surrounding for this remark, that is to say given it a context.) But if someone, in quite heterogeneous circumstances, called out with the most convincing mimicry: "Down with him!", one might say of these words (and their tone) that they were a pattern that does indeed have familiar applications, but that in this case it was not even clear what language the man in question was speaking. I might make with my hand the movement I should make if I were holding a hand-saw and sawing through a plank; but would one have any right to call this movement sawing out of all context?—(It might be something quite different!) (O.C., 350)

In this entry Wittgenstein is, in effect, comparing a person who says "I may be dreaming" when normal background conditions are not satisfied with a man who might suddenly shout, out of all context, "Down with him." In such a case, he says provocatively, "it would not even be clear what *language* the man was speaking." Wittgenstein's point here is that those words could be used by some-one to say something sensible in certain contexts, say in a revolutionary situa-tion. But just because they are familiar words, it does not follow that every utterance of them is sensible. This thesis is buttressed by an example that gives this passage its brilliance. Wittgenstein asks us how we would describe a person who is making a movement that one would normally make if one were holding a handsaw and sawing through a plank, but who at that particular moment is holding no saw and has before him no plank. Wittgenstein asks, "Would one have any right to call this movement sawing out of all context?" The answer is obviously no. Whatever the man is doing it is not sawing. And a man who utters certain words out of all context is making no statement. Though it is presented in a characteristically oblique fashion, there is thus an argument—indeed a pow-erful argument—embedded in the two quotations, and its application to Moore is evident.

If we add this familiar point about the background context to what he says in the two quotations, we can surface the submerged argument against Moore that is embedded in them. Here is my reconstruction of it (since the case where X is awake is not in the quoted passages, I shall leave it out here):

Insofar as X, the sceptic, wishes to make a certain kind of conceptual point, the utterance X uses to make it must be a genuine statement. Suppose X utters the sentence "I may be dreaming." If X is dreaming, the requirement of statement making is violated. For if X is dreaming, his remark is being dreamed as well. In that case X is not really talking or thinking, and therefore the utterance is not a genuine assertion. It is not a genuine assertion because the background conditions for genuine statement making have not been satisfied. These are that X be awake and is fully aware of what his words mean. But if X is asleep, these criteria remain unfulfilled. Therefore, X's words are senseless when uttered under those conditions, and because that is so, X's statement or formulation of scepticism lacks conceptual force.

The relevance of this argument to Moore's attempted proof is immediate. If the sceptic's position cannot be coherently stated, there is nothing that needs to be refuted. And indeed to offer a so-called proof by way of such a refutation is itself incoherent, since it assumes mistakenly that the sceptical position is a sensible one.

The preceding quotations illustrate the sorts of moves that Wittgenstein makes against Moore's comment that he cannot prove he is not dreaming. The text of *On Certainty* contains arguments (or implicit arguments) that not only seek to undermine Moore's assumption that "I may be dreaming" is sensible but that attempt to show that the sentence "I know I am dreaming" is also senseless. The implication to be drawn from arguments of the latter sort is that if "I know I am dreaming" is senseless, then "I know that I am not dreaming," *as Moore uses it*, is also senseless. The latter set of arguments are not so much simple contrast arguments as applications of the more general discussion of "I know" that runs through *On Certainty*. Some of that discussion concerns Moore's misuse of the term; some of it, in contrast, shows how the term is used in the course of our everyday activities—that is, in what Wittgenstein calls "the language-game." Moore's use and the proper use of the term are frequently contrasted with invidious consequences for Moore. This latter discussion itself is bound up with Wittgenstein's analysis of what it is to be mistaken and what it is to doubt something, so that the textual web that captures the sceptic's and Moore's talk about dreaming is very complicated.

What emerges from this approach is a powerful criticism of Moore's attempt to prove there is an external world. But something of greater importance also emerges: namely, the initial phases of Wittgenstein's attempts to characterize the nature of certainty—of that which stands fast for all of us, as he puts it. Wittgenstein is attempting to show, in opposition to Cartesian sceptics and dogmatists alike, that that which stands fast for all of us is not something about which we can be mistaken; it is not something even the dream hypothesis can call into question. So the rejection of Moore's attempt to prove there is an external world is tied to an account of why such a proof is both misguided and unnecessary. It is misguided because the existence of what stands fast is beyond doubt; and because it is beyond doubt, no proof of its existence is necessary.

But Wittgenstein's purpose in *On Certainty* is not merely negative. He sees it to be a challenge to give a positive account of the nature of certainty. This account issues in a series of notions, not all equivalent in meaning. He speaks of our inherited background, our world picture, the community, and so forth. Though these concepts differ, they have in common that what they refer to is not eliminable, revisable, justifiable, provable, true or false, or susceptible to doubt. No doubt had Wittgenstein lived long enough to polish his notes he might have arrived at a single conception of that which stands fast; but each of these is interesting in its own right, and in the endeavor to characterize this concept his powers of invention assume their highest forms. It is this positive contribution that constitutes the great achievement of *On Certainty*. His struggle to articulate this notion is something we shall follow in chapters 9 and 10, so we shall not pursue it further here. Instead, we shall set the stage for those later developments via his discussions of knowing and doubting.

It is important in initiating this discussion to emphasize that though Wittgenstein frequently talks about certain sorts of linguistic expressions, such as "I know," "I doubt," and so on, he is not merely talking about these expressions. He is doing something else as well. His ultimate aim is to distinguish believing from knowing and knowing from certainty. He does this in part by showing how they differentially relate to doubting. Accordingly, he is not merely speaking about the differences in the uses of the terms "believe," "know," "certain," and "doubt" (though he is surely doing that as well) but also and primarily about that which those words normally denote or pick out, that is, about belief, knowledge, certainty, and doubt. This is what Wittgenstein means, for example, when he says that knowledge and certainty are not two mental states like surmising and being sure. He writes in 308 of *On Certainty:* "What interests us now is not being sure but knowledge." And he says in 230: "We are asking ourselves: what do we do with a statement 'I *know.* . . '? For it is not a question of mental processes or mental states. And *that* is how one must decide whether something is knowledge or not."

The relationship between the use or uses of language and such features of human activity as knowing and doubting is, for Wittgenstein, a complicated one that cannot be encapsulated into a simple formula. But certain principles should be kept in mind in discussing that relationship. We should in certain cases distinguish words from what they are normally used to talk about; words, for example, as we have just seen, can be uttered out of context without making any sensible point. We can also, on the other side, as it were, distinguish that which is talked about from the idioms used to talk about it; so knowing and doubting, for example, are not in general to be identified with the uses of certain linguistic expressions. When Wittgenstein speaks of doubting as a practice he is talking about a certain social function human beings engage in and not just about the idioms one normally uses to mention or refer to that function. But it is also true that in certain cases or in certain situations the uses of such linguistic expressions are themselves instances or specimens of doubting and are not merely expressions of some underlying phenomenon that is wholly independent of those uses.

One might here compare these cases with types of speech acts in which the uttering of certain words or phrases is one standard way of doing something, such as marrying another (assuming, of course, that the standard background conditions, such as not already being married, have been satisfied). We shall therefore begin our investigation with what Wittgenstein calls "the correct uses" of "I know." We can then compare and contrast these with Moore's use of the term. The outcome of this process will be a delineation of the nature of knowledge and an account of how it differs from belief, on the one hand, and from certainty, on the other. Tied to that outcome will be a concomitant, negative, but highly important result. Wittgenstein will show that Moore's use of "I know" is not innocuous but leads to his saying something senseless. Wittgenstein will trace the genesis of this use to a misunderstanding that arises from Moore's adherence to a form of the Cartesian model. Let us see how the linguistic analysis leads to these substantive conclusions.

In 483 Wittgenstein writes:

> The correct use of the expression "I know." Someone with bad sight asks me: "do you believe that the thing we can see there is a tree?" I reply "I *know* it is; I can see it clearly and am familiar with it."—A: "Is N.N. at home?"—I: "I believe he is."—A: "Was he at home yesterday?"—"Yesterday he was—I know he was; I spoke to him."—A: "Do you know or only believe that this part of the house is built on later than the rest?"—I: "I *know* it is: I asked so and so about it."

In this passage we encounter three different examples in which "I know" is used correctly. "Used correctly" here means that the expression plays a specific role or set of roles in everyday human intercourse. In these scenarios, "I know" is used to draw a contrast with "I believe." It is important in everyday life to distinguish cases of belief from cases of knowledge. Imagine a case in which Smith is testifying at a trial. Does Smith believe that p or does Smith know that p? Clearly, the difference may be essential to the outcome of the case. In the examples Wittgenstein offers nothing as complicated as a trial is being described: the scenarios are much simpler. But that does not make them less important. In the conduct of our everyday affairs, it is still important for innumerable reasons to distinguish cases of belief from cases of knowledge.

By producing scenarios in which it is sometimes correct to say "I know" but not "I believe," and vice versa, Wittgenstein is helping us make this discrimination. In effect, his point is that it is correct usage to say "I know that p" when your ground or grounds for asserting p are stronger than they would be if you asserted "I believe that p." Depending on the status of such grounds, then (and certain other factors), we either have a case of belief or a case of knowledge. There is no general formula for determining how strong such grounds must be. Each case must be judged on its merits (here we see the method of cases in operation again as well as Wittgenstein's injunctions against theorizing in philosophy). Moreover, depending on the circumstances in which the question How do you know? arises, the response may convey different messages: it may give an explanation, a justification, or an emphasis to the affirmation, it may indicate the route by which one came to know, and so on. Wittgenstein describes each of these differing responses as cases of giving grounds, but the scenarios he provides suggest that we can and probably should make such further discriminations.

Such grounds are not to be identified or conflated with evidence—that is, the grounds one may have for correctly saying "I know" are not necessarily evidential in character. This is the case in each of his three examples. Consider the second. It states that I know that N.N. was at home yesterday because I spoke with him. I take it that Wittgenstein means that yesterday I was at N.N.'s home and spoke with him *there*. The example is to be contrasted with a case in which I am speaking with N.N. now. It suggests that even though a day has passed, I am still entitled to say that I know (and do not merely believe) that N.N. was at home yesterday. I am entitled to say this because I did speak with him then; but to offer that as a reason is not a case of providing evidence. Compare this case with one in which evidence is adduced. Suppose I assert "I know N.N. was at home yesterday because I spoke with him over the phone." My speaking with him by means of a mechanical device rather than in person changes the situation. Here I am offering evidence in referring to the sounds I heard on the phone. To be sure, mistakes are possible in both cases. My recollection of the date may have been erroneous, and my having heard N.N.'s voice is compatible with his not having been at home. I may well have heard a tape recording. What distinguishes a case of evidence from a case of non-evidence is thus not that mistakes are possible in the one case and not in the other but various other factors. But to expatiate on what those are would divert us from the main line we are following.

Let us just say that the contrast Wittgenstein wishes to draw in his description of the three scenarios is not between cases in which one has evidence and one does not but, rather, between cases in which the grounds justify one's saying "I know" in contrast to saying "I believe." Consider his third scenario. I say that I know that this part of the house was added later and give as my reason that I asked so and so about it. The assumption here is that so and so was in a position to respond authoritatively. This is neither a case of adducing evidence nor a case of direct perception. The contrast Wittgenstein is drawing is this. If on the basis of what I see when I look at the house and with no other information I infer that this part was added later, then I should say "I believe that it was." But now, because of what I have been told and the new information I have acquired, I am in a stronger position, and therefore I am entitled to say "I know." Likewise, in the first scenario when I say that I know this is a tree because I can see it clearly, I am not offering evidence—that is, doing something analogous to what I would be doing if I mentioned that I had spoken to N.N. over the phone. My observing the tree is stronger than evidence, and it justifies my saying "I know." In this situation it would be misleading to say "I believe it is a tree," for such a remark might lead another to infer that I suffer from defective vision. Thus, what allows one to distinguish cases of belief from cases of knowledge are the strengths of the grounds in each of the cases.

This last point is tied to another. In each of these cases I can be described as being in a position to know that p. Because I spoke with N.N. I am in a position to know that he was at home. Because my eyesight is good, I am in a position to know that the object is a tree. My being in the appropriate position also entitles me to answer the question, "How do you know that p?" Here the question can be understood as asking, "How did you come to know that p?" In responding to it my answer might give the route I took or the moves I made in getting into a position to know; in specifying what these are I am indicating to my interrogator why I am entitled to say "I know."

Let us consider this passage from a slightly different perspective. What the three cases have in common is that each of them excludes some measure of uncertainty; so if I could not see the tree clearly, then I might in that circumstance say "I believe it is a tree" rather than "I know it is a tree." Note that in each of these cases one is, as it were, in a state of belief when one possesses *some*, though not all or the right sorts of, grounds he might have in order to know that p. The person who has bad eyesight can see a certain tree-like shape in front of him but cannot clearly make out what it is. He does not disbelieve that it is a tree. Quite the contrary, he thinks it is, but isn't sure. Perhaps if he were closer he could decide the matter; but he is not closer, so in this case, he is not in a position to know. Or to put the matter differently, his reasons for thinking it a tree are not sufficiently strong to be grounds for knowledge. He would have stronger grounds if he could see the tree clearly. Therefore, in that situation, clarity of perception is the decisive factor in determining whether we are dealing with a case of belief or a case of knowledge. Note also that in each of these instances the issue of whether one knows or merely believes something arises in some context of puzzlement: there is an open question that must be decided. Someone with bad eyesight wonders whether it is a tree he is seeing; someone wonders whether this part of the house has been added to. These questions arise because the answers to them are not obvious. Some of Wittgenstein's sharpest criticisms of Moore make reference to this last point, as I shall indicate at the end of this chapter.

Yet this characterization of when it is correct to say "I know" rather than "I believe" is one Moore himself seems to have espoused. In "Certainty," as we noted earlier, he states that it would have been absurd to say that he thinks he has some clothes on when he knows that he does. As he puts it, "I don't merely think that I have, but know that I have." It would also seem that when Moore in "Proof of an External World" says "I know that this is my hand," he is using "I know" in contrast to "I believe" or "I think." So far, then, Wittgenstein and Moore seem to be in agreement. But the degree of agreement is very thin. Was there anyone who heard Moore give his lecture who doubted that he had clothes on? When he delivered "Proof of an External World" were persons unable to see whether he was holding up his hand? Wittgenstein, of course, answered these questions in the negative; and therefore, according to him, Moore was not using "I know" correctly. He would say that because some of the appropriate background conditions were not satisfied, Moore was not describing the difference between a case of belief and a case of knowledge.

Wittgenstein draws the distinction between knowledge and belief in another way: "If someone believes something, we needn't always be able to answer the question 'why he believes it'; but if he knows something, then the question 'how does he know?' must be capable of being answered" (*O.C.*, 550).

The distinction he is making here is philosophically important. He wishes to bring out that knowing involves a kind of objectivity that is not to be found in believing. One who claims to know that p, when challenged, must back up his claim with grounds that are open to non-subjective, interpersonal assessment. But such grounds are not necessary when one says one believes that p. One may believe for personal or subjective reasons, and one may legitimately refuse to divulge them. As Wittgenstein puts it: "It would be correct to say: 'I believe . . . ' has subjective truth; but 'I know . . .' not (*O.C.*, 176).

To ask "How do you know such and such?" brings out this distinction in a perspicuous way; it requires an answer that is not a description of one's personal motives. To be sure, an account of why one believes something may be an accurate description of the causal factors that induce such belief, and in that sense, "I believe" expresses a kind of "subjective truth." But to indicate how one knows is to describe something non-personal. It is to mention factors that are open to public scrutiny. Among these would be that one is in a position to know. That one is in such a position has nothing to do with one's psychology and is open to objective assessment. Unless one has and can give such grounds one cannot properly claim to know. Wittgenstein makes these points over and over again in *On Certainty*. Here are some typical quotations:

> It would not be enough to assure someone that I know what is going on at a certain place—without giving him grounds that satisfy him that I am in a position to know. (*O.C.*, 438)

> In a court of law the mere assurance "I know . . . " on the part of a witness would convince no one. It must be shown that he was in a position to know.
> Even the assurance "I know that that's a hand," said while someone looked at his own hand, would not be credible unless we knew the circumstances in which it was said. (*O.C.*, 441)

> In these cases, then, one says "I know" and mentions how one knows, or at least one can do so. (*O.C.*, 484)

We have previously emphasized that Moore's characteristic way of dealing with the sceptic is to refuse to say how he knows certain propositions to be true while asserting that he does know them to be true. (Sometimes Moore modifies this stance by saying he is less sure how he knows than that he does know.) Throughout *On Certainty* Wittgenstein challenges Moore's mode of dealing with the sceptic. This challenge is protean in its diversity. One of its sharpest forms appears in the question, "But if you cannot tell us how you know that p, or what special position you are in for making this claim, what reason do we have for believing that you *do* know that p?" The question presupposes that one might be mistaken in thinking one knows if one does not have reasons or the right sorts of reasons, and it also presupposes that one does not produce conviction simply by asserting something—one must be able to give reasons in support of his claim.

So how shall we describe someone like Moore who claims to know and yet gives no reasons at all? Without the availability of such reasons one is prescinded from determining whether Moore thinks, believes, or really knows that p. As Moore uses "I know" it is thus not playing any of its ordinary role or roles. But how serious is this deviation? For Wittgenstein it is profound. For when "I know" is used without the backup of supporting reasons *it is not playing any role at all.* It is no longer hooked into the language game but is freely floating. It is not doing its ordinary job of helping us discriminate among various kinds of common human propensities and activities. This is why Wittgenstein says that Moore's employment of the term is *senseless.*

We can see from this analysis how Wittgenstein is using the parlance of ordinary speech to make more than a linguistic point. From Wittgenstein's perspective Moore's claim to know is mistaken. But it is not an ordinary mistake. It is not, for example, the sort of mistake one makes when one says "I know" without having sufficient reasons or the right sorts of reasons. Suppose I thought N.N. was speaking from his house when he was calling from someone else's. In that case my inference that he was at home would be erroneous. But that is not Moore's *kind of* mistake. Moore thinks he can decide whether he knows p or merely believes p by introspection. By looking inward, he thinks he can decide whether he is in the mental state he would normally call knowing or in the mental state he would normally call believing. But I cannot decide whether I know that N.N. is home by introspection. I decide that question by seeing N.N. in his house. The difference between a case of knowledge and a case of belief (whether mistaken or not) is thus not a matter of my internal psychology. To think it is, as Moore does, is to misrepresent the logic of "I know." It is tantamount to using "I know" as if its logic were identical to that of "I am in pain." As Wittgenstein says: "The wrong use made by Moore of the proposition 'I know' lies in his regarding it as an utterance as little subject to doubt as 'I am in pain.' And since from 'I know it is so' there follows 'It is so,' then the latter can't be doubted either" (*O.C.*, 178).

Wittgenstein's remark that Moore thinks of "I know" on the analogy of "I am in pain" suggests another, very powerful reason for thinking that adherence to the Cartesian model is misguided. On that model, the human psyche embodies various states, faculties, and capacities, among them doubting, guessing, supposing, conjecturing, thinking, believing, and knowing. These form a range moving from incertitude toward certitude. As one slides along this range as one state replaces another; so one may move from doubt to belief and then from belief to knowledge. With each such movement one state disappears and another takes its place. A human being thus must introspect to see which state lies in the foreground of his psyche at any given moment.

This seems to be the picture Moore has adopted. But it raises an enormous difficulty—the identification problem. Suppose one looks inward; and suppose one wishes to determine whether one merely believes or knows that p. Which of these two states is currently present in one's psyche? Is it thinkable or possible that one could misidentify the state that is currently present? If the answer to this question is yes, then clearly the existence of the state cannot be identical to knowledge, for to correct the misidentification would require an appeal to something other than that particular state. Perhaps the appeal is to another internal state—but then the identification problem arises with respect to that— and so on, ad infinitum. The only alternative to this possibility is to invoke the notion that the recognition of such an internal state cannot be mistaken, and this amounts to assimilating it to one's awareness of one's own pains. This is, I believe, the point of the previous quotation. To use "I know" according to either alternative thus gives rise to insuperable difficulties engendered by the incoherence of the model.

The nonsensical use of "I know" derives from the Cartesian model because, in effect, it misdirects the philosopher's search for knowledge. The mistake is comparable to the category error of looking for the Fountain of Youth in Florida. This is, of course, a non-existent, fictive "entity." The explorer who has searched Florida for a fountain and does not find it has looked in the wrong place for it. But to say he has looked in the wrong place does not mean he should have looked for it in, say, Arizona. Since it does not exist, it is not the sort of thing that can be found in any territorial area. So the explorer is looking for the wrong sort of thing in the wrong place. That is Moore's situation. Moore is like an explorer, looking for a special inward state, but that is not what knowledge is, and that inward domain is not where it is be to located.

Wittgenstein's line of argument is compressed into a sentence we find in 569: "An inner experience cannot shew me that I *know* something."

The model has persuaded Moore that it is not necessary to offer reasons in support of a claim to know; he thinks he just has to consult his internal psychology in order to find the appropriate state. It is, of course, possible that when he claims to know that p he is indeed in a certain psychological state. His mistake is to identify that state with knowing. For a claim to know *entails* that one must go beyond one's personal psychological state and provide grounds in support of the claim, whatever such grounds may be—observational data, inference, and so forth. Such grounds are not identical to whatever psychological disposition or attitude one might find by looking inward.

This move of Wittgenstein's against Moore seems simple at first, merely a "linguistic point," as it were; but it is more than that, and its implications are profound. It entails that knowledge is not merely (i) a personal experience, (ii) a mental phenomenon, state, or process, or (iii) something to be discovered by looking inward. In expanding on these implications, Wittgenstein piles example upon example, covering an immense amount of conceptual space. Many of the examples are variants of the points just made. The requirement that we must be able to indicate how we know something by providing supporting reasons is often described by Wittgenstein in terms of the concept of justification. A claim without the possibility of justification cannot be a case of knowledge in this view. When taken as a group, this welter of examples thus issues in findings that tell us what knowledge is not. But they also tell us in a positive way what knowledge is.

The reader who first approaches the work of the later Wittgenstein may not understand that this is so. Such a reader may think that the approach is wholly negative. To be sure, there is no place in *On Certainty* where Wittgenstein poses and then in a sentence answers the question, What is knowledge? It may thus seem that he has failed to provide the single most important piece of information one wants: a neat and simple definition of knowledge. But as we have seen from earlier chapters, and from the examples we have provided in this one, his refusal to approach questions about the nature of knowledge in this way is not surprising. It is part of his general strategy to avoid replacing one model with another. Definitions look for the hidden essence in a multiplicity of surface features and thus always involve the imposition of a conceptual model.

That way of thinking about philosophy is retrograde, according to Wittgenstein. It is still searching for an explanation instead of a description, and thus modeling itself on science, where the aim is to provide a synoptic theory. To give such a description means to provide a host of examples taken from various actual situations in everyday life in which we make ascriptions of knowledge to persons: to ourselves and others. It is in reflecting upon this array of cases that we can achieve an understanding of what knowledge is. No simple definition will accommodate their variety. Instead of looking for such a simple definition or characterization, therefore, one should sensitize oneself to this multiplicity of cases, seeing how they resemble and differ from one another. What will emerge from this process will be a deeper understanding than any definition can provide. In particular, the insight obtained in this way can be contrasted with the simple conception espoused by Moore under the influence of the Cartesian model.

In the text of *On Certainty* Wittgenstein produces descriptions of at least a dozen different uses and corresponding misuses of "I know." Given space limitations, it would be impossible to discuss all of these cases here. Instead, I will consider three that are interesting in their own right and that are philosophically significant. I also select them because they will provide transitional bridges to the discussion of doubting that follows and to our treatment in chapter 10 of the relationship between knowledge and certitude. In analyzing these three cases, we shall return to the linguistic level again. Wittgenstein will now show, in ways that are different from those previously described, that Moore's use of "I know" is senseless, and why. An important lesson to be learned from his discussion is that senselessness takes many forms.

1. In normal conversation, one says "I know" in order to communicate information not known to others. Suppose you are asked, "Are you sure that Smith was there last night?" and you respond by saying, "I know he was." In that case your intention is to give the auditor information he did not previously possess. There is thus a subtle misuse of the idiom when you produce, as things you know, things that you also know that everyone knows. In a "Defense of Common Sense" Moore lists a number of propositions that he insists not only he but everyone knows—for example, that the earth exists, that the earth is very old, that most of us have lived at or near the surface of the earth. In asserting that he knows these things—and especially when he also asserts that he knows his auditors do, too—he is violating normal conversational implicatures for significant communication and thus indulging in a kind of nonsense. This is the point Wittgenstein is making when he writes: "But Moore chooses precisely a case in which we all seem to know the same as he . . ." (84). "The truths which Moore says he knows are such as, roughly speaking, all of us know, if he knows them" (100). "Why doesn't he mention a fact that is known to him and not to *every one* of us?" (462). "Thus, it seems to me that I have known something the whole

time, and yet there is no meaning in saying so, in uttering this truth" (466). (See A.P. Martinich, *Communication and Reference*, 1984, ch. 2, which contains an excellent discussion of conversational maxims and their violations.)

2. It has been argued that one must distinguish the truth of a sentence from the oddity of uttering it on some occasion. Failure to do so was named the "Assertion Fallacy" by John Searle in *Speech Acts* (1961, pp. 141–146). It might be odd to say without the appropriate contextual background, "That's a tree in front of me," but it might be true to say it. Searle's description of the fallacy implies that standard, non-peculiar utterances must conform to presupposed background conditions. So "That's a tree" would be odd if uttered when such conditions were not satisfied. Yet Searle states that from the oddity of the utterance it does not follow that the speaker's statement is not true. To believe that it does follow is thus a fallacy. In *On Certainty* Wittgenstein described and then neutralized what might be called an epistemological variant of the fallacy. Instead of speaking about oddity and truth, he speaks, in effect, about oddity and knowledge. Here are two passages that describe the fallacy. The reference in the first is to an entry in *Philosophical Investigations*: "In the language-game (2), can he say that he knows that those are building stones?—'No, but he *does* know it'" (*O.C.*, 396).

Wittgenstein's use of the word "can" indicates that he thinks it would be odd, inappropriate, or peculiar to say that one knows that those are building stones in the context of the language game (2). Yet the next sentence suggests it might be true to say that one knows that they are. Note that Wittgenstein puts the assertion that one does know that p in quotation marks, suggesting it is the kind of thing a philosopher like Moore would say. And indeed in the second passage he explicitly refers to Moore:

> Haven't I gone wrong and isn't Moore perfectly right? Haven't I made the elementary mistake of confusing one's thoughts with one's knowledge? Of course, I do not think to myself "The earth already existed some time before my birth" but do I *know* it any the less? Don't I show that I know it by always drawing its consequences? (*O.C.*, 397)

So, according to this variant, even if it is odd in a certain context, or out of any context, to say "I know that's a tree, " I might nonetheless know that it is. Hence one might conclude, paralleling Searle, that if I do know, it cannot be senseless to say that I do. But Wittgenstein disagrees that the sentence, as so used, is meaningful, since he holds that contextual satisfaction is one of the determinants of meaning. But if the sentence is senseless, then one who utters it does not know what he claims to know. In such a case there is no fallacy in concluding that the person does not know what he claims to know.

Wittgenstein describes his version of the fallacy in several places, for example, in 396–398 and 552, and responds to it in various ways, some of which allow that seemingly "odd" remarks are not necessarily meaningless. It might be that the background for an utterance is submerged in a particular conversational context and yet is playing its ordinary role, so that what seems like nonsense may not be. For example, a person who says in the middle of a conversation having nothing to do with trees "I know that's a tree," might have been thinking about trees all along and then suddenly blurts out this sentence. So there is a context in that situation that will help us make sense of the remark. But if we can trace no prior chain of thought and the person utters this sentence completely out of context, we would be dumbfounded to understand what the individual is getting at. Perhaps the speaker is deranged (423–424, 468–469). One might even conclude, Wittgenstein suggests, that "this fellow isn't insane. We are only doing philosophy" (467). So when Moore says outside of a normal context, and yet intending to make a significant comment, "I know that this is a hand," his utterance is correctly assessed as senseless.

3. As emphasized above, Wittgenstein contends that when a person correctly uses "I know" he must both have compelling grounds for this claim and be able to indicate to another what they are. Here I wish to mention a different, but related notion, namely, that when "I know" is used correctly those grounds cannot be less sure than the contention they are used to support. If they are, they do not serve to bolster the original claim. So if they are no stronger, or if they are weaker than the original claim, the speaker's employment of them would represent a kind of senselessness; it would be like the pointless activity of adding insubstantial packing to a box one wishes to fill. No matter how hard one tries, the box will remain empty. We find the point expressed in 243 of *On Certainty*, and especially in the second paragraph of that entry:

> One says "I know" when one is ready to give compelling grounds. "I know" relates to a possibility of demonstrating the truth. Whether someone knows something can come to light, assuming that he is convinced of it.
> But if what he believes is of such a kind that the grounds that he can give are no surer than his assertion, then he cannot say that he knows what he believes.

When Moore says "I know that I have two hands," and so forth, he implies that no grounds could be surer than his claim to know; so he gives no grounds. But to imply that no grounds could be surer than his claim to know is to misuse "I know." What Moore is trying to say is better expressed in a different idiom. He is trying to say that this proposition is exempt from doubt; but in such a case rather than saying "I know" it would be better to say "It stands fast for me" (*O.C.*, 116). Or one might say "That I have two hands is an irreversible belief." To use these idioms would explain why no ground could be surer than the asserted proposition. As Wittgenstein says:

> To whom does anyone say that he knows something? To himself, or to someone else. If he says it to himself, how is it distinguished from the assertion that he is *sure* that things are like that? There is no subjective sureness that I know something. The certainty is subjective, but not the knowledge. So if I say "I know I have two hands" and that is not supposed to express just my subjective certainty, I must be able to satisfy myself that I am right. But I can't do that, for my having two hands is not less certain before I have looked at them than afterwards. But I could say: "That I have two hands is an irreversible belief." That would express the fact that I am not ready to let anything count as a disproof of this proposition. (*O.C.*, 245)

This quotation is one of many in which Wittgenstein is driving a wedge between the notions of knowledge and certainty. We can see from the pair of passages just cited that the two concepts are to be characterized differently. In particular, he states that whereas a knowledge claim must be buttressed by grounds, and grounds that are no less sure than the claim, nothing can be more sure than that which is certain, and that is why the adducing of reasons is inapposite. As Wittgenstein puts it in 253, "At the foundation of well-founded belief lies belief that is not founded." In developing this theme in the early sections of *On Certainty*, Wittgenstein was thinking of certitude in propositional terms, but later he proposed a much more radical interpretation. But from that propositional perspective he put the difference this way: "That is to say, the questions that we raise and our doubts depend on the fact that some propositions are exempt from doubt, are as it were like hinges on which those turn" (*O.C.*, 341).

In chapters 9 and 10 we shall explore the difference between knowledge and certainty in greater detail. One way of delineating that distinction is to say, as Wittgenstein does, that some propositions stand fast for us and are exempt from doubt, whereas other propositions do not stand fast and are not exempt from doubt. The hinge metaphor brings out the point beautifully. It discriminates between two categories of propositions: those that are certain and not susceptible to doubt and those that express knowledge claims, where doubting is apposite. The idea that some propositions are beyond doubt gradually gives way in *On Certainty* to a different, non-propositional account of certainty. Unfortunately, then, the hinge metaphor will carry us only so far in distinguishing knowledge from certainty. Yet the importance of doubting is never abandoned as a key element in that endeavor. We shall therefore focus on it in the rest of the chapter.

It is obvious that doubting is intimately tied to knowing. One who doubts that p implies that he does not know that p, so there is an exclusionary relationship between the two notions. But Wittgenstein argues that there are even more profound connections. He shows that doubting is not a wholly internal state or process and that in this respect it is like and not different from knowing. This is what he means when he says that doubting is a societal practice. He also shows that doubting, like knowing, belongs *to* the language game and unlike certainty does not lie *outside* of it. On the basis of this analysis, he then argues that Moore's use of "doubt," and indeed the sceptic/idealist's use of that term, are both senseless. This last claim rests on a set of considerations very much like those we have just described, in which Moore has misidentified knowing by conflating it with an inner mental state.

Here we shall see that Moore and his sceptical opponents have misidentified doubt, confusing it with a notion that Wittgenstein calls "philosophical doubt." This doubt, as we mentioned earlier and as Wittgenstein will reaffirm, is not a case of doubting at all. We shall thus see how doubting is connected to the two main themes we have been exploring in this chapter: first, that knowing is not merely an inward state, process, or feature; and, second, that Moore's use of "I know" is, for a variety of reasons, senseless. We shall end this chapter with a description of the line of argumentation in *On Certainty* that leads to parallel conclusions about doubting.

We can begin by asking, How does Wittgenstein show that doubting is not to be identified with an inner state? The argument is similar to that in which he has shown that knowing is not simply a mental state—that is, an introspective felt experience, like a pain. He shows instead that it is part of a set of practices or activities that are constitutive of human communal life. These are practices similar to the playing of certain games. To play baseball is to engage in a set of complex activities involving other persons, sets of rules that they players follow, institutional arrangements, and so on. One cannot play baseball by simply looking inward—one must instead act in ways that are non-personal and as a member of a community. This complex set of activities, including the formative rules of the game and a certain kind of immersion in a human community, define what it is to play baseball.

Now doubting exhibits many of the same features, even though intuitively one may think of it as an inward state, something like a felt sensation. One could, surely, be correctly described as doubting such and such without feeling any inward sensation at all. This sort of case is not unfamiliar. Wittgenstein, of course, does not wish to deny that sometimes when in doubt one may feel a certain inward sensation, perhaps akin to hesitation. But his point is that it would be a mistake to identify doubting with that or any other sensation. In contrast to this Cartesian picture, Wittgenstein often refers to the "game of doubting": "We might describe his way of behaving as like the behavior of doubt, but his game would not be ours" (*O.C.,* 255).

What could he mean by the "game of doubting"? And why is the game of doubting not to be identified with an internal sensation? Let us take a specific example. Suppose a friend asserts in a friendly argument that Lou Gehrig holds the record for the most runs batted in during any 154-game major league baseball season. Your recollection is that it was Hack Wilson, which gives you a reason for doubting the claim. You say this to your friend, admitting that you are not sure. You have now begun the game of doubting; but like a baseball game that requires nine innings to be complete, you are only in the first inning and have just begun to play. You continue the game when you set out to discover the answer. There is an entire process to be completed before the game of doubting is finished. You check old newspapers, clippings in libraries, and baseball encyclopedias. All of them agree that the player was Hack Wilson. This set of activities begins with a problem, but it includes your going to libraries, looking for data, and so on.

That complex process is what Wittgenstein means by the game of doubting. It is a game designed to bring an open question to resolution. It is a game because it involves a set of practices, the analogs of rules, such as record keeping, the adducing of evidence, and so forth. It is a particular kind of game, more like baseball than solitaire in that it involves others, institutions such as libraries and law courts, and a communal background that rests upon uniformity of judgment and agreement. When you find the answer in these materials the game of doubting comes to an end. You now show the answer to your friend. At this point the friend should concede you are right. But suppose he refuses to accept your report. In that case he has resumed the game. For him to continue to play the game would mean that he would have to engage in a set of activities that paralleled your own—going to libraries, checking records, and so on. If the records confirm what you have told him, the game has come to termination.

Now suppose, however, that your friend continues to insist it is Lou Gehrig who holds the record for the most runs batted in and argues that his recollection cannot be mistaken. He might even argue that the so-called records are not to be trusted, that they may all emerge from the same source, that that source is possibly mistaken, and so on. In that case, what Wittgenstein would call serious doubting has stopped. The game your friend is playing is no longer rational; it is no longer being played according to established community rules. As Wittgenstein puts it, "these rules . . . only make sense if they come to an end somewhere. A doubt without an end is not even a doubt" (O.C., 625). Your friend is now "outside" the language game. This is precisely what the sceptic does when he insists that seeing is not a reliable criterion for believing that a chair is in the room. In that case, serious doubting has also come to an end, for there is no way of settling the question. This is a case of what Wittgenstein calls "philosophical doubt." It looks like ordinary doubt, and yet it isn't the same because even in principle it cannot be resolved. Like the person who refuses to accept records, the sceptic will insist that it is reasonable to doubt the reliability of all putative data, including those based upon vision. But why is this sort of obsessive doubt senseless? Wittgenstein answers with a parable about how to teach a pupil history. Here in part is what he says:

> A pupil and a teacher. The pupil will not let anything be explained to him, for he continually interrupts with doubts, for instance as to the existence of things, the meaning of words, etc. The teacher says "Stop interrupting me and do as I tell you. So far your doubts don't make sense at all."
>
> Or imagine that the boy questioned the truth of history (and everything that connects up with it)—and even whether the earth had existed at all a hundred years before. . . .
>
> Perhaps the teacher will get a bit impatient, but think that the boy will grow out of asking such questions.
>
> That is to say, the teacher will feel that this is not really a legitimate question at all.
>
> And it would be just the same if the pupil cast doubt on the uniformity of nature, that is to say on the justification of inductive arguments. The teacher would feel that this was only holding them up, that this way the pupil would only get stuck and make no progress. And he would be right. It would be as if someone were looking for some object in a room; he opens a drawer and doesn't see it there then he closes it again, waits, and opens it once more to see if perhaps it isn't there now, and keeps on like that. He has not learned to look for things. And in the same way this pupil has not learned how to ask questions. He has not learned *the* game we are trying to teach him. (O.C., 311–315)

As Wittgenstein says, the person who keeps looking in a drawer, opening and closing it again and again, searching for an object, say a button, has not learned how to look for things. *He has not learned the game of searching.* How could he be taught that game, and what would he learn? Roughly speaking, the answer is by early training, by living in a family as part of a community in which people search for lost objects. One comes to learn as a result of such training that it is *senseless* to continue to open and close a drawer obsessively; nothing can be gained after the first few tries. It is like checking the date by looking at hundreds of copies of the same newspaper. Such an obsessive process lacks a procedure for closure. That is why it can be continued endlessly, but that is also why it is senseless.

Wittgenstein's parables about doubting set the stage for his treatment of certainty. As he says: "Doubting and non-doubting behavior. There is the first only if there is the second" (*O.C.*, 354). "If you tried to doubt everything you would not get as far as doubting anything. The game of doubting itself presupposes certainty" (*O.C.*, 115). The notion that doubting presupposes certainty is an extraordinary insight—and we shall turn to its development now.

9

Wittgenstein's Foundationalism

We can say, then, that for Wittgenstein the applicability of doubt is one of the features that defines the language game. This is a complex thought with many ramifications. One is that where doubt is *inapplicable* we are dealing with matters that do not belong to the language game. A subcase of this is the subject matter of this chapter, namely, a highly original form of foundationalism that Wittgenstein develops in *On Certainty*. The foundations of the language game stand *outside of* and yet *support* the language game—exactly how is what we shall be discussing below. These foundations are identified in a series of metaphors as "the hinges on which others turn," "the rock bottom of our convictions," "the substratum of all my inquiring," and most pervasively "that which stands fast for us and for many others" (*O.C.*, 116). All of these expressions are metaphors for certainty. It is Wittgenstein's main thesis in *On Certainty* that what stands fast is not subject to justification, proof, the adducing of evidence, or doubt and is neither true nor false. Whatever is subject to these ascriptions belongs to the language game. But certitude is not so subject, and therefore it stands outside of the language game. It does so in two different forms, one relative, the other absolute. A proposition that is exempt from doubt in some contexts may become subject to doubt in others, and when it does it plays a role within the language game. This is the relativized form of certitude. But some propositions—that the earth exists, that the earth is very old—are beyond any doubt; their certitude is absolute.

A number of twentieth-century philosophers have advanced views that in certain respects resemble Wittgenstein's but that also differ substantially from his. I will briefly describe two of these.

Robin Collingwood, who was born in the same year as Wittgenstein but who died eight years before him, considered metaphysics to be a type of historical science whose subject matter was what he called "absolute presuppositions." According to Collingwood, every science, whether theoretical or applied, poses questions it attempts to answer. These questions and their answers rest upon presuppositions that are themselves not answers to questions. Since truth and falsity can be ascribed only to answers, such presuppositions are neither true nor false. Collingwood does not describe these "absolute presuppositions" in detail.

It is thus not clear what they are: whether they are types of dispositions or assumptions or latent thoughts or habits, though he does hold that they are "unconscious." They would seem, therefore, to be psychological in character and inexplicit in some sense. In discussing the relationship between science and its presuppositions, Collingwood's view is strikingly narrower than Wittgenstein's. He does not draw Wittgenstein's more general distinction between the language game and the communal practices that support it, for example. He also holds that such presuppositions vary from historical period to historical period, and this is why he claims that the philosophical study of such presuppositions is a branch of "historical science." From a Wittgensteinian perspective, his presuppositions would thus not be absolutistic in character, but would stand fast only in particular historical epochs. For Wittgenstein, as I have indicated, absolute presuppositions remain invariant under all historical transformations. So though Collingwood speaks of "absolute presuppositions," his view seems to have been a form of relativism, not unlike that which Charles Sanders Peirce advanced earlier in the century.

Peirce's relativism is explicit and seems closer to Wittgenstein's, but nonetheless differs from it in important respects. He affirms that whenever there is doubt something else is not doubted. But he denies what is not doubted is certain, for it too can be doubted in other contexts. So he agrees with Wittgenstein that not everything can be doubted at once, yet he denies that anything is certain. In that respect he differs from Wittgenstein, who states that on both the relativistic and absolutistic interpretations there is such a thing as certainty. Looked at from a Wittgensteinian perspective, Peirce seems to have held that we never get outside of the language game, that all contexts belong to it, and therefore that doubt is distributively possible over the totality of the items belonging to such contexts. Wittgenstein's notions that the language game is to be distinguished from its external supports and that certainty is to be identified with these are by comparison deep and original insights.

Wittgenstein describes the relationship among doubt, knowledge, and certainty in a number of different ways: "Some propositions are exempt from doubt" (341); "Doubt itself rests only on what is beyond doubt" (519); "Knowledge and certainty belong to different categories" (308); and so on. The inference to be drawn from his analysis is that knowledge and certitude are radically different from one another. In effect, Moore's error was to have conflated them. What he was talking about was that which stands fast for us, but he mistakenly used epistemic language in attempting to characterize it. He used language appropriate only to those practices occurring within the language game about something that was external to it. Wittgenstein's achievement in *On Certainty* consisted in correcting this category mistake: "To say of man, in Moore's sense, that he *knows* something; that what he says is therefore unconditionally the truth, seems wrong to me.—It is the truth only inasmuch as it is an unmoving foundation of his language-games" (*O.C.*, 403).

There are other important implications of the notion that the applicability of doubt has sharp limitations, and some of these may give rise to misunderstanding. Let us begin with one that is already familiar, namely, that so-called philosophical doubt is not a case of doubt at all. The sceptic, committed to ceaseless questioning, is not engaging in an activity whose rules of sensible employment require termination in principle. As Wittgenstein says in 450, "a doubt that doubted everything would not be a doubt," and again in 625, "a doubt without an end is not even a doubt." The sceptic thus stands "outside" the language game. But where is that? The question leads to a further ramification of the original distinction. The language game, as we have seen, is roughly that set of everyday human activities, institutions, and customs that define certain practices. The "game of doubting" is one of those practices, and its rules *presuppose* closure *in principle* for genuine cases of doubting. Closure in principle is another name for certainty. As Wittgenstein writes in 115, "The game of doubting itself presupposes certainty." But the game of doubting does not presuppose philosophical doubting.

So though both scepticism and certainty stand outside of the language game their relationships to it are distinct. The former threatens the game; the latter supports it and makes it possible. Accordingly, when Wittgenstein speaks about that which is beyond doubt, or affirms that the concept of doubt is inapplicable to some X, he is not alluding to scepticism but instead to that which is certain. We cannot say of scepticism that it is beyond doubt, even though the sceptic's practice does not belong to the language game. We must therefore exercise caution in our understanding of the idioms of applicability and inapplicability. Wittgenstein intends them to apply only to the foundational elements that support the language game.

This is not the only place where misunderstanding is possible. Sometimes Wittgenstein talks about the inapplicability of doubt in a way that can be misleading if not read in context. For example, he says, "absence of doubt belongs to the essence of the language-game." This phrase seems to suggest just the opposite of what I am asserting to be his main line of argumentation. But if one reads the whole passage in which this sentential fragment is encased, it is obvious that it is a variation on the theme being advanced here. This is what he says:

> But more correctly: The fact that I use the word "hand" and all the other words in my sentence without a second thought, indeed that I should stand before the abyss if I wanted so much as to try doubting their meanings—shews that absence of doubt belongs to the essence of the language-game, that the question "How do I know . . ." drags out the language-game, or else does away with it. (*O.C.*, 370)

In this passage Wittgenstein is stating that in normal human intercourse one generally acts habitually and not self-consciously—as he puts it: "Doubting and non-doubting behavior. There is the first only if there is the second" (354). If one's ordinary actions were always preceded by or accompanied by doubt, one would be paralyzed—one would "stand before the abyss," and ordinary behavior would be impossible. One does not doubt the meanings of the words one uses in normal circumstances, and it is in that sense that the "absence of doubt" belongs to the language game. But if one doubted everything—"dragged out the language-game" by unremitting doubt, one would soon do away with the language game itself—one could not even talk; and this is just the point Wittgenstein has been making throughout. So the locution he uses here is not inconsistent with the general thesis he is advancing but is another affirmation of it.

The original thought about the applicability of doubt has another important implication, namely, about a possible inconsistency in Wittgenstein's philosophical practice. That Wittgenstein should be a foundationalist, as I claim in this chapter, is surprising for a number of reasons. It suggests that he is advancing a philosophical thesis about everyday human activity and the conditions that make it possible—something like a transcendental argument. If so, it is a radical departure from the descriptivism he advocates as the correct philosophical method. It also suggests that the view he is advancing is similar to those one finds in Descartes, Locke, and others who hold that the human epistemic structure rests upon foundational items that are immune to doubt. But if this is his view, has he not been captured by a metaphysical picture that imposes a foundationalist gloss on human practice? Has he not become another Cartesian in search of impeccable foundations for knowledge, despite his protests to the contrary? These considerations raise the issue of whether he has been hoist on his own petard.

I will argue that despite appearances to the contrary the answer is no. We shall see both that Wittgenstein is a foundationalist *of sorts*, but not of a traditional sort, and that his form of foundationalism is consistent with his apothegm that description should replace explanation in philosophy. The main line of argumentation defending my interpretation will turn on a notion I call *homogeneous foundations*. I will explain later and in more detail what this term means. For the moment here is a brief characterization. I believe that most traditional forms of foundationalism, even those which are non-epistemological, assume or presuppose that what they identify as foundational items must belong to the same category as the items which rest upon them. Thus, for instance, the *cogito* is itself a piece of knowledge, though more fundamental than certain other pieces of knowledge that depend on it. This notion of homogeneous foundations will have to be modified slightly to accommodate non-epistemological forms of foundationalism, such as we find in logic, say. In such cases the axioms are not theorems, but they do conform to certain categorial constraints. Key ascriptions that apply to the theorems also apply to the axioms—for example, that they are true, susceptible to inferences via the application of *modus ponens*, and so on. We shall see below why traditional foundationalists have found it necessary to assume such a notion. The significance of this assumption for the interpretation of Wittgenstein is that he explicitly rejects this presupposition; in this respect, his is among the few epistemological versions of foundationalism in Western philosophy that does so. And it is for that reason that he will escape the allegation that he has been hoist upon his own petard.

Let us turn to what I call Wittgenstein's foundationalism. This is, on my reading, a view to the effect that certitude stands in a foundational relationship to the language game itself. Of course, if there is no such view in *On Certainty*, then the putative resemblance to traditional foundationalists will be just a red herring, and we can dismiss it. In that case our interpretation of what Wittgenstein is doing in *On Certainty* will require radical rethinking. But I think that Wittgenstein is a foundationalist in this sense. If I am right, then the question of what differentiates him from the tradition still remains to be addressed. But before we can explore that matter it remains to be shown that he is a foundationalist—and what is the evidence for that? In fact, it is overwhelming.

I have discovered more than sixty places in which Wittgenstein uses explicitly foundational language and where the contrast he is drawing is between the language game and the foundation or foundations (he uses both the singular and the plural, and I will follow his usage in what follows) that underlie and/or support it. Apart from these cases of explicit terminology, the text is replete with references that use a different idiom (e.g., *Gerust, feststehen, Ursache, festhalten,* etc.) but to the same foundational effect. By "explicitly foundational language," I mean he is using three German words (and certain grammatical variations of them). These are *Boden* ("ground," "soil") which occurs rarely; *Grund,* ("ground," "base," "bottom," "foundation"), which occurs frequently; and *Fundament* ("foundation," "basis"), which occurs more frequently than *Boden* and less frequently than *Grund.* Some of the grammatical variations we find on these nouns are *Fundamental, Grundlage, grundlos, unbegrundet, Grundlegung,* and *bodenlos.* One or the other of these three words or their cognates are to be found in the following passages: 87–88; 94; 103; 110; 112, 162; 166; 167; 204–205; 211; 225; 234; 245–246; 248; 253; 295–296; 307–308; 337; 341; 343; 347–348; 353; 358–359; 370–371; 380; 403; 411; 414–415; 449; 474; 475; 477; 492; 509; 512; 514; 516; 519; 558–560; 614; 670.

These sixty-plus citations represent approximately one tenth of the total number of entries in the published text of *On Certainty.* When foundational passages that do not explicitly use foundational language are added we can see that Wittgenstein's foundationalism is a major theme in this work. I recommend that the entire group of passages be read seriatim in order to feel the full impact of the foundationalism they express. Given space limitations, I will select only a few to illustrate what a more expansive treatment would reveal.

> Giving grounds, however, justifying the evidence, comes to an end;—but the end is not certain propositions striking us immediately as true, i.e., it is not a kind of seeing on our part; it is our acting, which lies at the bottom (*am Grund*) of the language game. (*O.C.,* 204)

> If the true is what is grounded (*Begrundete ist*), then the ground (*der Grund*) is not true, nor yet false. (205)

Those passages speak about *der Grund* of the language game and distinguish it from what occurs within the language game. What occurs within the language game may be either true or false, justified or not, but what grounds the game is neither. Entries 253 and 358–359 run typical variations on these themes. In 253 Wittgenstein writes that "at the foundation of well-founded belief lies belief that is not founded" and in 358–359, adds "But that means I want to conceive it as something that lies beyond being justified or unjustified; as it were, as something animal." He carries the idea expressed in 204 that certitude is non-propositional and that it is acting that lies at the bottom of the language game even further in 359. He now implies that it is something beyond intellection. This is a thought that becomes dominant as the work proceeds:

> I want to regard man here as an animal; as a primitive being to which one grants instinct but not ratiocination. As a creature in a primitive state. Any logic good enough for a primitive means of communication needs no apology from us. Language did not emerge from some kind of ratiocination. (*O.C.*, 475)

With these passages, the rupture between the foundations and the language game is as wide as it will become in the text. Language did not emerge from some kind of ratiocination but from "instinct" and from a primitive human state. In chapter 10 we shall indicate in distinguishing between his views and those of many contemporary cognitive scientists what Wittgenstein means by "ratiocination" and certain related terms. But as this passage indicates, he is stressing that the foundations of the language game do not arise from deliberation or the application of a theory but from much more primitive factors. And this is why they are not susceptible to epistemic evaluation. The language game in that sense has no justification; what supports it is beyond such assessments—it is just there like one's life.

The passages quoted are typical expressions of the foundationalist theme that runs through the text. I will therefore assume that the case for identifying Wittgenstein as a foundationalist has been made.

But what does it mean, at a deeper level of analysis, to say that Wittgenstein is a foundationalist? As I have indicated, I think he is a foundationalist, but of no conventional sort. Are these claims consistent, let alone true? I will now try to justify them. The remainder of this chapter will be dedicated to exploring the nature of foundationalism, and in the light of that investigation to establishing that Wittgenstein's version of this view is unique.

Let's start with a simple conceptual model. We shall presume that every foundationalist, traditional or otherwise, accepts this model, and then we shall explain where Wittgenstein deviates from it. The model is so simple and so general that it lacks the cognitive stuffing that has distinguished traditional foundationalists from one another. But it does capture certain formal features that can be used as the basis for such discriminations.

From at least the time of Aristotle many philosophers have asserted that some of the knowledge human beings possess is more fundamental or basic than the rest. If we call such primordial knowledge F and the remainder R, we can roughly express their intuition by saying that R depends on F but not conversely and that F depends on nothing. Let us sponge the epistemological gloss from this statement—that is, we shall leave F and R uninterpreted and in particular not take them to be pieces of knowledge. What remains is just a formal structure. It holds that there is some asymmetrical relationship of dependence between F and R, whatever these are taken to be, and that F is not dependent on anything else. So given some unanalyzed notion of "dependence" and some unanalyzed conception of what sorts of items F and R may be, we can say that this skeleton gives us the basic foundationalist intuition. The thrust of the model is that F somehow supports R and is itself not supported by anything. The idea that F is not supported by anything is generally taken to be another way of saying that F is foundational. Whether that is an ultimately correct inference we shall leave open at this time. But there is very little doubt that most foundationalist views have conformed to this simple model.

Still, if we want the model, even in this skeletal form, to be adequate to the historical tradition that begins with the Greeks we shall have to add another element to it. It is difficult to state this in a purely formal way and without giving specific examples, so some examples will follow. The formal point is that F will either be a single thing or a very limited number of things if there is more than one F, whereas R will be complex, possessing scope and amplitude. The formal point will thus flesh out the model, giving it topologically the shape of an inverted pyramid. The main body of the pyramid will rest on something equivalent to a simple base. It will be broader at its apex than at its base. We can call the base the foundation and what rests on it the mansion.

In the world of philosophy there are many mansions that conform to this model—both in epistemology and in other domains of the subject. A typical example is an axiomatic logical system, such as that developed by Whitehead and Russell in *Principia Mathematica (P.M.)*. As is well known, the system rests upon a set of primitives, five axioms that define them, and a principle of inference. This is the base of the system that expands upward and outward from it, forming a logical mansion that eventually allowed Russell and Whitehead to derive Peano's postulates from a set of ascending calculi. It is, of course, understood that a formula that is axiomatic within a particular system, such as *P.M.*, could be proved as a theorem in some other system with different axioms (or in a system of natural deduction). But every axiomatic system rests upon formulas that are not provable within that system. Some years later Sheffer showed that the five axioms of *P.M.* could be reduced to one, thus simplifying the base. The resulting picture was that of an inverted pyramid, with the sentential calculus being derived from the axioms, the predicate calculus later, and so on.

One can think of the Cartesian philosophy as giving rise to a parallel picture, whose elements are not theorems but epistemic propositions. Their base is the *cogito*—the F or foundation. The totality of propositions forming the inverted pyramid is R; these are propositions that Descartes claimed could be derived from F. With this additional feature we can say that this is the model that every traditional foundationalist accepts.

Even in this skeletal form, the model needs further explanation. For example, what does it mean to say that F *depends on nothing whatever?* Consider the *cogito* for a moment. It is the foundation of an epistemic superstructure. The items belonging to the superstructure are said to depend on the foundational item—Descartes seems to argue that their very existence as pieces of knowledge arises from that dependence. If the *cogito* were not known with certainty to be true, then nothing could be, and there could be no such pieces of knowledge. So let us agree that the dependence runs in the way that Descartes indicates. But now, a critic might ask, doesn't the *cogito* itself depend on something? For instance, doesn't it depend on someone's apprehending it with clarity and distinctness? And doesn't that depend on there being a language already in existence which that person speaks? But doesn't that entail that the person who speaks that language be alive and conscious, and doesn't that require that his or her heart be pumping blood, and doesn't that in turn necessitate the satisfaction of an infinite number of other conditions? So how can one say that the *cogito*—taken to be F in this context—depends on nothing?

I am sure that Descartes would have dismissed this objection. He would probably have said something like this:

> Look, I am distinguishing between specimens of knowledge, and the point I am making is that some of these—indeed a certain one I am calling the *cogito*—are more basic than others. It is irrelevant to talk about the notion of dependence in linguistic, physiological, or medical terms. They just do not apply to the case in point. It would be like asking, What color are the natural numbers? The question just makes no sense, for it violates certain categorial restraints. So when I talk about dependence and say that the *cogito* depends on nothing, I mean that it depends on no other piece of knowledge. The only question at stake is whether some other piece of knowledge is more basic than the *cogito*: and this I deny.

I believe that Descartes would be typical in giving this sort of answer. In doing so, he would be appealing to what I called above the doctrine of *homogeneous foundations*. He would be saying, in effect, that the notion of dependence applies to and is limited to putative pieces of knowledge. So F and R must be instances of knowledge before the notion of dependence can be sensibly applied to their relationship. Given this condition, his thesis would be that F does not depend on any piece of knowledge in order to be a piece of knowledge. That is what it means to say it is fundamental. Again, in a different domain of philosophy, Russell might have responded in much the same way. Of course, one would have to be alive in order to assume that the axioms of *P.M.* are true and indeed to initiate the process that resulted in the enormous number of constructive proofs that followed. But that would not mean the axioms could be said to be dependent on something. To say that they are not dependent on anything is to invoke the doctrine of homogeneous foundations. There is no theorem that they depend on, and that is the general category Russell would be presupposing in saying that the axioms of his system are not open to proof.

This line of reasoning brings us to Wittgenstein and to a major respect in which he differs from the tradition. As we have seen throughout this work, he rejects the idea that what is foundational is susceptible to proof, the adducing of evidence, truth or falsity, justification or non-justification. Whatever is so susceptible belongs to the language game and thus to a *different category* of human activity from *das Fundament*. Wittgenstein's genius consisted in constructing an account of human knowledge whose foundations, whose supporting presuppositions, were in no ways like knowledge. Knowledge belongs to the language game, and certitude does not. The base and the mansion resting on it are completely different. This is what Wittgenstein means when he says that knowledge and certainty belong to different *categories*. In saying this he realized that he was saying something philosophically insightful about the entire Western philosophical tradition. And it is his rejection of the thesis of homogeneous foundations that, to a great extent, separates him from that tradition.

These remarks raise a possible objection. As I have indicated in earlier chapters, there are two different accounts of F in *On Certainty*. One of these—the earlier—is propositional in character. It clearly derives from Wittgenstein's response to Moore, who thinks of certainty in propositional terms. As I stated earlier, when Wittgenstein speaks of hinge *propositions* as immune to justification, proof, and so on, we are dealing with the earlier account. The second account is completely different. It begins to develop gradually as the text was being written and comes to dominate it as it closes. On this view, there are several candidates for F, and all of them are non-intellectual. Among these are *acting, being trained in communal practices, instinct*, and so on.

We shall be discussing these two views below. The question we shall raise is whether the earlier view also rejects the doctrine of homogeneous foundations. A critic might deny this and argue as follows: Wittgenstein asserts (the critic will say) that hinge propositions are propositions. He also asserts they are foundational. But if they are propositions they do not differ in categorial kind from the ordinary propositions, that rest on them. And if so, the earlier view must be traditional in just the sense that the second is not. Therefore Wittgenstein does not differ from the tradition in the way that you claim. I think this is an interesting and important criticism, but I think it can be neutralized. I will be arguing that both views *reject* the thesis of homogeneous foundations and that the real difference between them is one of intellection. Or to put the point differently, that what Wittgenstein is calling *hinge propositions* are not ordinary propositions at all. Such concepts as being true or false, known or not known, justified or unjustified do not apply to them, and these are usually taken to be the defining features of propositions.

So Wittgenstein is using a familiar term—for special reasons—to refer to something that is not a proposition at all. As we saw earlier, even in the *Tractatus* he had recognized that such locutions are not straightforwardly about the world. The term he used for their "peculiar" status was "pseudo-proposition." Then later, as I indicated in previous chapters, he thought of these as "logical insights" and/or as "grammatical rules." The concept of a "hinge proposition" is his newest attempt to indicate their status. They are on this latest account proposition-like, and yet they are neither true nor false, not subject to evidence, proof, confirmation, or disconfirmation. They are thus not really propositions at all.

This is at least in part why Wittgenstein asserts that such "propositions" do not belong to the language game. We shall say more about this matter at the end of the chapter. But even here it is important to stress the difference between the earlier and later foundationalist accounts he gives us. Both reject the doctrine of homogeneous foundations, but they differ from one another in profound ways. Most commentators—I am thinking here explicitly of Marie McGinn—do not see the important difference between these two conceptions of certitude. But they are fundamental to understanding Wittgenstein's deepening understanding of certitude in *On Certainty*.

That both foundationalist accounts are not traditional is, then, the first point I wish to make here. But it still leaves open the petard question. Even if Wittgenstein is not advancing any traditional foundationalist model, the question remains whether description has replaced explanation in his account. In order to show that his account is descriptivist, we must deepen our exploration of the traditional foundationalist model. We shall see immediately that even in the simple form with which we have been working it leads to a set of puzzles or problems that Wittgenstein's approach is able to avoid. He is able to avoid the most obvious of these because of his descriptivist approach and the unique form of foundationalism it engenders.

What are the problems the traditional model produces? These arise from a set of natural questions—some of which are meat for the sceptic. According to the model, foundational F does not depend on anything and is said to be more fundamental than any R. But the sceptic will ask, How do we know that? How can you be sure there isn't something more fundamental than F upon which it depends?

Foundationalists meet such questions in a variety of ways, but they all insist that F cannot depend on anything—(and in so doing they assume the principle of homogenous foundations). F's lack of dependence is what it means to say that it is fundamental or basic. To put the matter in terms of certainty, foundationalists may say two things: that F is certain and that F is more certain than anything that could be invoked in its support. The notion that F is more certain than anything else is taken by them to be another way of saying that F does not depend on anything. For if some proposition, P, were more certain than F, then F could be derived from it and therefore would not be foundational. Though the propositions that F is certain and that F is more certain than any other P are not logically equivalent, they are generally taken to be so by traditionalists. Where they differ is in answering the probing sceptical question that this dual claim engenders, namely, How do you know that F is certain and especially more certain than anything that could be adduced in its support?

A variety of answers have historically been given to this question. Descartes stated that he could see clearly and distinctly that the *cogito* was true. Others have answered that by some act of rational intuition they can see that F is certain and more certain than any other proposition. One of the most interesting answers takes a general form. It is claimed that there *must be* such an F or one would be committed to an infinite and vicious epistemological regress. And if that were the case, then it would be impossible to have any present instances of knowledge. But since there are such instances, there must be a foundational F.

This line of reasoning apes the cosmological proof for the existence of God. The line of reasoning is familiar. If there were an infinite regress, there would be no first cause. If there were no first cause, there would be no second cause, and if no second cause then no third, and so on ad infinitum; and, accordingly, there would be no present cause. But since there is a present cause there cannot be an infinite regress and therefore there must be a first cause and that is God. By an analogical argument it is contended that because there are present pieces of knowledge there must be a foundational piece of knowledge (note again how the thesis of homogeneous foundations is presupposed by the argument), and from this the inverted pyramid of knowledge is developed.

Wittgenstein, as a foundationalist, also asserts that nothing could be more certain than that which stands fast for us, but in *On Certainty* his discussion makes no reference to the regress difficulty. Given his form of foundationalism the regress problem does not arise. It arises for traditionalists because they assume that the question, How do you know that that which stands fast for us is certain? is always applicable. And they assume that because they think that the foundation and what rests on it belong to the same category. But for Wittgenstein's form of foundationalism the question is not applicable and, in fact, embodies a category mistake. One cannot sensibly ask of that which is certain whether it is known (or not known) or true (or false); for what is meant by certitude is not susceptible to such ascriptions. The sceptical question thus need not be answered. This shows again how radically Wittgenstein's view differs from any traditional form of foundationalism.

Up to now we have been working with a formal sketch of the foundationalist model. I now want to show that, looked at both logically and historically, the model is much more complicated than I have depicted it. We need to add the substance I spoke about earlier in order to be able to distinguish various kinds of traditional foundationalists from one another and Wittgenstein from any of them. I believe that when fully fleshed out the model will contain nine strands. To my knowledge no traditional foundationalist philosophy exhibits all nine strands. Historically, foundationalist philosophies have differed from one another depending on how many and which strands they have adopted. Wittgenstein's two forms of foundationalism will exhibit all nine strands, and his adoption of them in each case will be defended on purely descriptive grounds. When the analysis is completed it will be seen that Wittgenstein is a descriptivist, is not offering an "explanation," and therefore is not imposing a conceptual model upon human behavior and communication. If this analysis is sound, it will dispose of the petard question.

The nine strands are (1) stratification, (2) aberrancy, (3) non-dependence, (4) particularism or methodism, (5) publicity, (6) negational absurdity, (7) absorption, (8) certitude, and (9) standing fast. This last strand will be divided into propositional and non-propositional versions. In order to simplify the discussion, and in particular to tie it into historical versions of foundationalism, we shall assume that the foundational items are propositional in character and that each of them is a specific piece of knowledge. Let us begin with the notion of stratification.

1. *Stratification.* This is a necessary but not a sufficient condition for foundationalism. It is the notion that the epistemic corpus is not all of a piece but has within it different levels or strata. This notion is necessary to foundationalism in the sense that no philosopher can be a foundationalist without holding that some of our knowledge has a different status than other bits or pieces of it. Our formula that R depends on F, but not conversely, captures this notion. Historically, the distinction among the strata has been drawn in different ways. For instance, some philosophers have held that only foundational knowledge is cer-

tain, the rest being only probable; and there have been other ways of distinguishing between the base and the superstructure.

We can show that stratification is a necessary but not sufficient condition by considering three brief historical examples. In the early dialogues Plato seems to have held the view that within the epistemic corpus there are no seams, that all knowledge is certain and that none is more certain than any other. On this view, all knowledge has exactly the same status. Clearly, if he did indeed hold such a view Plato would not be a foundationalist since no pieces of knowledge would have priority over any others. The example shows that stratification is a necessary condition for foundationalism, that some distinction between the base and what rests on it is requisite to any such view. As we saw in the preceding discussion, Wittgenstein is clearly a stratificationist. He holds that hinge propositions may take the form of empirical propositions but are not empirical propositions and adds: "This observation is not of the form 'I know. . . .' 'I know . . .' states what *I* know, and that is not of logical interest." (*O.C.*, 401).

But stratification is not a sufficient condition for foundationalism. The views of Quine and Popper can be described as stratificationist but not as foundationalist. Quine, as is well known, holds that the epistemic corpus has degrees of certitude. Some things we know—certain empirical laws—stand at or near the center of the epistemic corpus. They are the best-established pieces of knowledge we have and would be the last to be given up or be subject to revision. Other bits of knowledge fan out from the heartland, moving more and more toward the periphery of the epistemic penumbra. As they approach the periphery they have less evidential and conceptual support and thus in principle are those most susceptible to revision or abandonment.

In some of his papers, for example, in "Two Dogmas of Empiricism," Quine draws a distinction between the laws of logic, taken as uninterpreted formulas, and certain analytical sentences that can be derived from them via substitution. The difference between these analytic sentences and ordinary empirical statements is only one of degree. But the laws of logic have a different status; they seem to differ in kind from the analytical statements that can be constructed from them. If all statements, including the formal laws of logic, were distinguished only by degree, Quine would not be a stratificationist. To be that there must be a qualitative difference, or a difference in kind, between some propositions and others. I am here intepreting Quine as having held that there is such a difference with respect to the laws of identity and contradiction. If this is interpetation is correct (and I agree it is disputable), there is thus stratification within the holistic epistemic nexus. But for Quine not even the best-established propositions, including the fundamental laws of logic, stand absolutely fast in Wittgenstein's sense. This is so because in principle any of these laws could be revised or dropped depending on the path taken by future experience. Quine's position thus closely resembles that of his distinguished pragmatist precursor, Charles Sanders Peirce.

Popper's view, without Quine's holistic gloss, is not dissimilar. He argues that the body of knowledge lacks any sort of ultimate foundation, but also believes that some of its elements are qualitatively distinguishable from others.

For Popper the epistemic structure somehow pulls itself up by its bootstraps; it does not arise from foundations, for there are none. So here we have a pair of views that embody stratification but are non-foundational. So clearly stratification is not a sufficient condition for foundationalism but only a necessary one.

2. *Aberrancy*. The basic idea that Wittgenstein advances in this connection is that to be wrong about a foundational proposition is to be something other than mistaken; it is to suffer from some sort of serious conceptual aberration, a distinction I alluded to earlier. It is a key concept in *On Certainty* and worth mentioning again here, if only briefly.

In an amusing and yet insightful paper, "Certainty Made Simple," that appeared in *Certainty and Surface in Epistemology and Philosophical Method* (edited by A. P. Martinich and M. White, 1991), Wallace I. Matson describes an error Moore made while giving the Howison Lecture at Berkeley in 1941. Let's vary his example a bit for our purposes here. Suppose I enter a room with which I am perfectly familiar and say, as Moore did in "Certainty," "There are windows in this wall and a door in that one." But suppose that in the recent past the door had been removed and a painted decoration inserted in its place. Coming into the room I might with confidence say "There is a door in that wall." Wishing later to leave the room by that door, I might, as I approached it, begin to realize that what I had taken to be a door was not one. I might under those conditions be quite surprised. In such circumstances it would be entirely proper to say "I made a mistake; I thought there was a door here. There certainly used to be one . . . ," and so on. The point is that the language of mistakes is in order in this kind of situation. This sort of case is not so different from that in which I am adding up a long column of figures. Suppose the correct total is 561 but my calculation gives a total of 560. I realize that the total cannot be an even number and recalculate, finding the right answer. Again I can use the language of mistakes. I *just barely missed* getting the right amount, and this is where such language is appropriate.

But if my original "calculation" had given a figure of 10, then it would be puzzling to explain how I had gone so far astray. One would no longer say "You made a mistake in your calculation." The error would be of a different order, amounting to some kind of gross blunder. A person who holds that the earth is 2.5 billion years old when (let us suppose) the correct answer is 2.7 billion years is doing something akin to making a mistake. But one who holds that the earth came into existence only five minutes ago (as Russell suggested was logically possible) or 200 years ago or even 1,000 years ago is not making a mistake. There is a quantum difference involved. One who could be wrong about foundational propositions is not making a mistake but is suffering from an aberrancy with respect to our knowledge of the world. We can see with respect to this point that Descartes and Wittgenstein would be in fundamental agreement about the *cogito*. It states that I am thinking now and therefore I exist. If I am aware that I am thinking and yet deny that I exist, that would be a conceptual aberration and not a mistake. And because that is so it can be regarded as a hinge proposition in Wittgenstein's sense.

3. *Non-dependence*. We have indicated that foundational propositions by stip-

ulation cannot depend on other propositions or pieces of knowledge. So, clearly, non-dependence is a necessary condition for any such doctrine. But as the preceding remarks about a "seamless" view of knowledge, such as that held by Plato of the early dialogues, suggests, this is not a sufficient condition. For Plato no piece of knowledge depends on any other because they all have the same status. So we have the non-dependence condition satisfied, but the view is non-foundationalist since the body of knowledge is not stratified.

The other side of the question is perhaps more interesting. In what sense or senses do pieces of knowledge "depend on" others? In the case of a logical system, such as *Principia Mathematica*, whose theorems depend on the axioms, the answer is derivability through the application of principles of inference, such as *modus ponens* or *modus tollens*. In some epistemological theories the relationship would be evidential; for instance, in Hume the foundational base would consist of impressions that would provide evidence for a proposition such as "This is a red ball." But clearly neither of these constructions would capture Wittgenstein's view, as I interpret him. Of course some interpretation is necessary here since he does not speak to this issue directly. But a plausible suggestion is that the relationship between the foundations and what they support is one of presupposition.

By "presupposition" I do not mean the sort of thing that Strawson once characterized. For him the truth of a given presupposition, S, is a necessary condition for the truth or falsity of a related proposition, S'. This formulation will not do for Wittgenstein because it ascribes truth or falsity to the presupposition S. Let us illustrate the sense of "presupposing" that I think Wittgenstein has in mind by an example. Unless the world were, as we unreflectingly take it to be, of very great antiquity, certain sorts of human practices would make no sense. History as a practice depends on the fact that the earth has existed for many years. If this were not so, if the earth had just come into existence five minutes ago or even 200 years ago, historical inquiries of the sorts many persons have engaged in would be incomprehensible. We would be at a loss to explain what Thucydides or Gibbon was doing. We might say *that the earth is very old* is a proposition that is presupposed by persons engaging in any historical, anthropological, geological, or etymological inquiry. In that sense the propositions of history, geology, and so on, "depend on" it. But it in turn will not depend on them. The proposition "The Greek navy won the battle of Salamis in 480 B.C.," is not a presupposition for the earth is very old, but vice versa. A final note in this connection: Presupposing in this sense is not to be identified with assuming. As Wittgenstein says: "If I say '*we assume* that the earth has existed for many years past' (or something similar), then of course it sounds strange that we should *assume* such a thing. But in the entire system of our language games it belongs to the foundations" (*O.C.*, 411).

4. *Particularism or Methodism.* In a paper entitled "The Problem of the Criterion," Roderick Chisholm draws an important distinction between two forms of foundationalism. The terms he uses in this connection are "particularism" and "methodism." A methodist in his sense is someone who believes there is a method, technique, or procedure that will either generate or establish certain

things—for example, beliefs or propositions—to be foundational. Locke, according to Chisholm, is a methodist:

> Thus John Locke was a methodist—in our present, rather special sense of the term. He said, in effect, "The way you decide whether or not a belief is a good belief—that is to say, the way you decide whether a belief is likely to be a genuine case of knowledge—is to see whether it is derived from sense experience, to see, for example, whether it bears certain relations to your sensations.". . . This, of course, is the view that has become to be known as "empiricism." (The Aquinas Lecture, 1973, Marquette Univ. Press, pp. 15–16)

In contrast, Moore would be a "particularist" for Chisholm. Moore, as we saw, presents a list of propositions that he regards as components of the common sense view of the world. He does not tell us how he arrives at these "truisms," as he calls them, or how he knows them to be foundational. The suggestion is that there is no method for deciding such matters. His contention is that he is more sure of the truth of such propositions than he is of any explanation about how he comes to know them. Moore's list is only minimally, if at all, a system. We have no idea what the conceptual connections are between these propositions. Presumably the list could be extended, but Moore gives the no hint of what common feature connects its members. Perhaps there is no such connection. This would be an extreme form of particularism.

Chisholm states that every philosopher who can reasonably be called a foundationalist has been either a methodist or a particularist; and agreeing with this assertion, we can say that this complex condition is a necessary condition for somebody's being a foundationalist.

Wittgenstein seems to be a particularist. It is true that in *On Certainty* he frequently speaks about propositions and judgments forming a system (e.g., 140–142), but he never suggests there is a method for determining which propositions are to be regarded as foundational. I will therefore say that he belongs to the particularist category.

5. *Publicity*. It is not uncommon for philosophers to *equate* the search for certitude with the search for foundations—but this is a mistake. The moves in such cases are often Cartesian. One searches for an immediate experience about which one cannot be mistaken. This view has been advanced by Chisholm, who holds that such propositions as "I think that such and such" or "I believe that such and such," which directly describe one's internal psychology, are ground level. According to Chisholm, such propositions about one's beliefs and feelings are incorrigible. Moreover, such perceptual judgments as "I seem to see x" or "Yellow appears to me" are also certain. One cannot infer from them that one is seeing, for example, a yellow table; but one can be sure that a yellow presentation is in one's visual field.

Two points must be emphasized in speaking about certitude. First, it is a necessary condition for p's being foundational but not a sufficient condition. We must therefore distinguish p's being certain from p's being foundational. Suppose Moore's remark that he has had dreams is true and that he cannot be mistaken in making this claim. But from its certitude it does not follow that it is foundational. What would it be foundational for? Consider any general human practice, such as the study of history. How could Moore's statement be the basis for any sort of historical inquiry? Cartesians have always had difficulty in making their claims about "internal" certitude the basis for any sort of knowledge about the existence of the external world.

The second point is closely connected with the first. The previous objection was designed to show certain difficulties with Cartesianism. But the objection is more general. Norman Malcolm once held that the statement "This is an ink bottle" was known by him (in that context, of course) to be true with certainty. Let us grant this. But even if it is true, it would lack the generality needed to be foundational. One can see that by changing the scenario. Suppose Malcolm were mistaken and there was no ink bottle before him. Its absence would make virtually no difference to the everyday community activities we all engage in. Internality and specificity, even if they give rise to certitude, should be distinguished from certitude, which has a foundational character. The latter must be objective and interpersonal. That the earth is very old and that other persons exist are both certain and foundational. They are foundational presuppositions for *public* activities such as the study of history and geology. Whatever is foundational must not only be certain but other than private or personal as well. This is what the publicity criterion stipulates, and this is what Wittgenstein emphasizes against the Cartesians.

6. *Negational Absurdity.* I have spoken about this concept in earlier chapters in connection with Moore, so I shall mention it only briefly here. The point is connected with the criterion of aberrancy. Suppose it was somehow discovered that the earth had come into existence only two years ago. This is a discovery that might, let us say, be made by persons from another planet. They might find when they arrived on earth that all human beings were suffering from some sort of pervasive *distortion* of the nature of time—perhaps some terrestrial physical cause could be found to be responsible for such an *aberration*. On this account, human beings are *deluded* into thinking that such investigative activities as history and anthropology are really about distant past events. Our extraplanetary visitors, immune to such *distorting* physical phenomena, could discover that the earth is much younger than humans had supposed. The preceding hypothesis is perfectly consistent from a strictly logical point of view. It does not involve a contradiction in the way in which "Some bachelors are married" would. But it is nonetheless absurd.

What is the sense of *absurdity* that is involved here? One will note that the words "delusion," "aberration," and "distortion" were used in the preceding paragraph to generate that counter-factual account. They are required if one is to make sense of the fact that human beings could be wrong in very general ways about the way the world is. If such an hypothesis were true, our entire explanatory system would have to be abandoned. One could not speak of a revision in our state of knowledge in such a case. It is not like the *modification* of Newtonian mechanics that the Einsteinian revolution effected. "Modification," "revision," and "extension" are terms that apply to Einstein's discoveries, important as they are. But to find that the world had only recently come into existence would involve changes that would be incomprehensible to us. It is characteristic of foundational propositions that if they were imagined to be false the change involved would be of this order. No proposition that does not involve such a conceptual rupture can be foundational, and all that are foundational do. As Wittgenstein puts it, any such "revision" would amount to the annihilation of all yardsticks (*O.C.*, 492).

7. *Absorption*. Though not by this name—this is a concept found in *On Certainty*. When applied to the hinge propositions it explains their foundationalist status without appealing to the notion that we come to *know* these propositions through some sort of intellectual process. In an amusing passage Wittgenstein writes: "That I am a man and not a woman can be verified, but if I were to say that I was a woman, and then tried to explain the error by saying I hadn't checked the statement, the explanation would not be accepted" (*O.C.*, 79).

Why wouldn't the explanation be accepted? Wittgenstein is making the point that some propositions do not need checking or confirmation or justification. The passage gives rise to a hilarious image—that of someone checking to find out what sex he or she is. Why would he or she have to check? Could one forget what sex one was? To be sure, one can devise scenarios in which a process of checking would make sense, say after a sex-change operation or if one's mental faculties were impaired. But in normal circumstances, such as those Wittgenstein describes, if one had to confirm that one was a male, say, why would one trust the checking procedure? Could one be more sure of it than that one was male? "What reason have I, now, when I cannot see my toes, to assume that I have five toes on each foot? Is it right to say that my reason is that previous experience has always taught me so? Am I more certain of previous experience than that I have ten toes?" (*O.C.*, 429).

Consider some of Moore's examples: that human beings have lived and died upon the earth, that most of us have spent our lives at or near the surface of the earth. that there are objects in our environment. These are matters we absorb in the course of our lives, and they do not need confirmation or checking. How does one absorb them? Wittgenstein says by "observation and instruction." And then he adds significantly, "I intentionally do not say 'learns' (*O.C.*, 297). He is drawing a contrast between learning in some explicit manner and coming unreflectively and unself-consciously to be aware of something. One has not run an experiment to discover that the earth exists or that there are other people around or that one is male.

These propositions are not the products of intellection, reflection, trial and error, or experimentation; rather, they are aborbed by each of us in the course of our daily lives. The notion of absorption is intertwined with Wittgenstein's denial that ratiocination is the ground that supports the epistemic structure. This notion plays a major role in his account of the community. We acquire communal practices, such as being a native speaker, by absorption rather than by explicit learning. As Wittgenstein puts it elsewhere, we *inherit* our picture of the world. This is another way of saying that we absorb the foundations that make the language game possible. The emphasis upon inheritance or absorption sharply distinguishes him from traditional epistemologists who argue that our knowledge of foundational propositions is a matter of intellection or ratiocination.

8. *Certitude.* In chapter 10 we shall look at the views of some contemporary philosophers who deny there is such a thing as certitude. As we shall see, from Quine to the present they depict themselves as anti-foundationalists. It is thus an interesting question whether someone could hold a form of foundationalism while denying there is certitude. To my knowledge no notable philosopher has done so. It is also true that for those who hold the opposite position, such as Moore and Wittgenstein, there are a number of options concerning the relationship between the foundational items and certitude.

For Descartes, for example, certitude and foundationalism are not exactly equated. It is certain that God exists, but it is not obvious that this proposition is foundational in the way the *cogito* is. Wittgenstein clearly equates the two. But one principle that all foundationalists, including Wittgenstein, accept is that if p is foundational, p is certain. It follows that if p is not certain, then p is not foundational, and this entails that being certain is a necessary condition for p's being foundational. Moore also accepts this principle. So at least Moore and Wittgenstein agree in this respect. Where they differ is over the question of whether the foundations are knowable.

I mention these by now familiar points in order to make another point that is less obvious. Why did Wittgenstein eventually discard the propositional account in favor of one that is not propositional? I believe the answer is that he recognized that if one thinks of certitude in propositional terms—as Descartes and Moore did—the tendency to think of such propositions as being *known* would be irresistible. And this is the inference he wished to resist. To trace the course of this rejection in *On Certainty* is fascinating. On a first reading one would never suspect that Moore and Wittgenstein would disagree about this point. Wittgenstein ascribes certitude to propositions, just as Moore does when he asserts that he knows this p or that q to be true with certainty.

It would thus appear that their basic disagreement is over whether it makes sense to say that such propositions can be known. That is, of course, a central point of disagreement. But it is not the only one. As one reads on, and more deeply, one can see that the propositional account is also an issue, though not wholly independent of the epistemic question. It is no accident, therefore, that Wittgenstein began to move away from the propositional account. His first reaction consisted in asserting that what he was calling hinge propositions are not propositions in any traditional sense of that term and, in particular, that they are not mental—a "kind of seeing, as it were." Neither are they straightforwardly empirical—though they look as if they are. Even the idea that they are "grammatical rules" was seen to over-intellectualize the point he was trying to make. Instead he began to conceive of certainty as a mode of acting. The idea that acting lies at the bottom of the language game (instead of any system of propositions) is a new and radical conception of certainty. Certainty stems from one's immersion in a human community in which rote training and the inculcation of habits create the substratum upon which the language game rests. This non-propositional conception of certitude thus sharply separates Wittgenstein from the tradition.

9. *Standing Fast.* We have seen that one metaphor Wittgenstein uses for certainty is "standing fast." I believe this concept is ambiguous as he employs it,

that it denotes two different notions. On the one hand, it is hinge propositions that are said to stand fast; on the other, each in a set of non-propositional features is said to stand fast. We shall begin with the propositional account. It is marked by three characteristics: (i) that foundational propositions form a system and (ii) that some hinge propositions do not stand absolutely but only relatively fast, and (iii) that some hinge propositions—"that the earth exists," for example, stand absolutely fast. The emphasis he gives to the propositional theory stresses its relativistic character; the absolutist version is more hinted at than explicitly stated. In holding this propositional account, Wittgenstein thus differs from Descartes, who thinks of the *cogito* as the sole foundational item and from Moore, whose common sense propositions do not form a system, and from both Descartes and Moore, who think that all foundational propositions hold abolustely. In his later view Wittgenstein's foundationalism abandons principles (i) and (ii) of the propositional account. Since the new view is non-propositional, it cannot be a system of propositions, and the foundations it describes are absolutist in character.

The notion that hinge propositions form a system is to be found in the following quotations (which, of course, are only a subset of a larger number making the same point). The first contains an implicit reference to Descartes.

> What I hold fast to is not *one* proposition but a nest of propositions. (*O.C.*, 225)

> When we first begin to *believe* anything, what we believe is not a single proposition, it is a whole system of propositions. (Light dawns gradually over the whole.) (*O.C.*, 141)

> It is not single axioms that strike me as obvious, it is a system in which consequences and premises give one another mutual support. (*O.C.*, 142)

> The child learns to believe a host of things. I.e. it learns to act according to these beliefs. Bit by bit there forms a system of what is believed, and in that system some things stand unshakeably fast and some are more or less liable to shift. What stands fast does so, not because it is intrinsically obvious or convincing; it is rather held fast by what lies around it. (*O.C.*, 144)

The last quotation expresses the relativism theme. According to this idea what stands fast at one time may not stand fast at another. A hinge proposition is not under consideration at one moment, yet it may be at another. When it is it no longer stands fast—at that point it is no longer a hinge proposition; instead, it will depend on one. Unlike Peirce, Wittgenstein, of course, maintains that when a proposition is functioning as a hinge proposition it is not part of the language game and it is certain. He compares propositions to pieces of apparatus. When we are surveying the night sky with a telescope, the telescope is assumed to be reliable. It does not come under scrutiny and thus stands fast (we can count on it) in those circumstances. In that context it is like a hinge proposition. But if something goes wrong with the procedure, we may wish to examine the telescope itself. In that case it no longer stands fast but instead has become an object of inquiry. In such a case something else will stand fast if one is to make a proper examination of the telescope. Standing fast is thus relativized to context:

p is not intrinsically certain, but it is held fast by what surrounds it. Here are some quotations that illustrate Wittgenstein's relativism:

> It might be imagined that some propositions, of the form of empirical propositions, were hardened and functioned as channels for such empirical propositions as were not hardened but fluid; and that this relation altered with time, in that fluid propositions hardened, and hard ones became fluid. (*O.C.*, 96)

The metaphor he is working with, of water flowing through channels that begin as hardened and later become fluid, and conversely, is expanded in the next citation. In a wonderful conceit he speaks of "the river-bed of thoughts" and how they may shift:

> The mythology may change back into a state of flux, the river-bed of thoughts may shift. But I distinguish between the movement of the waters on the river-bed and the shift of the bed itself; though there is not a sharp division of the one from the other. (*O.C.*, 97)

> But if someone were to say "So logic too is an empirical science," he would be wrong. Yet this is right: the same proposition may get treated at one time as something to test by experience, at another as a rule of testing. (*O.C.*, 98)

The later view, by way of contrast, is both absolutistic and non-systematic. Wittgenstein did not have this view in mind when he began to write the notes that comprise *On Certainty*, probably because his focus was on Moore's work, with its propositional emphasis. It is also probable that he was influenced by Malcolm's paper, "Defending Common Sense," which attacks Moore's use of "I know" and which Malcolm read to him in 1949. But as the work proceeds the second view begins to emerge. That it begins to emerge only slowly is in some ways surprising. It is already implied in the *Investigations*, and a plausible argument can be made that it is found, or at least anticipated, in his 1936 "Lectures on Private Experience." Still, it does not exist in the early entries at all and becomes prominent only in the later sections of *On Certainty*. What is important is that the second view becomes the dominant view in the later passages.

The exegetical situation is complicated here. Even the propositional view turns up in some late passages (e.g., 653), so it is possible that Wittgenstein never abandoned the earlier doctrine, especially with its absolutistic tinges, and that he vacillated between them. Nonetheless, the direction of his thinking is clear; so I shall continue to refer to the later view as the dominant one. That they are at least contrasting is undeniable, one having a relativistic thrust, the other not; one taking an anti-intellectual form and the other not.

Like many views that are developed in opposition to another, this second account of certainty takes many different forms depending upon the particular contrast Wittgenstein wishes to highlight. There are three such main forms: (1) that certainty is something primitive, instinctual, or animal, (2) that it is acting, and (3) that it derives from rote training in communal practices. In all of these the major contrast with his former view is that what stands fast is the product of reasoning or intellection. Insofar as propositions or even pseudo-propositions or grammatical rules are conceived of as the products of rational activity, the new view stands in opposition to any such account. Here are the main citations that mention these three strands:

> I want to regard man here as an animal; as a primitive being to which one grants instinct but not ratiocination. As a creature in a primitive state. . . . Language did not emerge from some kind of ratiocination. (*O.C.*, 475)

> Giving grounds, however, justifying the evidence, comes to an end;—but the end is not certain propositions striking us immediately as true, i.e., it is not a kind of *seeing* on our part; it is our *acting* which lies at the bottom of the language game. (*O.C.*, 204)

> The child, I should like to say, learns to react in such-and-such a way; and in so reacting it doesn't so far know anything. Knowing only begins at a later level. (*O.C.*, 538)

> From a child up I learnt to judge like this. *This is* judging. (*O.C.*, 128)

> "We are quite sure of it" does not mean just that every single person is certain of it, but that we belong to a community which is bound together by science and education. (*O.C.*, 298)

These three strands—*instinct, acting,* and *training*—are different. If they were to be analyzed further, which Wittgenstein, of course, never had time to do, they might well turn out (as I believe) to be in tension with one another. But I think that Wittgenstein meant them to be part of a single complex idea that he wishes to contrast with the propositional account. It is thus possible to find an interpretation that welds them into a single (admittedly complex) conception of that which stands fast. On this interpretation, what Wittgenstein takes to be foundational is a picture of the world we all inherit as members of a human community. We have been trained from birth in ways of acting that are non-reflective to accept a picture of the world that is ruthlessly realistic: that there is an earth, persons on it, objects in our environment, and so forth. (In this connection see Cora Diamond, *The Realistic Spirit*, 1991.) This picture is manifested in action. When we open a door our lives show that we are certain. Certainty is thus not a matter of reflection about the door but a way of acting with respect to it. All animals, including humans, inherit their picture of the world, and like other animals much of our inheritance derives from early training—-"something must be taught us as a foundation" (*O.C.*, 449).

It is no accident that the reference to children plays such a prominent role in the later sections of the text.

> For how can a child immediately doubt what it is taught? That could mean only that he was incapable of learning certain language games. (*O.C.*, 283)

> We teach a child "that is your hand," not "that is perhaps (or 'probably') your hand." That is how a child learns the innumerable language-games that are concerned with his hand. . . . Nor, on the other hand, does he learn that he *knows* this is a hand. (*O.C.*, 374)

> Children do not learn that books exist, that armchairs exist, etc., etc.,—they learn to fetch books, sit in armchairs, etc. etc. (*O.C.*, 476).

> So is this it: I must recognize certain authorities in order to make judgments at all? (*O.C.*, 493)

In these passages we see an explicit rejection of the notion that what stands fast for us is the product of reason and ratiocination. Insofar as hinge propositions are taken to be the products of reason, the newer account opposes any such view. The foundations are neither known nor unknown, neither reasonable nor unreasonable. They are there, just like our lives. In the preceding passages Wittgenstein's examples make it clear that his foundationalism is non-relative. The existence of the earth and the communities which nurture us are not like pieces of apparatus that can be discarded or repaired if they do not work correctly. The notion of "working correctly" has no application to these cases. We cannot revise, alter, or question the existence of the earth. It and the communities that live on it stand absolutely fast. We shall say more about this matter in chapter 10.

I conclude this chapter by reverting to the petard question. That question was, Is Wittgenstein imposing a traditional foundationalist model upon human behavior and thus engaging in explanation rather than description? At the outset of the chapter I stated that in my view he was not. There is both textual and non- textual support for this judgment. "At some point," he writes in *On Certainty* (189), "one has to pass from explanation to mere description." "Somewhere we must be finished with justification, and then there remains the proposition that this is how we calculate" (212). And he says:

> "We could doubt every single one of these facts, but we could not doubt them *all*."
> Wouldn't it be more correct to say: "we do not doubt them *all*."
> Our not doubting them all is simply our manner of judging and therefore of acting. (*O.C.*, 232)

In this last passage, Wittgenstein's interlocutor, a clever philosopher, suggests that although we can doubt every single fact, we cannot doubt all of them. His remark makes a philosophical or logical point. It suggests that logic or analysis can tell us what we can or cannot do. It thus imposes a conceptual model upon human practice. Wittgenstein corrects the philosopher here. He says, in contrast, that it would be more correct to say "we do not doubt them all." He is describing what we actually do. This is his approach throughout the work. In saying that human persons inherit a picture of the world from birth he is describing what they inherit. He is not telling us what must be the case, but what is the case. It is this powerful descriptive account that is the basis for his rejection of scepticism, which imposes a distorting model upon human practice. That account can also be used to show what is wrong with certain contemporary theories we find among cognitive scientists and their philosophical congeners. We shall now, in the final chapter, turn to these matters.

10

Folk Theory, Standing Fast, and Scepticism

I mentioned at the beginning of this book that despite their differences Moore and Wittgenstein shared a philosophical outlook that is still relevant: a conviction that there is such a thing as certainty and that an accurate description of the world must take account of it. In Anglo-American philosophy this continues to be a minority point of view, though it has a substantial number of adherents. The converse, majority position has taken widely differing configurations in the twentieth century—beginning with semi-sceptics like Russell who saw philosophy as mostly dealing with undecidable questions through the logical positivists with their claim that any certain proposition is empty of factual content to the early anti-foundationalists, Popper and Quine.

On the contemporary scene we have Hilary Putnam and Paul Churchland, who (following Quine) aver that all significant propositions, including the best-established physical laws and even some of the basic laws of logic, are open to reassessment and revision in the light of future experience. There are also extreme relativists like Stephen Stich, who argues in *The Fragmentation of Reason* (1990) that what is traditionally called truth is to be replaced by a number of pragmatic notions that do not presuppose a search for objectivity.

These recent rejections of certainty borrow from a common fund of suppositions that, surprisingly, still reflect positivist influences: (i) that science will ultimately solve all philosophical problems, including those concerning the mind, (ii) that philosophy should therefore model itself on science, and (iii) that scientific inquiry leads at most to probability with respect to our understanding of the world. Putnam is typical in his commitment to these principles. What he finds "seductive," he tells us,

> is the idea that the way to *solve philosophical problems is to construct a better scientific picture of the world.* That idea retains the ancient principle that Being is prior to Knowledge, while giving it a distinctively modern twist: all the philosopher has to do, in essence, is be a good "futurist"—anticipate for us *how* science will solve our philosophical problems. (*Representation and Reality*, MIT Press, Cambridge, Mass., 1989, p. 107)

A direct implication of this point of view is that philosophy is not, as has often been assumed, an autonomous discipline with its own special subject matter and unique procedures for apprehending reality. As Quine puts it, philosophy "is an extension of science." Another pronouncement with the same thrust is Patricia Churchland's statement that "there is no First and Inviolable Philosophy." I will argue in this chapter that Wittgenstein's account of that which stands fast undermines all such views. All of them, from a Wittgensteinian perspective—and from mine—confuse such epistemic notions as knowledge and justified belief with a non-epistemic concept, certitude.

These types of views embody three different sorts of challenges to Wittgenstein's position. The first two we have already addressed in previous chapters, but it will be useful to summarize Wittgenstein's reaction to and refutation of them. First, there is the issue of relativism. We have seen that Peirce argued that a proposition that is presupposed in one context can be contested in another. He inferred from this fact that no proposition is intrinsically or absolutely certain. In his propositional account Wittgenstein also develops a form of relativism, but in contrast to Peirce he holds that what he calls "hinge propositions" are certain. As we shall see below, Quine, Stich, the Churchlands, and others follow Peirce in holding that a proposition assumed to be true in one context can be challenged in another; and, like Peirce, they deny that any proposition is instrinsically certain or immune to future revision. Their relativism is also buttressed by their scientism. According to them, scientific claims to knowledge achieve at most probability but never certitude. This conclusion follows, of course, from their suppositions that any scientific statement or theory is in principle revisable and that if any such statement were certain it would not be revisable. Wittgenstein's position differs from these in a striking way. He holds that hinge propositions are neither true nor false, are neither confirmable nor disconfirmable. Such ascriptions do not apply to them. Their standing fast in some circumstances but not in others does therefore not entail that when they do hold fast they are probable only. So his relativism does not imply the non-existence of certainty.

Second, there is a sceptical challenge to his views that might be expressed as follows. A sceptic might concede that Wittgenstein's views about the non-revisability of the common sense *framework* (whether that is conceived in propositional or non-propositional terms) are correct. The sceptic would thus agree that ascriptions of truth or falsity, provability, confirmability, and so on, do not apply to the framework. In making this concession the sceptic would thus be conceding that the common sense framework is certain. But then he could go on to argue that his challenge is not to the existence of certainty but to the existence of *knowledge*, that is, to the existence of something that supposedly occurs within the language game. He might argue that Wittgenstein's views do not bear on the question of whether any knowledge claim can be true; and it is this sort of claim he wishes to challenge. He might also argue that this is what the historical sceptical challenge has always been. Accordingly, the sceptic's position might be summarized as contending that Wittgenstein has engaged in a long *non sequitur*, attacking a position that nobody has ever disputed.

Wittgenstein would disagree with the sceptic's historical thesis. He would hold that there have been sceptical challenges to the existence of certitude as well as to the existence of knowledge. But more important he would disagree that the sceptical challenge, in either respect, is cogent. As we shall show at the end of the chapter, Wittgenstein's analysis is that scepticism is incoherent, that is, that the sort of question the sceptic wishes to raise about the existence of knowledge or about the existence of certainty is self-refuting. Wittgenstein is arguing that, in effect, the sceptic is questioning the existence of the language game and its supportive foundations, which together generate the rules that define what counts as cases of knowledge. To raise such a challenge is to employ linguistic idioms whose very meanings derive from the rules of the language game and from the presuppositions that make the game possible. The sceptic is thus engaged in an activity that is sensible only if he rejects the conditions that make that activity sensible.

The third objection is the deepest, inasmuch as it incorporates to some extent the previous two while engendering a more fundamental problem. This is the issue raised by the kind of scientism espoused by Quine, Putnam, and the Churchlands, that is, whether *the common sense framework* itself is eliminable or revisable. If they are correct in asserting that it is, then clearly there would be no such thing as certainty. In the remainder of the chapter we shall concentrate on Wittgenstein's response to and rejection of this point of view. We shall turn to that task now.

It would obviously be impossible to address all the variants of these differing forms of scientism: relativism, probabilism, conventionalism, neopositivism, and anti-foundationalism in this chapter. I will therefore concentrate on what is currently the most popular version of the majority position, one that is espoused by philosophers with strong ties to the cognitive sciences. Whether the cognitive sciences, as practiced by non-philosophers, entail or even suggest any philosophical thesis is a matter I shall set aside here. But, clearly, many philosophers believe that they do and, in particular, that they give strong support to corrigibilist doctrines.

These philosophers assert that recent developments within cognitive science put in question "our common sense framework." What they mean by "our common sense framework" is not very clear; they use it mostly in contrast to "science." But we can ferret out something from the contrast. The common sense framework seems on their conception to be a broad-ranging view that most ordinary persons have about the world and certain of its features. Unfortunately, the exact nature of this view is not spelled out. As we shall see below, bits and pieces of it are mentioned; these suggest that it is both a *Weltanschauung* and a kind of theory having an explanatory thrust. The term "framework" also suggests that it is not merely a collection of discrete propositions or thoughts but that it has an organizational structure and is therefore a system. Its components include observational data, generalizations, prejudices, old saws, some scientific information that has trickled down to the average man, and rules of thumb. Some of these components may be true, some false. But belief modification is also possible, so various false beliefs may eventually be replaced by true ones.

From these descriptions it would seem that there are overlaps between "our common sense framework" and what Moore called the common sense view of the world. But there are also seminal differences. As we noted earlier, Moore asserts that each proposition belonging to the common sense view is true and is wholly so, and therefore that the common sense view in an important sense is not modifiable. For example, such propositions as "The earth has existed for many years past" and "I [Moore] am a human being" are not revisable in the light of future experience. His view thus diverges from that just described. Moore also thinks of the common sense view as as non-scientific and, moreover, would assign the task of describing the common sense view to philosophy. In that sense he would defend its autonomy.

Curiously enough, with respect to this last point these scientistically oriented philosophers agree with Moore, for they also see the common sense framework as embodying a world outlook that is to be contrasted with that of science. But they also see the relationship, as Wittgenstein and Moore do not, as adversarial, as providing incompatible accounts about a common subject matter. That is, they think of the common sense framework as embedding a theory about the same aspects or features of the world as science and therefore as being in competition with it. We thus face a pair of alternatives between which we must choose. This is why these philosophers describe the common sense framework as "folk theory." The contrast they wish to draw is between two different types of theoretical positions, one of them scientific and the other not.

As they use the term, "folk theory" refers to any non-technical, pre-scientific explanatory system of the world. Further, again aping the sciences, they subdivide folk theory into folk physics, folk semantics, folk psychology, and so forth, depending on the nature of the phenomena to be explained. Thus, those who at one time held that thunder and lightning were caused by the anger of the gods were doing folk physics, and those who held that certain people, called witches, were possessed by demons were giving folk psychological explanations. In both cases we were being presented with inchoate theories, no longer scientifically acceptable, to explain such phenomena as the weather or types of idiosyncratic behavior. Generalizing from such examples, these philosophers have produced powerful arguments to the effect that, like any explanatory system, folk theory is always subject to revision or even replacement in the light of subsequent scientific discoveries.

In particular, many of of them, so-called eliminative materialists, assert that recent discoveries in brain neurophysiology cast doubt upon all folk psychological explanations, inasmuch as those assume the existence of mental phenomena, such as beliefs, thoughts, intentions, and doubts. Without trying in any detail to lay out the basis for this assertion—a matter that by itself would fill the chapter—let me say that eliminative materialists contend that the "items" or "entities" supposedly referred to by such folk psychological notions have, from a contemporary scientific standpoint, the same status as demons and witches— namely, they just don't exist. These notions and the common sense framework in which they are embedded are, accordingly, to be eliminated from any scientific account of the world. As Paul Churchland explains:

> As the eliminative materialists see it, the one-to-one match-ups will not be found, and our common-sense psychological framework will not enjoy an

intertheoretic reduction, *because our common-sense psychological framework is a false and radically misleading conception of the causes of human behavior and the nature of cognitive activity.* On this view, folk psychology is not just an incomplete representation of our inner natures; it is an outright misrepresentation of our internal states and activities. Consequently, we cannot expect a truly adequate neuro-scientific account of our inner lives to provide theoretical categories that match up nicely with the categories of our common-sense framework. Accordingly, we must expect that the older framework will simply be eliminated, rather than be reduced, by a matured neuroscience. (*Matter and Consciousness*, MIT Press, Cambridge, Mass., 1988, p. 43)

If these philosophers are right, their doctrines raise profound challenges for an outlook such as we find in *On Certainty*. First, as we have seen, Wittgenstein holds that each of us has a grasp of the world that is not open to alteration, remediation, or replacement. Using the parlance of eliminative materialism, we can say that for Wittgenstein *the common sense framework* will stand fast, come what may. Second, Wittgenstein (like Moore) believes in the autonomy of philosophy. To be sure, he does not use this expression; but I take it he would have agreed that there are aspects of the world that are uniquely characterizable by philosophy and that the common sense framework is one of these aspects. In his view, philosophy is not a science but a *sui generis* activity, one of whose functions (but not the only one) is to describe the presuppositional relationship between that which stands fast and the language games of daily life. In this respect Wittgenstein differs profoundly from Collingwood, who depicted philosophy as being a branch of historical science. For Wittgenstein philosophy and science do not necessarily stand in an adversarial relationship. Each has its proper domain, though, of course, the two may impinge upon one another. The eliminativists, in contrast, see the common sense framework as standing in an exclusionary relationship to science. On their view, each is trying to give a different, all-encompassing account of reality, and therefore both cannot be right. Who is right, then? Patricia Churchland responds with this answer: "In the idealized long run, the completed science is a true description of reality, there is no other Truth and no other Reality" (*Neurophilosophy*, MIT Press, Cambridge, Mass., 1986, p. 249).

If the eliminativists are right, then Wittgenstein is wrong. Philosophy cannot give us an autonomous account of reality. But as I shall now argue, it is he who is right. To focus the discussion let us contrast their differing treatments of belief, keeping in mind that the eliminativists contend that strictly speaking there are no such things. Since common sense believes there are, then common sense should be rejected in favor of cognitive science, which "needs no such hypothesis." But Wittgenstein's treatment of belief stands in sharp contrast to such a view. His discussion is complex; let us begin with his distinction between believing and knowing. As we indicated earlier, the latter is not something mental in the way that believing or surmising is: "We are asking ourselves: what do we do with a statement "I know . . ."? For it is not a question of mental processes or mental states" (*O.C.*, 230).

Furthermore, believing has a different logic from knowing. This is somewhat masked by ordinary language. We can ask both why A believes that p and why A knows that p, and we can also ask how A believes that p and how A knows that p. But the questions require different orders of responses. To ask why A believes that p is generally to elicit an answer in causal terms (e.g., because A read it somewhere, had an earlier experience like that, and so on). In contrast, to ask why A knows that p is to challenge his right to know. It suggests that the information A has was supposed to be kept secret. Thus, the question might mean, What enabled him know that, given the security precautions we took? The answer would typically provide an excuse or a justification, (e.g., he knows it because he received our fax by mistake; he overheard a confidential conversation; we thought he was included). To ask how does A know that p is—as we saw in chapter 9—to speak about the grounds A has for knowing, such as being in the right position. "He could see it clearly." But to ask how does A believe that p suggests an answer of a different logical type: "He believes it fervently (though not completely, with a grain of salt, etc.)." It thus elicits a response that talks about how p is entertained: firmly or with reservations, and so on. These considerations show that belief and knowledge differ categorially.

In *On Certainty*, Wittgenstein is consistent in distinguishing knowledge from certainty. The former is an epistemic concept, belonging to the language game; the latter is non-epistemic and stands in a presuppositional, supportive relationship to the language game. Knowledge is part of a conceptual system whose other members include guessing, hypothesizing, thinking, believing, and doubting. They together form a web of related and intertwined notions that play roles in everyday human intercourse and interaction. But certainty does not belong to this system; it stands outside of it. It makes the language game, that is, this set of activities, possible. That the earth exists is certain. Such certitude is thus a presupposition for the study of history. If the earth did not exist history as a human activity would not exist either. In that sense, the one is a condition for the other. The study of history takes place within the language game and involves such activities as forming hypotheses, gathering evidence, asserting conclusions, judging, doubting, believing, and knowing.

This compact summary does not, however, do justice to Wittgenstein's complex use of the term "belief" in *On Certainty.* Sometimes Wittgenstein uses it as if the concept it denotes belongs within the language game, and sometimes he uses it as a foundational expression. The first usage is typified by "'Is N.N. at home'"—I: 'I believe he is'" (*O.C.*, 483). The second occurs in passages such as these:

> When we first begin to believe anything, what we believe is not a single proposition, it is a whole system of propositions. (*O.C.*, 141)

> The existence of the earth is rather part of the whole *picture* which forms the starting point of belief for me. (*O.C.*, 209)

> At the foundation of well-founded belief lies belief that is not founded (*O.C.*, 253)

The two uses of "belief" are explicitly contrasted in the last quotation. Belief that is well founded is supported by evidence, discovered by playing according to the rules of the language game and thus belongs to the language game. But belief that is not founded belongs to the foundations and lies outside the language game. These distinct uses of "belief" show that Wittgenstein not only makes reference to what common sense would call mental functions—and his talk about doubting, judging surmising would provide further evidence for this asseveration—but also to a foundational system of beliefs that he describes in various ways: as "my picture of the world" or "the inherited background." As he says in 94, "But I did not get my picture of the world by satisfying myself of its correctness. No: it is the inherited background against which I distinguish between true and false."

I submit on the basis of such textual evidence that Wittgenstein is sometimes thinking of beliefs as foundational and sometimes as not. In effect, the reference to beliefs as foundational belongs to the "propositional account" of that which stands fast for us. Propositions on that view are types of beliefs. This view was eventually superseded by a deeper, non-propositional account, as I mentioned in chapter 9. But for our discussion of eliminativism let us assume for the moment that his foundationalism is a type of belief/propositional system.

Let us also assume that in such idioms as "my picture of the world" or "the inherited background" Wittgenstein is speaking about what eliminative materialists call "the common sense framework of the world." *Then in what sense is such a belief system open to the criticism that it is a species of folk psychology and is, accordingly, susceptible to revision or elimination?* The question is both interesting and important and will have significant implications for Wittgenstein's treatment of scepticism, as we shall see below.

As I have formulated it, the query raises a terminological point. In ordinary discourse we distinguish between the terms "revisable" and "eliminable." To say that T is revisable entails that T will still exist after certain changes have been made. To say that T is eliminable implies that after certain changes have been made T may no longer exist. Quine and his followers tend to conflate these expressions. I will conform to their practice in order to simplify the discussion. The central issue is whether there is something that stands fast in the sense that it is neither eliminable nor revisable. Since I want to focus on that basic contrast, I will use the expressions interchangeably in what follows.

I will now argue in responding to the question that what Wittgenstein is describing as our "picture of the world"—even construed as a system of beliefs—is not a specimen of folk psychology, is not a theory, and is not, even in principle, revisable in the light of any scientific findings. If I am right, then Quine, the Churchlands, and Putnam et al. are wrong. Now in saying this, one must also concede that there may well be something that is characterizable as folk psychology. This may be a set of commonly held beliefs, ranging from rule of thumb explanations based on human experience to various maxims and apothegms, some of them being instances of sheer superstition that have no factual basis. Considered as a unified system folk psychology may well be revisable. Some of its beliefs may eventually be discarded as by-products of scientific progress; others may be retained but given a scientific explanation—as in the cases of lightning and psychotic behavior—so that with respect to such cases it is correct to say that they are susceptible to scientific advance. But none of those beliefs is part of what Wittgenstein means by our "inherited background." That background is not amenable to revision or rejection at all ' alone by science.

My argument will be divided into two steps. First, I shall sho Wittgenstein's foundationalism is not a species of folk psychology—in p lar, why it is not a theory—and, second, I will argue that in his foundatio Wittgenstein has identified an ineliminable, non-modifiable aspect of h life that his critics have missed. It takes considerable talent to notice the ob and considerable talent to miss it because one is blinded by theory. I thin critics fall into the second category.

For brevity's sake I shall refer to reductive materialists, eliminative mater ists, neurophilosophers, empirical philosophers, and similar folk as graduali By this term I mean to bring out that they are committed to three principles: that no sharp distinction can be drawn between folk views and scientific view or to put the same point in slightly different ways, that folk views and scientific views subtly merge into one another or that the differences between them are matters of degree rather than of kind, and so forth; (ii) that in both cases the views in question can be characterized as "theories"; and (iii) that insofar as both purport to be speaking about the same world or the same features, science will always give us the better theory.

Thus, from a gradualist perspective what Wittgenstein means by our "world-picture" is not different in kind from the theoretical "world-picture" that science proffers except that it is more primitive and suffers from liabilities that the scientific account does not. The following lengthy quotation from Patricia Churchland's *Neurophilosophy* (1986) beautifully exemplifies these three principles. The passage begins with a statement of the first of our three principles, namely, that no sharp line can be drawn between common sense and science: "Our knowledge is a richly interconnected whole, and it resists a principled epistemic division between scientific beliefs and non-scientific beliefs. As Einstein put it, 'The whole of science is nothing more than a refinement of everyday thinking'" (264).

In the rest of the quotation Churchland identifies what she calls here "everyday thinking" with "the common sense system." Note that she gives everyday thinking (the common sense system) an epistemic status: that it is dedicated to the production of knowledge in just the way "the whole of science" is except that it is less refined. This is a clear example of the sort of conflation of epistemic concepts with certainty that I alluded to at the beginning of this chapter. Wittgenstein denies, of course, that the common sense system (that which stands fast) is committed to epistemic goals. It is rather something that makes epistemic activity possible. That is the major difference between knowledge and certainty for him.

Churchland's quotation continues with affirmations of the other two gradualist principles, namely, that both common sense and science are theories and that the latter is superior to the former. Note also that she infers from the superiority of science that philosophy is not an autonomous discipline.

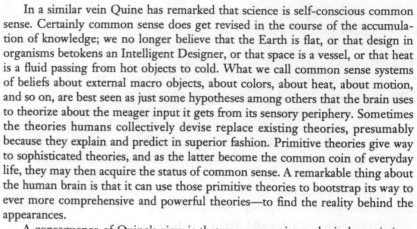

In a similar vein Quine has remarked that science is self-conscious common sense. Certainly common sense does get revised in the course of the accumulation of knowledge; we no longer believe that the Earth is flat, or that design in organisms betokens an Intelligent Designer, or that space is a vessel, or that heat is a fluid passing from hot objects to cold. What we call common sense systems of beliefs about external macro objects, about colors, about heat, about motion, and so on, are best seen as just some hypotheses among others that the brain uses to theorize about the meager input it gets from its sensory periphery. Sometimes the theories humans collectively devise replace existing theories, presumably because they explain and predict in superior fashion. Primitive theories give way to sophisticated theories, and as the latter become the common coin of everyday life, they may then acquire the status of common sense. A remarkable thing about the human brain is that it can use those primitive theories to bootstrap its way to ever more comprehensive and powerful theories—to find the reality behind the appearances.

A consequence of Quine's view is that even our epistemological convictions about what it is to acquire knowledge and about the nature of explanation, justification, and confirmation—about the nature of the scientific enterprise itself—are subject to revision and correction. As we come to understand how the brain works, we will come to learn about what it is for a brain to "theorize," to be "rational," and to "understand." We will discover general principles of brain operation that may change, and change radically, our existing epistemological conceptions.

It is in this sense that there is no *first* philosophy. There is no corpus of philosophical doctrine concerning science and epistemology such that we can be sure it is the Truth to which all science must conform. There is, as Quine remarks, no Archimedean point outside all science from which we can pronounce upon the acceptibility of scientific theories. In abandoning the view that there is a First and Inviolable Philosophy, Quine urges us to adopt a metaphor coined by Neurath: "Science is like a boat, which we rebuild plank by plank while afloat in it. The philosopher and the scientist are in the same boat." (264–265)

I said that theory can blind one to the obvious. There are two important metaphors in the preceding quotation that exhibit such myopia: the bootstrap and boat metaphors. Churchland says that the brain "can use those primitive theories to bootstrap its way to ever more comprehensive theories." This suggests that without any support or foundation the brain can somehow elevate itself to some higher theoretical position. But, clearly, the brain requires some support—it is "held fast" by things around it, by the body, by the rest of the nervous system, by the external environment that impinges on it, and most important by its status as a part of a person. It is not the brain that theorizes or understands but the person who has it. By focusing so intently on the brain Churchland overlooks the *obvious* fact that the brain is part of a complex system, other units of which also play roles when a person theorizes and understands. What she describes as "the meager input it [the brain] gets from its sensory periphery" is not so meager at all. There is an an enormous quantity of stimuli that arise from the environment, and these are picked up by mechanisms other than the brain, as J.J. Gibson has demonstrated in *An Ecological Approach to Visual Perception* (1979).

The Neurath conceit also overlooks the obvious. The boat of science rests upon water, and something, including the water and other parts of the boat, must remain fast while this or that plank is being replaced. The boat is not simply suspended in midair; it must be supported by something. It is *obvious* that the metaphor presupposes an external and independent world. There must be such a world if one is to obtain the planks that are used to rebuild the vessel. That world includes trees, persons to cut them, vehicles to transport them, mills and carpenters to shape them, and so on. Science requires and makes use of these facilities. But that world also provides data for scientific thought. Science does not merely bootstrap itself; it must go beyond itself to access such data and facilities. The ship does not exist in a vacuum, as Neurath's metaphor suggests. It implies that each and every plank can be replaced without support from an external source, but this is clearly unrealistic.

Neurath's metaphor when taken literally is thus a caricature of scientific activity, the sort of thing one might find in *Gulliver's Travels*. In that work Swift writes that the architects in Laputa, driven by theory, build their houses from the roof down. This is a prescient inversion of the bootstrap metaphor, showing by contrast just how implausible it is. The point Swift is making applies to Neurath and anticipates Wittgenstein: one must start every activity from some foundation. The true view is that there is an independent, objective reality that underlies the kind of probative activity we call science. It is that reality which supports Neurath's boat and the activities of its crew and is thus the Archimedean point from which science must begin and to which it must conform. Any scientific theory that denied the existence of the earth, for example, would not be acceptable. Neurath's metaphor ignores that reality. To call attention to this omission is to begin to explain why Wittgenstein is right.

But the explanation can be buttressed by the following considerations. According to gradualists, science never gives us certainty but at most probability, and, further, it is science and science alone that will give us a true picture of reality. Wittgenstein would not (nor would I) contest the claim that science gives us only probability. We shall stipulate that this part of the gradualist view is correct. One can make that concession in order to bring out the difference between Wittgenstein's views and any form of gradualism or relativism of the Peircian type. For it is the further contention that science alone can give us a true picture of reality that Wittgenstein rejects. Let us follow his reasoning.

In 162, we find an important passage containing two metaphors: "I have a world picture. Is it true or false? Above all it is the substratum of all my enquiring and asserting. The propositions describing it are not all equally subject to testing."

This quotation brings us to our last and perhaps most difficult exegetical hurdle if we are to grasp the structure of his argument. What is the substratum in this case? Wittgenstein says it is our world picture. This term suggests that one has a mental image of the world, say something like a picture of a round ball floating in space. If that is what Wittgenstein means, how could such a picture be the substratum of all our inquiring and asserting? What possible connection could it have with such human practices? The answer seems to me to be clear.

This is not what Wittgenstein means when he speaks of a world picture. But then what could he mean? What sort of thing could function as such a substratum? The question is difficult. As I have stressed in this work, Wittgenstein is grappling with the problem of giving a positive account of that which stands fast for us. In various contexts he uses different metaphors: "our world picture," "our inherited background," "the scaffolding of our thoughts," and so on. Taken literally, these are not logically equivalent. But we should not press him too hard about that which he did not have time to explore further.

What he is driving at in each case is that the metaphor describes something that is not part of the language game and therefore is not susceptible to certain sorts of ascriptions: such as being true or false, known or not known, justifiable, revisable, and so forth. One might say, following Austin, that it is the negative use that wears the trousers here. So when Wittgenstein calls our world picture "the substratum of all my enquiring and asserting" he means that one's description of the world has reached its deepest level. One cannot go further; one has reached bedrock (another metaphor). Let us grant him this. But can we elicit any hint of a coherent, positive account of that which stands fast from this array of metaphors? I think we can.

For such an interpretation let us start at the other end, as it were, and ask, What sort of thing could support such activities as inquiring and asserting? To this I think the answer is not a mental image or a proposition such as *I exist* but rather the human community that embeds such activities. These activities are engaged in from infancy; they are absorbed rather than learned by trial and error. In this sense we inherit our background. It is thus the community that stands fast for us.

Let us therefore fix on the locution "our inherited background" and take it to be identical with the community. This will bring us as close to a literal description of that which stands fast as we shall find in the text. But now what could be meant by "the community"? The text offers some clues. Wittgenstein says "the existence of the earth is the starting point of belief for us." We should, therefore, distinguish the earth—or, more generally, the inorganic world—from the community. But part of that inorganic world will be part of the community: the land we occupy and build structures on, the topographical environment that has been there before humanity existed, and so forth. Given this distinction between "the earth" and the "community," but including at least part of the former in the latter, we can describe the community as constituting our inherited background.

Such a description will have three different levels of depth. There is a totality consisting of human beings and other animals, their activities, interactions, practices, and institutions. This is the community proper. This totality will also include, as mentioned above, inorganic components—the bricks and stones out of which habitations are made, for example. At a second level we can distinguish within this totality a subunit, which we can call the set of human practices—customs, habits, traditions, and so on. Finally, we can distinguish within the set of practices individual practices—such as asserting, inquiring, judging, and so on.

It is the community that supports both the total set of practices, and *pari*

passu, this or that particular practice. The relationship in this case is presuppositional; the community makes that set of practices possible. If it didn't exist they
wouldn't either. On the other hand, there is an important logical relationship in
the opposite direction. These practices are essential to the existence of the community: we can think of them as necessary conditions. Everything we call a
human community must have such practices. We would find it incomprehensible if something were defined as a human community that lacked such practices
as inquiring, asserting, judging, doubting.

So if they were eliminated or were absent, the community as we know it
would disappear. It would be like removing the king and queen and calling the
resulting game chess. What then is the language game on this analysis? It, I take
it, is another name for the set of practices—the set that includes such particular
practices as inquiring, asserting, and so on. The community (our inherited background) is thus not identical to the set of practices (the language game) but
makes them possible and in this sense is the substratum that supports them.
Whether this account actually captures Wittgenstein's thoughts is surely open
to discussion, but given the inconclusive nature of the textual evidence it is the
best we can do.

If we accept this account, we can make sense of Wittgenstein's analysis of
science and thus begin to see how his argument against the gradualists develops.
Science is one of those community practices, dedicated to the search for truth
and understanding. Wittgenstein is thus using the substratum metaphor to
bring out the difference between a benthic, presuppositional, communal foundation—our common sense framework—and the structure of scientific inquiry it
supports. Consider the following passage:

> Think of chemical investigations. Lavoisier makes experiments with sub-
> stances in his laboratory and now he concludes that this and that takes place
> when there is burning. He does not say that it might happen otherwise, another
> time. He has got hold of a definite world-picture—not of course one that he
> invented: he learned it as a child. I say world-picture and not hypothesis, because
> it is the matter-of-course foundation for his research and as such also goes
> unmentioned. (*O.C.*, 167)

The contrast Wittgenstein is drawing between Lavoisier's chemical investigations and the "world-picture" that Lavoisier "has got hold of" is designed to
establish that the common sense framework supports such investigations without being overturned by their findings. The foundational metaphor is an effective way of expressing the point; it creates a virtual visual image, thus acting as a
powerful reminder to those philosophers co-opted by a model that science is not
the be-all and end-all of intellectual activity. No matter what science discovers,
the foundations upon which its investigative activities depend are exempt from
doubt, proof, justification, and therefore revision. Put in literal language the
point would be obvious. Said metaphorically it contains a significant message.
Since gradualists hold that our conceptual framework is in principle subject to
perpetual modification, Wittgenstein's rupturalism is clearly incompatible with
such a view.

In contrast to Patricia Churchland's gradualism and for the sake of symmetry I will call a philosopher like Wittgenstein, or indeed myself, a rupturalist. As I interpret him, Wittgenstein would deny that the difference between the common sense framework and science is merely one of degree. Instead he would insist that there is a rupture or discontinuity between them. He would also deny that the common sense framework is a theory, and especially that it is a theory in the sense or senses intended by gradualists. As Wittgenstein says: "The difficulty is to realize the groundlessness of our believing" (O.C., 166).

This is just what the gradualists do not realize. If our believing is groundless, then it cannot be a theory. A theory is an intellectual construction, with premises and a conclusion. Its premises are the grounds that support its conclusion. That which stands fast—our inherited background—is nothing like that. Being bedrock it is not supported, and not having an argumentative structure it lacks premises and a conclusion. It is not *the sort of thing* that can be construed as a theory, and it is a mistake to characterize it as such.

To be sure, for Wittgenstein the philosophical depiction of the common sense framework and the philosophical depiction of science are in some sense incommensurable—what they differentially depict cannot be put into the same boat, including Neurath's. It is a case of apples and pears. Because that is so he would deny the gradualist claim that science is superior to philosophy, and he would not assert the converse either. Each has its own autonomous status. In contemporary philosophy the difference between Wittgenstein and philosophers like Quine, Neurath, and the Churchlands roughly corresponds to the difference in outlook between those who believe in the autonomy of philosophy, as Wittgenstein and I do, and those who see philosophy as the handmaiden of the sciences. In particular, a rupturalist believes that the investigation of the common sense framework does not fall within the scope of science; instead, it is a task that philosophy is *uniquely* qualified to pursue. There is for the rupturalist a First and Inviolable Philosophy.

Let us carry these differences still further, deepening the argument against the gradualists. We have stated that when Wittgenstein speaks of a system of beliefs he is thinking of beliefs as propositions. To formulate his view in this way suggests that he is talking about certain sorts of mental entities. If so, his view would run counter to the eliminativist position, for its proponents deny that there are any mental entities. But the term "mental entity" is complex. Are they denying that there are any mental activities at all, such as believing or thinking, or are they denying that the description of such activities commits one to a realm of corresponding entities?

It is difficult to decide, for the writings of the eliminativists show a vacillation between these alternatives. But if they intend the first, then they must confront the objection that they cannot, without inconsistency, even state their view. Their position can be formulated as follows: They believe or think that there are no beliefs or thoughts—and clearly that is a self-contradictory proposition. So it is more plausible that they intend the second. That is the thesis that any supporter of the common sense framework must reify the concept of belief. But if that is their view how does it apply to Wittgenstein? It is true that he distinguishes between knowledge and belief, denying that the former is mental and affirming that the latter is. But does he ever think of beliefs as *entities* in the way the eliminativists suppose? I deny that he does.

In all of his later philosophy Wittgenstein attacks such hypostatization. Consider his discussions of the meaning of a word in the *Blue Book* and in the *Investigations* or his account of belief in *Zettel* (e.g., in 437). In speaking of meaning, for example, he is denying that it is to be *identified* with what Frege would have called a "thought" or a "mental state"—that is, something like a Platonic essence. The family resemblance account, for example, is developed in opposition to such a view. I previously distinguished two different senses in which Wittgenstein uses the term "belief" in *On Certainty*. Even in the first of these, when the role of the concept is confined to the language game, Wittgenstein would deny that belief is to be identified with any sort of Platonic essence. But his view is even stronger when he is speaking about that which stands fast as a system of beliefs or propositions. Thus when Wittgenstein says "The child learns by believing the adult. Doubt comes after belief" (*O.C.*, 160), he is not talking about Platonic entities children putatively grasp in conversation with adults but about their unreflective willingness, as a result of training, to act upon orders or commands from their elders. It is that sort of upbringing in a community that stands fast for each of us.

This dispositional account is carried over to his later discussion of what stands fast; it is what he is alluding to when he says that acting lies at the bottom of the language game. This, as I read it, is an alternative formulation about the foundational status of the community. Wittgenstein, as much as the gradualist, thus disavows the need to assume the existence of mental entities in order to give an accurate description of human mental activity.

What separates him and the gradualist is not the issue of entityhood but rather their differing conceptions of beliefs and propositions. This is especially true when they are talking about the kinds of beliefs that comprise the common sense framework. For gradualists the correct explanation of belief is (or will be) given by cognitive science. Now this assertion is made by philosophers and not by scientists. As I have indicated, Wittgenstein has no objection to any strictly scientific theory.

What he rejects are certain philosophical accounts about belief that model themselves on science. He wishes to give an alternative to those philosophical "theories." In contrast to them his account derives from a description of the sorts of practices that constitute a community or society. Belief at that level is not a matter of knowing various propositions to be true or a kind of intellectual grasping. Instead, it is embedded in habitual action, in such ordinary behavior as opening and closing doors. When I leave the house my unhesitating movements exhibit the certitude that the front door is there. The belief or certitude I have in that case is not a thought in any Fregean or mentalistic sense.

It is thus clear that Wittgenstein's account of beliefs that stand fast is incompatible with gradualism. For Quine or Patricia Churchland the common sense framework is a theory—an inferential system expressed in propositional structures, best analyzed by cognitive science. For them, one's switching on a light is the outcome of a complicated, self-conscious intellectual process that includes sequences of assumptions, conjectures, beliefs, and inferences—for example, that what one sees there is a switch, that being a physical object it will not vanish as one approaches it, and that when it is pushed it will move in accordance with Hooke's law and cause a light bulb to illuminate. Everyone is thus a kind of neophyte Newton, applying in such cases physical laws to the world and drawing specific inferences from them. But not only do they assert that one is applying theories every time one does anything but they also claim that any theory, be it folk psychological or physical, is open to revision, just as Newton's was. It follows that in their view no theory is certain, for if it were certain it is a necessary truth that it could not be enhanced. Hence, certitude and gradualism are incompatible.

In previous chapters I described Wittgenstein's reaction that this is an over-intellectualized view of human behavior. It is true that in a regimented situation a clever interrogator can elicit an account of what seems to be theory-driven behavior from an ordinary person: This is indeed what the Churchlands in effect do in arguing their case. But the situation is reminiscent of that between Socrates and the slave boy in the *Meno*. It is dubious that the slave boy knew geometry all along, as the experiment seems to suggest. Like the Churchlands' reconstructions of the presumed thought processes of ordinary persons when they open a door or switch on a light, Socrates created an artificial, misleading situation. Most basic action is unreflective, habitual, instinctive, and non-self conscious; it is not theory laden. So Wittgenstein, in referring to our common sense framework, is not talking about a theory at all—that is, about a set of conjectures that one can suppose to be true; instead, he is talking about action at a primitive level and stressing that this is not to be identified with self-conscious propositional attitudes.

I interpret Wittgenstein's denial that the common sense framework is a theory to be the first step in an argument we can elicit from his writings (and which, of course, he never makes explicit) in defense of the thesis that certitude exists. The second step in the argument is the proposition that the common sense framework is not revisable. The two steps, taken in conjunction, entail that gradualism is mistaken.

The argument, as it develops in *On Certainty* in Wittgenstein's characteristically diffuse way, is of general import, for it also entails that scepticism is mistaken. The sceptic presupposes that certainty is presumably ascribable only to theories, that every such theory is revisable in principle, and that such revisability implies the non-existence of certainty. But Wittgenstein argues that that which stands fast is not a theory, so the sceptic begins with a mistake that is like the gradualist's. Moreover, since there is something that stands fast and is not revisable, the sceptic is mistaken in that respect as well. The second part of Wittgenstein's argument promotes the case for non-revisability. Let us begin our discussion of it by returning to eliminativism.

We have seen that eliminativists believe that our ordinary ways of characterizing human life are deeply mistaken, that what ordinary persons call beliefs, thoughts, intentions, desires, and doubts do not denote any entities in the mind-brain. If a developing cognitive science finds these terms otiose in its theory about how the mind-brain operates, the eliminativists predict that they will ultimately be dropped from our folk-psychological descriptive vocabulary. Here they point to the disappearance of such terms as "witch" and "demon," except as terms of abuse. Further, they argue that the disappearance of this vocabulary would amount to a massive revision of the common sense framework. On this point their view is that this vocabulary is tied in inextricable ways to the common sense outlook. Some of these writers, Paul Churchland, for instance, speculate that when the common sense framework is eliminated, C-fiber talk, or its equivalent, will replace our everyday mental vocabulary.

Suppose we agree that this will happen, that the whole range of psychological terms will eventually disappear from everyday discourse and be replaced by scientific idioms of a sort unpredictable at the moment. Would that affect Wittgenstein's claim that our common sense system of beliefs—our inherited background—is not revisable? The answer is that it would not. I will give two arguments in support of this claim.

Let us begin by following the steps an eliminativist would take to establish his case. We can then see how the Wittgensteinian argument counters it. In order to prove that no mental entities exist when certain brain operations are occurring a scientist would have to begin by identifying cases of what ordinary persons call doubting and belief. He would do this in order to show that on the occasions when an ordinary person claims to be believing or doubting something, no entity in the brain corresponds to the state that person claims to be in. He would go about this task by collecting and assessing evidence that refers to the observable behavior, including the verbal behavior, of that individual and to certain of that person's neural processes. But from this base it would not be easy to establish the conclusion he wishes to reach. Where in the brain would he look for such entities, and how would he ascertain that none exists there at that moment? I believe these difficulties are insurmountable, but to pursue that line here would not be germane since the argument does not depend on it.

It is sufficient to recognize that our scientist would be engaging in a number of familiar community practices: doubting a commonly held opinion; identifying, collating, and sorting data relevant to it; and making judgments and assertions based on his findings. Now how would a Wittgensteinian describe these activities? From his perspective, the scientist would be playing the doubting game. In this particular case he would be playing the game called the scientific method. This is a societal activity with well-defined rules designed to establish or disconfirm any scientific hypothesis. To establish his thesis it would be necessary for the scientist to follow such stipulated procedures. But if so, how does that show that the common sense framework is not revisable?

It shows it as follows. The eliminativist proposes that the disappearance of our everyday mental vocabulary would entail the revision or elimination of our common sense framework. But what the hypothesis would also entail, if correct, is that much of our inherited background, namely the totality of such practices, would then be revised or disappear since, as we have seen, it is these practices that are essential components of the common sense framework. And that in turn would entail that such specific practices as doubting, asserting, and judging would also be revised or disappear. But to believe they will is a profound mistake.

Take the English word "doubt," for instance. It is translated into Italian as *dubbio.* The locutions are different, but they refer to the same practice. If through some Common Market magic *dubbio* should disappear from Italian and be replaced by a new epithet, or by nothing at all, there would be no effect on the practice of doubting or on the framework which includes that practice. The situation is analogous to what would be the case if the lira were replaced by a new currency, the Eurodollar, say. The change in nomenclature would not result in the disappearance of such traditional economic activities as buying, selling, trading, and banking.

Those practices have existed in recognizable forms since time immemorial, and they would continue to exist after the lira had disappeared. The eliminativist is thus wrong in thinking that if our ordinary vocabulary of mental terms were replaced by a new scientific parlance, the change would entail the disappearance or the massive revision of the common sense framework. Clearly, it would not. Even the historical evidence runs counter to the conjecture. When words like "witch" and "demon" lost their descriptive uses those changes had no effect upon the common sense framework. The set of traditional practices essential to that framework continued unaltered. There is thus no reason to believe that future changes in our mental vocabulary will affect those practices. The eliminativist hypothesis leads to the falsehood that they would. It is therefore to be rejected.

It follows from these considerations that scientific practice is not correctly described by eliminative theory, since doubting is an essential ingredient of that practice. In effect, eliminativism is self-refuting, for *the practice of revising in science* would not exist unless the practice of doubting did as well. No scientist would revise or reject the received theory unless he was in some doubt about it. The practice of doubting (as distinct from the use of the word "doubt" or its cognates in other languages) is thus an inexpungible part of our common sense framework. If it is not eliminable, then neither is the framework itself. So no change in our ordinary vocabulary would affect the revisability of the common sense outlook. The conclusion of the argument is that Wittgenstein is right after all.

The second argument attacks the revisability thesis from a different perspective. Like the first, it begins by affirming that human communal life is defined by a spectrum of personal and institutional interactions, which we can call practices. Among these are believing, doubting, judging, and asserting. The spectrum also includes the familiar and important practice of revising. The process of revision is typically a complicated activity with many steps. Given that this is so, one can now pose the following question: *What would it be like to revise the practice of revising itself? How would one go about doing this? Indeed, is the notion of revising that practice sensible?*

I submit that it is not, that the endeavor would require engaging in the very practice it seeks to emend. The suggestion that such a revision is possible (which underlies both sceptical and gradualist attitudes) is self-refuting. In Wittgensteinian language, it would not engender a world picture one can comprehend. Insofar as any "community" lacked the practice of revising, it would not be a human community. It would lack all investigative procedures, not only those of the sciences and social sciences but those of everyday life as well, including those that contribute directly to human survival. "Such a 'revision,'" Wittgenstein writes, putting the word "revision" in quotes, "would amount to the annihilation of all yardsticks" (*O.C.*, 492).

This same lack of cogency will apply to the suggestion that we can revise or eliminate such practices as doubting, judging, and asserting and still be left with a human community. To make such claims is to presuppose that human society would be what it now is and yet to presuppose by these essential modifications that it would not be. Such a conjunction of presuppositions is clearly absurd. There is thus a sensible limit to revisability; it has its parameters and rules. One of these is that not everything is revisable, including revisability itself. There is thus something that does stand fast. We conclude that Wittgenstein's affirmation of this thesis is correct.

The previous lengthy discussion can be summarized briefly, and in that form it will allow us to pinpoint the exact differences between Wittgenstein and the gradualists. The latter argue as follows:

1. All theories are open to revision in the light of future experience.
2. The common sense framework is a theory (of a primitive type).
3. The common sense framework is therefore revisable in the light of future experience.
4. If a theory is revisable it is not certain.
5. Therefore, the common sense framework is not certain.

Wittgenstein meets this argument by rejecting several of its premises and adding others. He is willing to accept (1) for purposes of the argument but denies (2), namely, that the common sense framework is a theory. He replaces it with 2′, so that the counter-argument runs as follows:

1′. All theories are open to revision in the light of future experience.
2′. The common sense framework is not a theory; it is our inherited background.
3′. That background includes community practices that we absorb at an early age.
4′. These practices are essential ingredients of the common sense framework.
5′. If they were revisable or eliminable the common sense framework would be revisable or eliminable.
6′. But they are not revisable or eliminable.
7′. Hence, the common sense framework is not revisable or eliminable.
8′. Therefore, the common sense framework is certain.

Wittgenstein's argument thus turns on three premises: that the common sense framework is not a theory, that communal practices are essential (i.e., necessary) components of the common sense framework, and that such communal practices are not revisable. In this chapter I have constructed arguments having a textual basis to support these propositions. They demonstrate that Wittgenstein's reasoning is cogent and, accordingly, that there is such a thing as certitude.

The bearing of Wittgenstein's argument on scepticism is direct, and its import is destructive. We can now succinctly indicate why. To begin with, it must be emphasized that in speaking of "the sceptic" Wittgenstein is not referring to so-called ordinary persons but to intellectuals and in particular to philosophers. His application of the locution must thus be distinguished from one of its common employments. There is an everyday use of the term that does apply to ordinary persons.

For example, some journalists are said to be sceptical—and indeed are—of the promises made by the politicians whose campaigns they are covering. They realize that "there is many a slip betwixt objective cup and subjective lip," as Quine once put it. But the journalists do not doubt that the politicians exist, that they speak English, have had two parents, and so forth. They do not question our inherited background. In being sceptical of political pronouncements they are appealing to the past record of the candidates or to the feasibility of their prospective programs. Their kind of scepticism thus belongs to the language game and in principle is capable of resolution. But the sort of "sceptic" against whom Wittgenstein's argument is directed is more radical. His worries are obsessive and non-terminating. What differentiates him from the ordinary man?

We have given Wittgenstein's answer—in a general form—in chapter 6. He contends that the sceptic, like the traditional epistemologist, is in the grip of a conceptual model or picture. The model is composed of two parts, one of which his dogmatic opponent also accepts. Because of this common acceptance sceptical challenges are relevant to the dogmatist position. Both in effect agree on the conditions that any knowledge claim must satisfy: to say that A knows that p entails that p is true, that A cannot be mistaken, and that A's grounds for asserting p are airtight (i.e., there can be no gap between ground and assertion to allow for the possibility of error). They thus agree conceptually. But they differ over the facts, for the dogmatist holds, as the sceptic does not, that there are cases that satisfy these criteria.

What differentiates the sceptic's picture from that of his opponent is the second component. Moreover, it is internally complex. It has a foothold in the kind of scepticism that belongs to the language game and yet is not satisfied with such a grounding. The sceptic notices that humans often err with respect to claims they advance. The more he looks into such claims the less compelling they seem. Error is commonplace and is often compensated for or ignored in the give and take of everyday life.

There is thus a common sense basis for what finally becomes an anticommonsensical, full-blown, radical outlook. For what the sceptic also notices in deeply reflecting on such cases is something quite general: that neither the senses nor human reason can be counted on to guarantee, *in any arbitrarily selected case*, that it satisfies the conditions for knowing. This insight, if the sceptic were willing to formulate it explicitly, embeds a line of reasoning which holds that since in this case or in that case one might be mistaken, it is possible to be mistaken in every case. The sceptical insight thus consists *in seeing a connection between the notions of any case and every case*.

It is this addition that fleshes out the sceptical model, and such familiar arguments as the dream and demon hypotheses or their variants are used to reinforce it. They support the notion that since one might be mistaken in any given case it follows that one might be mistaken in every case. If so, nothing can be certain since every case is subject to doubt. The sceptic is thus not distinguishing between cases but is absorbing their variety into the model. He is thus imposing a philosophical picture on a diversity of features that should be distinguished. The outcome is a theory justifying obsessive doubt. The conclusion reached is thus very radical. It makes no difference what the case is: whether it is the existence of the external world or of other minds or of the veracity of memory—it is subject to doubt.

Wittgenstein's text shows great sensitivity to this set of moves. He thinks it shows intellectual power and insight and yet is profoundly wrong. His basic thesis that doubt is not possible in some cases is set in opposition to it. We can identify at least five levels of increasing depth that his response takes. These are, of course, expanded in the text in subtle and complicated ways, and to expatiate on them would require more space than we have at our disposal. I will therefore present them seriatim with minimal commentary. The list hardly does justice to the power and impact of Wittgenstein's treatment of scepticism, but our discussion in previous chapters should help in that appreciation.

1. At the simplest level Wittgenstein contests the facts from which the sceptical model is generated. He denies that human beings do doubt in every case. As he says, "The reasonable man does *not have* certain doubts" (*O.C.*, 220); "A doubt is not necessary even when it is possible" (392); and "One doubts on specific grounds" (458). His denial here is reminiscent of Moore's claim to know this or that p. Moore asserts that, in fact, he knows this or that p to be true. Wittgenstein is saying, in fact, we do not doubt this or that p. The difference between Moore's "I" and Wittgenstein's "we" is important. Moore is telling us what he knows to be true with certainty. Wittgenstein is asking the philosopher not to theorize but to look and see what we human beings actually do or do not doubt. That we do not doubt some things is significant; in opposition to the sceptic's model, it allows us to see how the language game is actually played.

2. A more powerful point, expressed in a variety of ways, carries us to a deeper level. It is the notion, familiar from our discussion in chapter 9, that what the sceptic is calling doubt is not really a case of doubt. What determines something to be such a case is its conformity to community practice. Real doubt thus presupposes the existence of the community. The sceptic does not engage in any such communal practice, and hence his supposititious worries are not really doubts at all. The important point Wittgenstein is making is that such worries do not apply to and therefore do not affect human life. They do not raise real questions and therefore do not require real answers. One might call them countfeit doubts, *fausse monnaie* that cannot be used to buy real goods. Recall some of the ways he expresses this thought: "A doubt that doubted everything would not be a doubt" (*O.C.*, 450) and "A doubt without an end is not even a doubt" (625). In a lengthy passage he writes:

> Doubting has certain characteristic manifestations, but they are only characteristic of it in particular circumstances. If someone said that he doubted the existence of his hands, kept looking at them from all sides, tried to make sure it wasn't "all done by mirrors," etc., we should not be sure whether we ought to call that doubting. We might describe his behavior as like the behavior of doubt, but his game would not be ours. (*O.C.*, 255)

The idea that the sceptic's game would not be ours is one we have emphasized throughout this work. Sceptical doubts do not belong to the language
game; they stand outside of it. In Wittgensteinian language, "they lie apart from
the route travelled by human inquiry." They are thus impotent with respect to
any significant investigation carried out by persons playing the language game,
including the scientist.

3. Wittgenstein explicitly rejects the sceptical leap from any case to every
case. In a passage I cited in the previous chapter, his interlocutor, now in the
guise of a therapeutic philosopher who notes this mistake, says: "We could
doubt every single one of these facts, but we could not doubt them *all*."
Wittgenstein agrees but adds: "Wouldn't it be more correct to say: 'we do not
doubt them *all*.'" And then, most significantly, he states: "Our not doubting
them all is simply our manner of judging, and therefore of acting" (232).

The argument Wittgenstein uses against the move from any case to every
case is that it would be equivalent to saying that we have always played a certain
game (chess, say) incorrectly. From the fact that one might play an arbitrarily
selected game incorrectly it does not follow that one might play every game
incorrectly. The idea that we might always be mistaken, that we could always be
adding incorrectly or playing a familiar game incorrectly, is a special form of
nonsense in which the wheels of language spin idly and do no work. Once again
his comment "our not doubting them all is simply our manner of judging" takes
us back to his basic idea that description should replace explanation. We could
not be said to be engaging in the community practice called judging if we were
always mistaken. And judging exists. A description of that practice includes, as
an essential part, that most judgments are correct. The point has been recognized by many contemporary philosophers, notably Donald Davidson in his
principle of charity.

4. One of Wittgenstein's deepest criticisms of scepticism stems from the
notion that all of us are reared in a community. In this ambience we learn to
recognize certain persons, our parents and others, learn to speak a language, and
eventually come to participate unself-consciously in a wide range of human
interactions, practices, and institutions. Wittgenstein says that such an immersion in the community constitutes our inherited background. This background
is deeply ingrained—so deeply as to be inexpugnable. There is no possible way
that one can reject or revise it. Yet the sceptic wishes to question its existence.
But even the form the sceptic's challenge takes—the linguistic format to which
it must conform so that another can understand it—presupposes the existence of
the community and its linguistic practices. The sceptic's doubts are thus self-
defeating. They presuppose the very existence of that which he wishes to challenge as possibly non-existent, namely, the inherited societal background which
stands fast for all of us. They thus serve as an ironic reminder that there is such a
thing as certainty.

5. Finally, Wittgenstein wishes to emphasize that it is the existence of the
world that is the starting point of belief for every human being. Most of the
world is inorganic. There are thus two different components to our inherited
background. There is the community, as described above, which includes both
organic and non-organic components, and there is the world. Their interrela-

tionship is complex. The world, taken as a totality, represents the deepest level of certitude, having a kind of priority with respect to the community. For unless the inorganic world existed there would be no human communities.

Wittgenstein's foundationalism, even in its absolutist form, thus differs from those of the tradition in being striated. These two features—the world and the community—thus stand fast in different ways, that is, in having somewhat different presuppositional relationships to the language game. Taken together they are what philosophers have called the external world. Both aspects exhibit a kind of objectivity—an intruding presence—that impinges upon human beings and to which in diverse ways they must conform. Neither aspect is open to obsessive doubt or to revision. Wittgenstein's "solution" to the problem of the existence of the external world is that no sensible question can be raised with respect to either of these aspects. Their existence is presupposed in any formulation of the problem. Therefore to question their existence, as the sceptic presumably wishes to do, is self-defeating. In even trying to formulate its challenge scepticism initiates the process of its own destruction.

Scepticism is thus not a possible position, resting upon or embedding a set of consistent beliefs. Contrary to what Moore thought, no counter-argument to it need be mounted. If there is a philosophical task it is to show why scepticism is plausible and yet why it is impotent. But the task is not wholly negative. It faces two positive challenges. The first is to delineate how the language game is played: how such terms as "knowledge," "belief," "doubt," "judgment," and so forth, are actually used, an effort that will include an account of the rules that govern such uses. The second is to describe the presuppositions that make the language game possible at all. In *On Certainty* Wittgenstein does both of these things.

I said at the beginning of this book that a persuasive case can be made for regarding Wittgenstein as the greatest philosopher of the twentieth century and perhaps as the greatest Western philosopher since Kant. If he had not written *On Certainty* this assessment would still stand. But for anyone who has carefully worked through this work there can be little doubt about the support it adds to this evaluation. Both its critical and positive achievements are of the highest order. In the former respect we can say that one of Wittgenstein's greatest contributions to philosophy is to have shown the self-defeating nature of radical scepticism, why it cannot even get off the ground. In developing this insight his grasp of scepticism is palpably more profound than Moore's. Moore presupposes that the sceptic's doubts make sense and can be answered by asserting that he (Moore) knows this or that p with certainty. But Wittgenstein's understanding is deeper. He shows that what the sceptic wishes to say cannot be said without violating the constraints that would make the question sensible. No such answer as Moore wishes to provide is thus possible or needed. Scepticism is not merely mistaken, as Moore thinks; it is, as Wittgenstein demonstrates, conceptually aberrant.

When to this achievement is added the development of a new method, the descriptions of the ways that conceptual models exercise their ineluctable grips upon thinkers, and accurate characterizations of our everyday linguistic uses, we are—and have been throughout this study—in the presence of genius.

Selected Bibliography

Ambrose, Alice. "The Defense of Common Sense," *Philosophical Investigations*, 1:3 (1978), 1–11.

_____. "Moore and Wittgenstein as Teachers," *Teaching Philosophy*, 12 (1989), 107–113.

Apel, Karl Otto. "Das Problem der philosophischen Letztbegruendung im Lichte einer transzendentalen Sprachpragmatik," in B. Kanistscheider (ed.), *Sprache und Erkenntnis*. (Innsbruck: 1976), 55–82.

Ayer, A.J. *Wittgenstein* (New York: 1985).

Baker, Gordon P. *Scepticism, Rules and Language* (Oxford: 1985).

Baker, G.P., and P.M.S. Hacker. *Wittgenstein: Rules, Grammar and Necessity* (Oxford: 1985).

Baker, Lynne Rudder. "On the Very Idea of a Form of Life," *Inquiry*, 27 (1984), 277–289.

_____. *Saving Belief* (Princeton, N.J.: 1987).

Baldwin, Thomas. *G.E. Moore*. (London: 1992).

Bennett, Philip W. "Wittgenstein's Theory of Knowledge in *On Certainty*," *Philosophical Investigations*, 3:4 (1980), 38–46.

Black, Carolyn. "Taking," *Theoria*, 40 (1974), 66–75.

Bogen, James. "Wittgenstein and Scepticism," *Philosophical Review*, 83 (1974), 364–373.

Bouwsma, O.K. *Philosophical Essays*. (Lincoln, Neb.: 1965).

Carr, Brian. "The Grounds of Uncertainty," *Philosophical Inquiry*, 1 (1979), 205–214.

Cavell, Stanley. "The Availability of Wittgenstein's Later Philosophy," in G. Pitcher (ed.), *Wittgenstein: The Philosophical Investigations* (New York: 1966), 151–186.

Churchill, John. "The Certainty of Worldpictures," *Philosophical Investigations*, 11:1 (1988), 28–47.

Conway, Gertrude D. *Wittgenstein On Foundations* (Atlantic Highlands, New Jersey: 1989).

Cook, John W. "The Metaphysics of Wittgenstein's *On Certainty*," *Philosophical Investigations*, 8:2 (1985), 81–119.

De Martalaere, Patricia. "Wittgenstein, critique de Moore: de la certitude sans savoir," *Revue Internationale de Louvain*, 84:2 (1986), 208–228.

Diamond, Cora. *The Realistic Spirit* (Cambridge, Mass.: 1991).

Dilman, Ilham. "On Wittgenstein's Last Notes (1950–51)," *Philosophy*, 46:176 (1971), 162–167.

Duffy, Bruce. *The World As I Found It* (New York: 1987).

Emmett, Kathleen. "Forms of Life," *Philosophical Investigations*, 13:3 (1990), 213–231.

Finch, Henry LeRoy. *Wittgenstein—The Later Philosophy*. (Atlantic Highlands, New Jersey: 1977).

Fogelin, Robert J. "Wittgenstein and Classical Skepticism," *International Philosophical Quarterly* (1981), 3–15.

French, Peter A. "Wittgenstein's Limits of the World," *Midwest Studies in Philosophy*, 1 (1976), 114–124.

Frongia, Guido. *Wittgenstein: Regole E Sistema* (Milano: 1983).

Gill, Jerry H. "On Reaching Bedrock," *Metaphilosophy*, 5 (1974), 272–282.

_____. "What Wittgenstein Wasn't," *International Philosophical Quarterly*, 30:2 (1990), 207–220.

Glock, Hans-Johann. *A Wittgenstein Dictionary* (Oxford: 1993).

Goldstein, Laurence. "Wittgenstein's Late View on Belief, Paradox, and Contradiction," *Philosophical Investigations*, 11 (1988), 49–73.

Gullvag, Ingemund. "Remarks on Wittgenstein's *Ueber Gewissheit* and a Norwegian Discussion," *Inquiry*, 31:3 (1988), 371–386.

Hacker, P.M.S. *Insight and Illusion* (Oxford: rev. ed., 1986).

Haller, Rudolf. "Justification and Praxeological Foundationalism," *Inquiry*, 31:3 (1988), 335–345.

_____. *Questions on Wittgenstein* (Lincoln, Neb.: 1988).

Hanfling, Oswald. "On the Meaning and Use of 'I Know,'" *Philosophical Investigations*, 5 (1982), 190–204.

_____. "Was Wittgenstein a Sceptic?" *Philosophical Investigations*, 8 (1985), 1–16.

_____. *Wittgenstein's Later Philosophy* (Albany, N.Y.: 1989).

Hannay, Alastair. *Human Consciousness* (London: 1990).

_____. "New Foundations and Philosophers," in A.P. Martinich and M. White (eds.), *Certainty and Surface in Epistemology and Philosophical Method*, (Lewiston, N.Y.: 1991), 25–40.

Harwood, Sterling. "Taking Scepticism Seriously—and in Context," *Philosophical Investigations*, 12 (1989), 223–233.

Hertzberg, Lars. "On the Attitude of Trust," *Inquiry*, 31:3 (1988), 307–322.

Hilmy, Stephen S. *The Later Wittgenstein* (New York: 1987).

Hinman, Lawrence M. "Can a Form of Life Be Wrong?" *Philosophy*, 58 (1983), 339–352.

Hintikka, Merrill B., and Jaakko Hintikka. *Investigating Wittgenstein* (New York: 1986).

Hudson, W.D. "Language Games and Presuppositions," *Philosophy*, 53 (1978), 94–99.

_____. "The Light Wittgenstein Sheds on Religion," *Midwest Studies in Philosophy*, VI (1981), 275–292.

Janik, Allan. "Self-deception, Naturalism and Certainty," *Inquiry*, 31:3 (1988), 295–306.

Johannessen, Kjell S. "The Concept of Practice in Wittgenstein's Later Philosophy," *Inquiry*, 31:3 (1988), 357–369.

Kenny, Anthony. *Wittgenstein* (Cambridge, Mass: 1973).

Klein, Peter D. *Certainty: A Refutation of Scepticism* (Minneapolis, Minn.: 1981).

Klemke, E.D. *Essays on Wittgenstein* (Chicago: 1971).

Kripke, Saul A. *Wittgenstein on Rules and Private Language* (Cambridge, Mass.: 1982).

Lazerowitz, Morris, and Alice Ambrose. *Essays in the Unknown Wittgenstein* (New York: 1984).

Lear, Jonathan. "Leaving the World Alone," *Journal of Philosophy*, 79 (1982), 382–403.

Leinfellner, Elisabeth, Werner Leinfellner, Hal Berghil, and Adolf Hubner. *Wittgenstein and His Impact on Contemporary Thought* (Vienna: 1980).

Leyvraz, Jean-Pierre. "Logic and Experience in Wittgenstein's Later Work: *On Certainty*," *Man and World*, 11 (1978), 257–269.

Lloyd, A.C. "Wittgenstein's Last Epistemology," *Philosophical Inquiry*, 1 (1979), 195–204.

Luckhardt, C.G. "Beyond Knowledge: Paradigms in Wittgenstein's Later Philosophy," *Philosophy and Phenomenological Research*, 39:2 (1978).

McGinn, Marie. *Sense and Certainty.* (Oxford: 1989).

McGuinness, Brian. *Wittgenstein: A Life. Young Ludwig 1889–1921* (London: 1988).

Malcolm, Norman. *Thought and Knowledge* (Ithaca, N.Y.: 1977).

_____. "Wittgenstein: The Relation of Language to Instinctive Behavior," *Philosophical Investigations*, 5:1 (1982), 3–22.

_____. *Ludwig Wittgenstein: A Memoir*, 2nd ed. (New York: 1984).

_____. *Nothing Is Hidden: Wittgenstein's Criticism of his Early Thought* (Oxford: 1986).

_____. "Wittgenstein's 'Scepticism' in *On Certainty*," *Inquiry*, 31:3 (1988) 277–293.

_____. "Wittgenstein on Language and Rules," *Philosophy*, 64 (1989), 5–28.

Malgren, Helge. *Intentionality and Knowledge: Studies in the Philosophy of G.E. Moore and Ludwig Wittgenstein* (Goteborg: 1971).

Martinich, A.P. and M. White, (eds.), *Certainty and Surface in Epistemology and Philosophical Method* (Lewiston, N.Y.: 1991).

Meynell, Hugo. "Doubts About Wittgenstein's Influence," *Philosophy*, 57 (1982), 251–259.

Monk, Ray. *Ludwig Wittgenstein: The Duty of Genius* (New York: 1990).

Moore, G.E. "Wittgenstein's Lectures in 1930–33," in *Philosophical Papers* (London: 1959), 252–324.

Morawetz, Thomas. "Wittgenstein and Synthetic *A Priori* Judgments," *Philosophy*, 49 (1974), 429–434.

_____. *Wittgenstein and Knowledge: The Importance of "On Certainty"* (Amherst, Mass.: 1978).

Newell, R.W. *Objectivity, Empiricism and Truth* (New York: 1987).

Odegard, Douglas. "Two Types of Scepticism," *Philosophy*, 54 (1979), 459–472.

Orr, Deborah Jane. "Did Wittgenstein Have a Theory of Hinge Propositions?" *Philosophical Investigations*, 12:2 (1989) 134–153.

Pears, David. *Ludwig Wittgenstein* (Cambridge, Mass.: 1986).

_____. *The False Prison: A Study of the Development of Wittgenstein's Philosophy*, 1–2 (Oxford: 1987–1988).

Perkins, R. "Moore's Moral Rules," *Journal of the History of Philosophy* (Oct. 1990), 595–599.

Rorty, Richard. *Philosophy and the Mirror of Nature* (Princeton, N.J.: 1979).

Ross, Jacob Joshua. "Rationality and Common Sense," *Philosophy*, 53 (1978), 374–381.

Schilpp, P.A. ed. *The Philosophy of G.E. Moore* in the Library of Living Philosophers Series. (LaSalle, Ill: 1942).

Schulte, Joachim. "World-picture and Mythology," *Inquiry*, 31:3 (1988), 323–334.

Seabright, Paul. "Explaining Cultural Divergence: A Wittgensteinian Paradox," *Journal of Philosophy*, 84:1 (1987), 11–27.

Searle, John R. *Intentionality: An Essay in the Philosophy of Mind* (New York: 1983).

Shanker, Stuart G. "Wittgenstein's Solution of the 'Hermeneutic Problem,'" *Conceptus*, XVIII (1984), 50–61.

Sharrock, W.W., and R.J. Anderson. "Criticizing Forms of Life," *Philosophy*, 60:233 (1985), 394–400.

Shekleton, James. "Rules and 'Lebensformen,'" *Midwest Studies in Philosophy*, 1 (1976), 124–132.

Shiner, Roger. "Two River Images: Wittgenstein and Heraclitus," *Philosophy*, 49 (1974), 191–197.

_____. "Wittgenstein and the Foundations of Knowledge," *Proceedings of the Aristotelian Society*," 78 (1978), 103–124.

Smith, Barry. "On the Origins of Analytic Philosophy," *Grazer Philosophische Studien*, 35 (1989), 153–173.

_____. "Wittgensteinian Philosophy and the Culture of the Commentary," in R. Haller and J. Brandl (eds.), *Wittgenstein: a Re-Evaluation* (Vienna: 1990), 247–254.

Soles, Deborah H. "Some Ways of Going Wrong: On Mistakes in *On Certainty*," *Philosophy and Phenomenological Research*, 42:4 (1982), 555–571.

Stroll, Avrum. "Some Different Ways That Things Stand Fast for Us," *Grazer Philosophische Studien*, 22 (1984), 69–89.

_____. "Foundationalism and Common Sense," *Philosophical Investigations*, 10:4 (1987), 279–298.

_____. "Wittgenstein and Folk Psychology," *Proceedings of the 12th International Wittgenstein Symposium* (1988), 264–270.

_____. "Wittgenstein's Nose," in B. McGuinness and R. Haller (eds.), *Wittgenstein in Focus* (Amsterdam: 1989), 395–414.

_____. "How I See Philosophy: Common Sense and the Common Sense View of the World," in A.P. Martinich and M. White (eds.), *Certainty and Surface in Epistemology and Philosophical Method* (Lewiston, N.Y.: 1991), 185–201.

Stroud, Barry. *The Significance of Philosophical Scepticism* (New York: 1984).

Suter, Ronald. *Interpreting Wittgenstein: A Cloud of Philosophy, a Drop of Grammar* (Philadelphia: 1989).

Svensson, Gunnar. *On Doubting the Reality of Reality: Moore and Wittgenstein on Sceptical Doubts* (Stockholm: 1981).

Triplett, Trimm. "Recent Work on Foundationalism," *American Philosophical Quarterly*, 27:2 (1990), 93–111.

Von Wright, G.H. "Wittgenstein on Certainty," in *Wittgenstein* (Minneapolis, Minn.: 1982), 165–181.

White, Alan R. "Common Sense: Moore and Wittgenstein," *Revue Internationale de Philosophie*, 40:7 (1986), 313–330.

Wilde, Carolyn. *Certainty: A Discussion of Wittgenstein's Notes on Certainty* (London: 1976).

Winch, Peter. *Trying to Make Sense* (New York: 1987).

_____. "True or False?," *Inquiry*, 31:3 (1988), 265–277.

Wittgenstein, Ludwig. *Philosophical Investigations* (Oxford: 1958).

_____. *The Blue and Brown Books* (Oxford: 1960).

_____. *Philosophische Bemerkungen* (Oxford: 1964).

_____. *Zettel* (Oxford: 1967).

_____. *On Certainty* (Oxford: 1969).

_____. *Remarks on Colour*. (Berkeley and Los Angeles: 1977).

_____. *Last Writings on the Philosophy of Psychology* (Oxford: 1982).

Wolgast, Elizabeth. *Paradoxes of Knowledge* (Ithaca, N.Y.: 1977).

Index